DATE DUE

GOVERNING THE EMPIRE ST

D1058268

Governing the Empire State:

An Insider's Guide

State of New York

Management Resources Project

1988

Library of Congress Cataloging-in-Publication Data

Governing the Empire State.

    Bibliography: p.
    Includes index.
    1. New York (State)—Politics and government—
1951–   . 2. Administrative agencies—New York
(State) I. Management Resources Project (N.Y.)
JK3441.G68   1988   353.9747   88–8426

    ISBN 0-9621102-0-5

Credits

Cover design: John Moore Graphic Design, Inc.

Cover illustration: Tom Payne

Cartoons: Tom Payne

Graphic Illustrations: John Moore Graphic Design, Inc.

Copy Editor: Caroline Eastman

Manufactured and printed by Williams Press, Inc.

Table of Contents

Foreword

State government plays a vital role in our lives, each day providing essential services to millions of New Yorkers. Decisions regarding the direction, shape and cost of State services involve the Governor and his staff, legislators, leaders of State agencies, budget specialists, and many others. Deliberations among these officials can be difficult and time consuming, and must address the needs of a variety of competing interests. It is this complicated process of public administration that is the substance of *Governing the Empire State: An Insider's Guide*.

Although an abundance of literature exists about government, generally little is available that provides the public manager, interested citizen or student with a clear and concise perspective about how New York State government functions and how the various internal control systems and leaders interact. The *Insider's Guide* fills this gap, portraying a clear picture of the processes that guide and control State government while offering a balanced look at the organizational environment that shapes policies and programs.

While the *Insider's Guide* is an authoritative source book on how State government works, using this knowledge to make government fit the needs of its people is the task of the public servant. Whether the reader is a public manager, legislator, or citizen, I hope that this book is a springboard for effective action. It is only through the participation of all New Yorkers that we can achieve the essential purpose of government: to improve the conditions of peoples' lives.

Henrik N. Dullea
Director of State Operations
and Policy Management
Executive Chamber
State of New York

Acknowledgments

Governing the Empire State: An Insider's Guide would not have been possible without the assistance of many officials in New York State government. Although not every individual's name is listed here, due to space limitations, we are grateful to all for their help and support.

The *Guide* is a product of the Management Resources Project, jointly sponsored by the Governor's Office of Employee Relations (GOER) and the Rockefeller Institute of Government, State University of New York (SUNY). The Project's responsibilities include creating and making available materials that will help State managers make better informed decisions on public policy issues. Development of the *Guide* was continuously encouraged and supported by the Project's Board of Directors: Nancy L. Hodes, Chair; V. James Gutowski, Donald Giek, and William Sullivan of GOER; and David Andersen, Warren Ilchman, and James Morrell of the Rockefeller Institute.

An Editorial Advisory Board, composed of Jane Gould, T. Norman Hurd, Kearney Jones, Vincent LaFleche, and Richard Torkelson, was of great assistance in helping to shape the *Guide*'s outline, providing guidance during the course of writing the volume, and in reviewing the final manuscript.

The following people agreed to serve on chapter review committees in addition to giving us interview time during chapter preparation and revision: Joseph Bress, Candy Carter, Joyce Chupka, Robert Davison, Lawrence DeLong, Russell DiBello, Jerry Dudak, Dall Forsythe, Mary Hanak, Joseph Hilton, Ronald Hoskins, Vincent LaFleche, Richard Lynch, Richard Nunez, Arthur O'Neil, Seymour Peltin, William Redmond, Michael Reger, James Ruhl, Richard Spaulding, Philip Sperry, Paul Veillette, and John Wilson. Their comments and suggestions were most helpful.

Catherine Gerard, Paul Shatsoff, and Onnolee Smith of GOER reviewed draft chapters and offered many useful suggestions.

The following people gave freely of their time for personal interviews and were available for queries that often followed as chapters were being drafted and modified: Judith Avner, David Axelrod, Bruce Bailey, James Baldwin, Sally Barkevich, Joseph Bierman, Lloyd Bishop, John Burke, Sidney Burke, Anne Carr, Alan Chartock, Jeffrey Cohen, Mollyo Cohen, Rand Condell, Edwin Crawford, J. Robert Daggett, Christopher Dammer, Audrey Davis, William Davis, Andrè Dawkins, Richard Decker, Donna Dedrick, Wilma DeLucco, Margaret Doolin, Henrik Dullea, Kenneth Edlund, John Ennis, Edward Farrell, Cynthia Feiden-Warsh, Frederick Fields, Sidney Firestone, Andrew Fleck, John Flynn, Cornelius Foley, Amy Fulstern, Lionel Galarneau, George Gamble, Mark Ganz, John Gleason, Herbert Gordon, Charlotte Gray, Anne Grebert, Frank Greco, Jeffrey Haber, Steven Hancox, Elizabeth Houlihan, John Hudacs, Barry Isenberg, Brad Johnson, John Kaelin, Samuel Kawola, John Kelliher, Charles Klaer, Sheldon Kramer, Mary Ann Krupsak, Robert Kurtter, Joan Kutcher, Richard Leckerling, Alfred Manzella, Ilene Margolin, Peter Martino, Frank Mauro, Lorna McBarnette, Robert McEvoy, William McGowan, James McSparron, Robert Mitler, Elizabeth Moore, Paul Moore, Charles Palmer, Robert Parrish, Jovan Paunovitch, Vincent Perfetto, Linda Randolph, Paul Reuss, Harold Rubin, Michael Rush, Joseph Schmitt, Joan Senter, Gail Shaffer, Gloria Shepard, Nancy Spiegle, Joseph Spinelli, Brian Stenson, Ronald Stout, Ronald Tarwater, Joseph Tomkowski, Daniel Tworek, Lee VanDeCarr, Brent Wallace, Jay Walsh, Arthur Webb, James Whitney, Lois Wilson, Laurel Winegar, and Theodore Winnie.

We are indebted to V. James Gutowski, currently Deputy Commissioner of Labor (but Deputy Director of GOER for Management/Confidential Affairs during the period when this Guide was conceived and prepared), for writing Chapter I, which puts New York State government into proper perspective. We are also indebted to Vincent E. LaFleche and several members of his staff, who drafted part of Chapter VI on management control systems, and who kindly (and quickly) provided us updated materials for this section.

Special thanks go to William Sullivan, Acting Director of the Committee on the Work Environment and Productivity, who first suggested several years ago that a guide to the basic New York State governmental processes be prepared, and who provided continual support and encouragement throughout the project.

We are especially grateful to the Division of Management/Confidential Affairs of the Governor's Office of Employee Relations, the Civil Service Employees Association, and the Public Employees Federation for providing the financial support necessary for the preparation and publication of the Guide.

Finally, this Guide would not have been completed without the tireless efforts of two graduate interns, Suzanne Felt and Carrie Lamitie. They conducted many of the interviews, sifted through large amounts of printed materials, drafted and revised chapters, and never lost interest in the project. In the course of preparing the *Guide*, we all learned a great deal about New York State Government processes.

Jane Zacek
Director
Management Resources Project

Special Thanks

As the Chair of the Management Resources Project's Board of Directors, I am delighted that the *Guide* is now in print and available for all those who want to know how our State's government works. I want to publicly thank a few of the many dedicated State managers who in particular contributed their time and talents to the *Guide*: Bill Sullivan, Acting Director of the Committee on the Work Environment and Productivity, who first proposed that such a volume be created, and who willingly read and reread drafts of the manuscript; Jim Gutowski, who as Deputy Director of the Governor's Office of Employee Relations, supported the idea of the *Guide* from its inception, was willing to read and comment on chapter drafts as they appeared, and wrote Chapter I; Ramon Rodriguez and Catherine Gerard of the Division of Management/Confidential Affairs at GOER, who consistently supported the creation of the volume and assisted in every way possible in helping to finalize the text; Don Giek, Director, Program Planning and Employee Development at GOER, who served as liaison with several public employee unions and ensured that union officials had input into chapter drafts; and Jane Zacek, Director of the Management Resources Project, who guided this project through to completion. It is a product of which we can all be proud.

Nancy L. Hodes
Executive Deputy Director
Governor's Office of
Employee Relations

Introduction

New York State government is large and complex. Limited by the State Constitution to twenty executive departments, the Executive Branch has established a number of divisions, offices, commissions, and boards, so that today almost sixty executive agencies respond to citizens' identified needs in one way or another. There are also a large and increasing number of public benefit corporations, ranging from the New York State Thruway Authority to the Municipal Bond Bank Authority. In addition, there are the 211-member State Legislature, with its large (and growing) staff, and a multitiered and complex court system.

The executive branch of State government is composed of approximately 200,000 full-time employees, fifty-two correctional facilities with 37,000 inmates, and thirty-two psychiatric centers serving 23,000 inpatients and 72,000 nonresident individuals annually. The Executive Branch is responsible for the maintenance and supervision of 110,000 miles of roads and highways. To support these functions, it had a 1987-88 budget of $41 billion, an amount that represents only a portion of what is actually spent on all public services throughout the State.

Managers in executive agencies, especially those new to State service, are frequently confronted with a need to know more about various state systems and processes, but do not have a handy guide to which to refer. Typically, inquiry to the office that specializes in a particular process provides such a myriad of detail that the inquirer is likely to be overwhelmed. Reviewing procedures manuals with constant updates and modifications, not always written for the nonspecialist to comprehend readily, is likely to produce similar results. This *Guide* is designed to avoid unnecessary detail. Its purpose is to provide an overview of New York State systems that have been identified as important for managers to know without getting bogged down in detailed and tedious compilations. Offering an overview of general concepts and actual (rather than formal) procedures in a clearly written style, with numerous examples of the system in action, fills an identified gap in the available descriptive or analytical materials about State government.

The outline for the *Guide* was developed after in-depth interviews with more than a dozen senior managers. Further, we had the collective advice of an editorial advisory board, drawn from a variety of State agencies, with extensive knowledge of how State government really works. Based on the strong recommendations of both these groups, the following nine chapters were developed:

- The Context of New York State Government
- The Governor's Office
- The Executive Budget Process
- Human Resources Management
- Agency–Legislative Relations and the Legislature
- Internal Control, Oversight, and External Review
- Contracting and Purchasing
- Administrative Law and Agency Limitations
- State Government in an Intergovernmental Setting

The material included in each chapter is based on extensive interviews with dozens of managers in a broad cross-section of agencies as well as review of vast amounts of printed materials.

Each chapter strives to

- provide a concise but accurate description of how the system really works;
- include examples of the system in action that serve as a useful guide;
- identify those State agencies responsible for ensuring that the system is operating in accord with the State Constitution, legislative mandates, and properly established rules and regulations;
- make available additional materials in an appendix or glossary, as well as to list useful sources for further details.

The *Guide* was designed originally for managers and other executive branch personnel interested in knowing more about State governmental processes. It will also be useful for legislative staff and local governmental managers and staff who want to learn more about State governmental systems. Further, the *Guide* is eminently suitable for college and university students and for faculty who want to become familiar with how State government really operates.

What Publications are Currently Available?

Of the published materials that describe New York State government operations, none focuses on major state systems, and none provides a comprehensive overview of these systems.

Joseph Zimmerman, *Government And Politics of New York State* (1981), offers an historical perspective to New York State government, but largely reviews institutions rather than systems. Peter Colby, ed., *New York State Today* (1985), includes a number of useful essays that consider various aspects of state government. Gerald Benjamin and T. Norman Hurd's volume, *Making Experience Count* (1985), based on oral interviews with a number of leading officials in the administration of Governor Hugh Carey, provides useful insights into the Executive Chamber and the varied responsibilities of agency heads trying to get the job done. Alan Hevesi's *Legislative Politics in New York State* (1975), although dated, examines the informal as well as the formal operating procedures of the Legislature. Hevesi, an assemblyman since 1971, has the advantage of being a knowledgeable insider. Abdo Baaklini's *The Politics of Legislation in New York State* (1979) describes the legislative process from the vantage point of that branch of government. Robert Kerker's *The Executive Budget in New York: A Half-Century Perspective* (1981) includes a great deal of detail as well as historical background on budgeting from a formal point of view. The League of Women Voters, *New York State: A Citizen's Handbook* (1979) is informative on various institutions of state government but does not consider the governmental processes within the executive branch.

There are a number of useful general references on laws, rules and regulations, facts and figures about state organizations and personnel, and socio-economic data about the State. These are listed and annotated in the appendix entitled "Some Handy References."

Publications and memoranda issued periodically by the agencies proved especially helpful in preparing this *Guide*. Agencies and legislative offices were also helpful in providing information that we could incorporate into charts and other graphic materials.

Finally, the idea for this volume came from one prepared for the Massachusetts Department of Personnel Administration, *Credibility and the Public Trust* (1983), by Harvard University's Kennedy School of Government under the direction of Eileen McDonough-Rogers.

Chapter I

The Context of New York State Government

Introduction

In elementary school New Yorkers learn that their state, the Empire State, was settled in 1614 by Dutch and English colonists. Instruction on the American Revolution reveals that one-third of the battles in that war were fought on New York State soil and that British-held New York City provided a haven for loyalists. Perhaps the most important lessons about New York center on its role as a hub for immigrants of yesterday and today, home for millions of adopted Americans who contribute to the wealth and diversity of both the State and the nation.

In middle school, New Yorkers learn that a bicameral legislature convenes each year in Albany, the locus of State government where laws are passed and public policy matters are debated and decided. They discover an apparent inconsistency in the judicial system, since the nation's Supreme Court is the highest court in the land, while New York State's Supreme Court is the district or trial court where original matters are heard, and the Court of Appeals is the highest court in the State.

In high school, New Yorkers learn how a bill becomes a law and some sense of the responsibilities of certain State agencies. If they're lucky, they may participate in a mock legislative session or follow the progress of a particular bill or issue in order to learn more about the legislative process.

And, in time, New Yorkers discover more about their state through personal experience. Metropolitan New Yorkers explore the remote beauty of the Catskills, Adirondacks, and Finger Lakes regions, while "Upstaters" venture below the Westchester County line

2

to experience the cultural treasures and striking contrasts of one of the world's most remarkable cities. Through this process, one begins to get a sense of the State's dramatic diversity.

For far too many citizens, this is the extent of their understanding of New York State, its governmental workings, and its vitality as an economic contributor to the nation's economy. Many citizens don't realize that New York has one of the most progressive and responsible state governments in the nation, or that New York places a high value on the needs of those who live or work within its borders, giving emphasis to the most unfortunate among us.

Large, By Any Measure—And Unique

New York State has the second largest population of the fifty states—nearly 18 million people. It is the seventh most densely populated state [Statistical Yearbook (1985-86), p. 5.], and its population includes an unusually broad spectrum of races and religions.

New York is one of the world's major financial centers. The total assets held by commercial bankers in the State represent one-fifth of the total assets of all such banks in the nation. Wall Street is the focal point for the world's securities and commodity exchanges, and New York City has more foreign bank branches than any other city or state [Statistical Yearbook (1985-86), p. 208.]. New York State ranks second in the nation in manufacturing with 1,383,300 employees (1983).

Although the State ranks thirtieth in land area, it is the fourteenth largest agricultural producer and supplier, making agriculture New York's single largest industry. It is the second largest dairy state and is a major producer of fruit, vegetables, livestock, and poultry [Statistical Yearbook (1985-86), p. 208.]. Its state park system, the most extensive in the U.S., serves as a model for other states.

New York's progressive government has made it a state of firsts. It was the first state to establish a free public school system, an electric power company, a uniformed police force, and a civil service system based on merit. And, especially relevant to the theme of this Guide, it was first to implement a strong executive budget system.

The State of New York is a microcosm of the diversity of the nation. For that reason, a good deal of New York's heritage and many of its resources have been immortalized in history, art, and entertainment that transcend the State and truly belong to the nation.* It has been and remains a national and international center of finance, industry and the arts. But, for the very same reasons

---

*See Chapter Appendix I.

3

that the State is so special, it has had its share of problems and crises. And yet New York's government has a tradition of being willing and able to deal with the most serious kinds of problems in imaginative and constructive ways.

New York State's Bureaucracy is Large, Diverse and Complex

There is no question that New York State's government is extensive. The fifty-seven executive branch agencies listed in Appendix A are only the tip of the bureaucratic iceberg. The term "state agency" is often used loosely to refer to the State's boards, commissions, offices, divisions, departments, councils and committees. When legislative entities are included, the State encompasses at least eighty-six commissions, fifty-six boards, ninety-eight committees, and sixty-three councils, in addition to the divisions, departments and offices included in Appendix A.

Although many of these organizations are headquartered in Albany and New York City, their regional offices and facilities form a statewide network. Currently, state staff are employed in at least two hundred regional offices, and operate 191 health, human service, and correctional institutions around the State. The State University system (SUNY) comprises sixty-four university and college campuses statewide. Finally, scores of other state facilities provide residents with recreational, cultural and other opportunities.

There are also approximately 130 independent authorities and quasi-public corporations that have been established by statute to provide services for the benefit of the general public. Examples of authorities include large ones such as the Port Authority of New York and New Jersey, the Power Authority of the State of New York, the Dormitory Authority, and the Thruway Authority; and smaller ones such as the Job Development Authority, the New York State Bridge Authority, the Battery Park City Authority and the Project Finance Agency. Altogether, New York State's various governmental entities employ more than 240,000 full and part-time employees, making it the eleventh largest employer in the nation—public or private.

The legislative branch has also become a significant bureaucracy. Its approximately 3,250 full-time employees provide staff assistance and support for the 61 members of the Senate and the 150 members of the Assembly. Over time, the Legislature has evolved from being part-time, with two three-month sessions, to a seven- or eight-month operation.

4

The judicial branch has also grown dramatically and the demands on it continue to far outstrip the available resources. There are now 1,100 judges and justices and 11,000 support and administrative personnel in the state courts. But both the human resources of the court system and the courts themselves clearly remain overburdened.

The State's overall budget has grown dramatically over the past quarter century (see Chart 1.1). The source of each proposed budget dollar is identified in the pie-chart on the left of Chart 1.2, and dollars are distributed for the purposes indicated in the chart on the right.

Part of the growth shown in Chart 1.1 is inflationary. Most of the increase, however, is attributable to a dramatic, continuing growth in the nature, scope, and extent of services provided to the general public by government organizations. Some of these services affect all citizens while others affect only small segments of the State's population.

1.1 Total State Expenditures
(in billons)

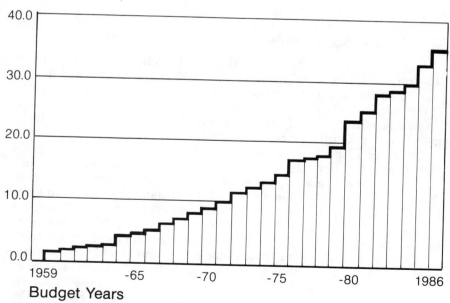

Budget Years

*Cash disbursements for all state sources-cash based accounting.
From *Comptroller's Annual Report to the Legislature.*

1.2 The State Budget
WHERE IT COMES FROM—WHERE IT GOES
(by percent)

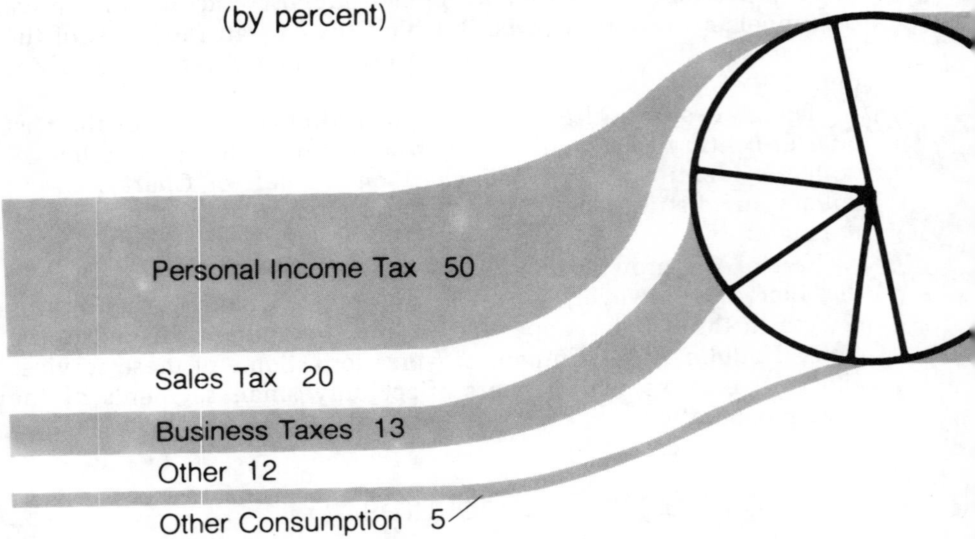

Personal Income Tax   50

Sales Tax   20

Business Taxes   13

Other   12

Other Consumption   5

The Private Sector/Public Sector Comparison

There is a widely held myth that the private sector knows what it's doing, while the public sector is inefficient and wasteful. In the private sector, success is typically measured by the size and color of the bottom line. In the public sector, programs are funded through taxes and other public financing methods, and "success" is admittedly more difficult to evaluate or measure.

In many respects, however, the two sectors are not really all that different. Although often pictured as leaner and more efficient than government, many private sector firms are more bureaucratic than a well-managed state agency that has had to retrench and has become more efficient as the result of the fiscal crises of the last decade. And while government is renowned for its byzantine complexity, corporate decision-making too has become increasingly complex due to increased regulation, consumer and stockholder awareness, automation and the resulting availability of huge amounts of data, and to the impact of legislation, rules, regulations and public policy on corporate activities. Whatever inefficiencies exist in the private sector may be passed along to consumers, not as taxes as they would be by government, but in the prices paid for goods and services. Even the reprehensible behavior of the handful of public

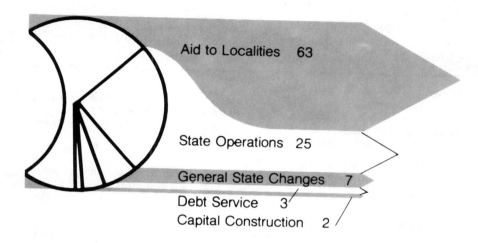

Aid to Localities 63

State Operations 25

General State Changes 7

Debt Service 3

Capital Construction 2

sector officials who betray the public trust has its private sector counterpart in the activities of the few corporate officials found to be responsible for toxic waste dumps, insider trading scandals, or the sale of dangerous products.

The debate over which sector is more efficient, productive, or socially beneficial is not useful. There is a growing awareness of the interrelatedness of government and business. And there is an important need to improve communication, increase mutual awareness, and create inter-sector coalitions to deal effectively with specific issues and problems.

Functions of New York State Government

The services provided by New York State government involve unique functions and tasks. In many instances, they include essential programs that are inherently unprofitable, such as hospitals for the severely retarded and for the criminally insane; institutions that provide medical, recreational, and rehabilitative services for mentally ill adults who cannot function in society; correctional and youth facilities; and highway snow removal and maintenance.

7

It is critical to understand the variety and scope of New York State government services. The following listing doesn't attempt to include all executive branch state agencies, but rather to organize the largest ones into functional categories, to provide a sampling of more specialized institutions, and to summarize briefly the mission of each.

CORRECTIONAL SERVICES

Correctional Service agencies work to enforce the penal code while preparing incarcerated adults and youths to reenter society. Research and data generated and collected by these agencies are the basis for the development of new inmate rehabilitation programs and services.

Department of Correctional Services
Operates fifty-two (1986) facilities (including minimum, medium and maximum security facilities) for the custody and rehabilitation of over 37,000 inmates.

Division for Youth
Recommends and coordinates services, educational programs and research for the prevention of juvenile delinquency; also provides technical support, planning and funding to communities to help meet the needs of their youth, and operates a comprehensive system of programs for youth who have been placed in its charge by the courts.

Division of Parole
Assists prospective releasees and parolees in obtaining education or vocational training, employment and residential arrangements; also surveys parolee activities to prevent and detect further criminal behavior.

Division of Probation and Correctional Alternatives
Supervises the administration of probation services and correctional alternatives programs, enforces probation laws and promulgates necessary rules and regulations; also administers a program of state aid for local probation services.

Commission of Correction
Regulates and investigates correctional facilities and is involved in correction policy development.

Division of Criminal Justice Services
Conducts research, monitors program effectiveness and acts as a clearinghouse in disseminating information concerning research studies and criminal justice administration; also serves as a central depository of fingerprints and personal data for the identification of arrested persons.

PROTECTIVE SERVICES FOR THE GENERAL PUBLIC
Collectively, these programs ensure the safety and well-being of all New Yorkers by monitoring the physical environment, controlling disease, regulating food producers, and enforcing the laws of the state.

Division of State Police

Enforces the law, and supports other federal, state and local law enforcement agencies.

Division of Military and Naval Affairs

Includes the New York Air National Guard, the New York Army National Guard, the New York Naval Militia, the New York State Emergency Management Office, the Radiological Emergency Preparedness Group, the US Marine Corps Reserve, and the New York Guard; mobilizes at the call of the Governor to aid in local disasters and emergencies.

Department of Health

Enforces and administers the Public Health Law, the State Hospital Code, and the State Sanitary Code; conducts research; regulates the health care industry, and supervises and provides state aid to local health authorities.

Department of Environmental Conservation

Administers wildlife and fish laws and manages two forest preserves; regulates the disposal, treatment and transport of toxic wastes; provides for abatement of water, land and air pollution; and administers all other state programs created to protect and enhance the environment.

Department of Agriculture and Markets

Develops programs for the revitalization of rural areas and the expansion of agriculture; protects consumers by inspecting food; administers programs to protect plant and animal health; and performs a number of other services as an advocate of agriculture.

Consumer Protection Board

Acts as coordinator of all state consumer protection activities; also assists local governments in developing consumer protection activities, intervenes in Public Service Commission proceedings, and represents consumers before state, federal and local agencies.

Department of Law

Defends suits against the state, its officials or agencies, and prosecutes violations of state law; also concerned with protection from consumer frauds, civil rights violations, workers' rights and utility rate cases; initiates legal action to protect the environment.

REGULATORY AGENCIES

By controlling the services available to New Yorkers, regulatory agencies ensure that those services meet legal standards and operate toward the benefit of clients.

Public Service Commission

Regulates rates and service of gas and electric corporations (including municipally operated plants), steam corporations, privately owned water corporations, telephone corporations, environmental planning for gas and electric transmission lines, and safety of liquid petroleum pipelines; also investigates utility accidents and complaints and inspects gas and electric meters.

Banking Department
Supervises and examines savings banks, trust companies, state banks, safe deposit companies, credit unions, licensed lenders, sales finance companies, private bankers, savings and loan associations, and licensed cashiers of checks.

Insurance Department
Supervises the insurance business by determining the qualifications of insurers, issuing licenses, examining licenses and conduct of insurers; regulates rates, availability, policies, advertising, and claims service.

Department of Economic Development
Promotes development and retention of business and industry; focuses attention on new programs to assist the business and industrial community; furthers tourism; and encourages export trade.

Department of State
Provides technical assistance to local government, administers fire prevention and control services, licenses and regulates a variety of occupational organizations and individuals, and publishes documents on State and local government operations.

State Energy Office
Develops and coordinates energy policy within the State, including energy conservation, data collection, and information dissemination; develops and implements strategies to maximize the use of energy resources and meet shortages.

AGENCIES PROVIDING SERVICES DIRECTLY TO THE GENERAL PUBLIC
These agencies provide New Yorkers with safe transportation and a wide variety of recreational opportunities and educational and training programs. Direct provision entails assessing need and then designing, implementing and evaluating programs to meet that need.

Department of Motor Vehicles
Registers motor vehicles, motorboats and snowmobiles; licenses all motor vehicle operators, dealers, and driver schools; registers vehicle repair shops and inspection stations; promotes traffic safety.

Department of Transportation
Coordinates and assists in the construction and operation of highway, rail, mass transit, marine and aviation facilities and service; regulates rail and motor carriers in interstate commerce.

Office of Parks, Recreation, and Historic Preservation
Operates State parks, historic sites, marine and recreational vehicles programs and facilities; coordinates the statewide program of public and private historic preservation.

Department of Education
Responsible for all public and private education in the State; administers State aid for local schools; operates schools for the blind and the deaf; conducts vocational rehabilitation programs; and supervises admission to practice for certain professions and occupations.

State University of New York
Encompasses sixty-four campuses statewide, including university centers, health science centers, colleges of arts and sciences, agricultural and technical colleges, and locally sponsored community colleges.

AGENCIES PROVIDING SPECIALIZED SERVICES TO THE PUBLIC
These agencies provide specialized services to populations with acute service needs. The aging, veterans, the unemployed, the handicapped, and persons addicted to drugs and/or alcohol all receive attention through these agencies.

Department of Labor
Charged with improving working conditions, protecting the safety and health of public employees and certain other workers; ensures compliance with minimum wage laws; and administers a statewide employment service, unemployment insurance, disability benefits and workers' compensation.

Department of Social Services
Supervises and regulates federally or state mandated welfare and health programs administered at the local level to serve people in economic need;

promulgates regulations to assure proper public assistance and care, administers State programs, and enforces related laws and regulations.

Division of Substance Abuse Services
Responsible for planning, developing, administering, regulating and funding over 400 substance abuse programs statewide; also conducts research, promotes public awareness of the substance abuse problem, and monitors trends in abuse.

Division of Veterans' Affairs
Assists and advises veterans on services, benefits, preferences and entitlements, and administers payment of bonuses and annuities to blind veterans.

Office of Vocational Rehabilitation (Education Department)
Develops individualized plans for handicapped individuals (except the legally blind) who have vocational objectives; contracts with the appropriate service provider; and provides placement and follow-up services.

Office for the Aging
Administers activities under the federal Older Americans Act, Community Services for the Elderly Program, Nutrition Assistance Programs for the Elderly, expanded In-Home Services for the Elderly and other programs; also recommends programs and policies affecting the elderly to the Governor.

DIRECT CARE AND CLIENT SERVICES
These services provide state residents who suffer from long- or short-term debilitating illnesses with rehabilitation or recovery programs while conducting medical research and developing state-of-the-art treatment approaches.

Office of Mental Health
Develops plans and programs, provides services in the areas of prevention, care, research, treatment, education and training of the mentally ill.

Office of Mental Retardation and Developmental Disabilities
Develops plans and programs, provides services in the areas of prevention, care, research, treatment, rehabilitation, education and training of the mentally retarded and developmentally disabled.

Helen Hayes Hospital (Health Department)
Provides complete treatment for adults and children suffering from disabling orthopedic and related defects or handicaps, with emphasis on maximizing the functional rehabilitation of patients.

Roswell Park Memorial Institute (Health Department)
Conducts clinical and laboratory research on the causes, mortality, prevention, and treatment of cancer.

New York State School for the Blind at Batavia (Education Department)
Enrolls legally blind children from kindergarten to age 21.

Health Science Centers at Brooklyn, Stony Brook and Syracuse (SUNY)

Each includes a medical school and a teaching and research hospital which serves the communities of Brooklyn, Stony Brook and Syracuse, respectively.

SUPPORT OR INFRASTRUCTURE AGENCIES

Together, these agencies ensure that the work of New York State government is done as efficiently as possible and that agencies have the human and financial resources they require.

Department of Taxation and Finance

Administers the State's tax laws and the treasury; responsible for collecting most of the State's revenues and for issuing regulations to clarify tax requirements.

Division of the Budget

Assists the Governor with formulation of the Executive Budget by examining and revising agency budget requests; it also assists with budget implementation and in investigating, supervising and coordinating the fiscal operations of State agencies.

Department of Civil Service

Acts as the central personnel agency for State agencies; assures adherence to the "merit and fitness" standard of employment; adopts rules pertaining to civil service matters; provides local civil service commissions with technical assistance; and hears and determines appeals relating to personnel issues.

Office of Employee Relations

Coordinates and directs the State's implementation of the Public Employees' Fair Employment Act, and serves as the agent of the Governor to conduct collective negotiations with the public sector unions; also assures adherence to the negotiated agreements; responsible for development and implementation of all programs for management/confidential (non-unionized) employees.

Office of the State Comptroller

Maintains the State's accounts; pays the State's payrolls and bills; invests the funds of the State; audits State agencies and local governments; and administers the State's Social Security and Employee Retirement agencies within the Office.

Office of General Services

Provides support services for State agencies, including centralized purchasing, data processing, construction, maintenance, design and protection of State buildings, printing, transportation and communication systems.

The Policy Making Process

The making and enactment of public policy can be a complex and protracted process. It may include any or all of the following: problem identification, data gathering, public hearings, demonstrations by constituent groups, draft legislation in both houses of the Legislature, budget hearings, legislative hearings, compromise legislation, media involvement, federal and local level involvement, enactment of legislation, securing funds and staff for implementation, competitive bidding, and, finally, implementation. Depending on the nature of the issue, implementation may begin quickly, or it may be phased in over a number of years. As circumstances change or unanticipated problems result from the policy, adjustments must be made or new policy developed, and the policy making process begins again. At any stage an interested party may litigate the entire issue or a particular element of it in the courts. While this cumbersome process may seem absurd to those who don't participate, it is nevertheless one that is open and allows for input from virtually everyone affected by a public policy decision. If it is cumbersome, that is in part because it represents the very essence of a democratic society.

In critical situations, however, government can and does move swiftly. For example, in response to the New York City fiscal crisis of 1975–77, all of the elements of New York State government moved together quickly to deal with a potentially disastrous economic situation. The Love Canal land pollution episode was brought to light by residents who alerted local officials to chemical odors in their house basements. The Governor's Office mobilized several State agencies (primarily the Department of Health and the Department of Environmental Conservation) to conduct testing and research on the community impact of land pollution from buried chemical wastes. The Legislature and local governments involved worked together with State agencies to eliminate the immediate health hazards posed by that situation.

But, generally, public policy decisions aren't measured by how quickly they're enacted. Instead, they are evaluated on their equity and on their long-lasting impact on society. The debate and controversy that surround public policy matters are of immeasurable value because they force decision makers to examine the most minute aspects of their decisions, and to anticipate their impact on the citizens of the State.

Conclusion

This *Guide* focuses primarily on State government processes in the support or infrastructure agencies in areas such as budgeting, personnel, and internal controls, functions that provide support to the main work of government—the delivery of services to the citizens of the State of New York. The information in this book should be helpful in understanding how government in New York State works, how decisions are reached, and how change is accomplished.

APPENDIX I*
Places and People

The following list of places and people represent only a fraction of the State's resources and only a handful of the thousands of native New Yorkers who have distinguished themselves in their respective fields of endeavor.

Structures

Statue of Liberty
Brooklyn Bridge
Empire State Building
World Trade Center
Yankee Stadium
Shea Stadium
Rockefeller Center

St. Lawrence Seaway
Madison Square Garden
Nelson A. Rockefeller Empire
    State Plaza
State Capitol
Fort Ticonderoga

Places

Ellis Island
Saratoga Springs
Broadway
Wall Street
The Adirondacks
The Hudson River
Lake Champlain/Lake George
The Thousands Islands
The Finger Lakes—Wine Country
Cooperstown—Baseball Hall of Fame
Lake Placid—The Winter Olympic Village 1932/1980

The Hamptons
Long Island Sound
Central Park
The Bowery
The Catskills
Niagara Falls

Aphorisms

"O.K." refers to "Old Kinderhook" and was Martin Van Buren's
    campaign slogan
"Up the river" refers to Sing-Sing Prison
"The Great White Way" refers to Broadway
"The Big Apple" refers to New York

Cultural Centers and Institutions

Metropolitan Museum of Art
The Metropolitan Opera
Lincoln Center
Eastman House

Carnegie Hall
Munson-Williams-Proctor Institute
The Guggenheim Museum of Art
Albright-Knox Art Gallery

Industrialists

Vanderbilts
Whitneys

Rockefellers
Schuylers

---

*The appendix was compiled with the research assistance of Karen Knapp and Barry Ford.

15

Athletes

Jeffrey Blatnick
Kareem Abdul-Jabbar
Julius Irving
Vince Lombardi
Shirley Muldowney
Whitey Ford
Lou Gehrig
Sandy Koufax

Bruce Jenner
Kathy Horvath
Phil Rizzuto
Bob Cousy
Mike Tyson
Bob Beamon
Nancy Lieberman

Nobel Prize Winners

Theodore Roosevelt (1906)—Peace
Eugene O'Neil (1936)—Literature
Kenneth J. Arrow (1972)—Economics
Burton Richter (1976)—Physics
Hamilton Smith (1978)—Medicine

Inventors

George Steinmetz
Thomas Edison

George Eastman
Samuel Morse

New York Governors Who Became Presidents

Martin Van Buren
Grover Cleveland

Roosevelts (Theodore and
  Franklin)

Entertainers

Bernadette Peters
Barbra Streisand
Maureen Stapleton
Lena Horne
George Gershwin
Marvin Hamlisch
Kirk Douglas
Carole King
Zero Mostel

Jane Fonda
Fannie Brice
Gregory Hines
Eddie Murphy
Henry Fonda
Madonna
Diahann Carroll
Beverly Sills
Harry Belafonte

Authors

Herman Melville
William Kennedy
Washington Irving
Eugene O'Neill
James Fenimore Cooper
Toni Morrison
Neil Simon
Toni Bambara

Walt Whitman
Henry James
Margaret Mead
James Baldwin
Pearl S. Buck
Alex Haley
Richard Wright

Chapter II

The Governor's Office

The Governor's Office, variously referred to as the Executive Chamber, "the Chamber," or "the second floor," is the engine behind the process of state policy formation. The second floor at the Capitol is the meeting ground where the multitude of players who affect State policy discuss, compromise, weigh, fight over, create, and reject program ideas.

The Governor, unquestionably the most critical single decision-maker in State government, gives the Office a particular personal leadership and management style. Although there are some structural characteristics that span administrations, it is difficult to describe a "generic administration," for the routes of access to the Chamber and the dynamics of the policy formation process differ significantly, depending on the incumbent. In any administration, the many competing interests in the State must be weighed in order to develop a package of programs (the Governor's program) that the Governor will include in the annual State-of-the-State message. Having an agency-proposed bill included in the Governor's program means that the Governor is publicly committed to it and considers it a State priority.

To understand the process of policy development for the Governor's annual State-of-the-State message, a description of the current structure of the Executive Chamber and the functions of the various offices within it is useful. The idea that the Governor's staff should be specialized in order to best manage the many agencies began under Governor Averell Harriman in the mid-1950s. Today, the Chamber includes the Program Office, the Office of the Counsel, the Press Office, the Appointments Office, the Office of Contract Compliance and Minority-and Women-Owned Business Enterprises, the Office of Hispanic Affairs, the Advisory Committee for Black Affairs, the Office of Management and Productivity, the Division for Women, and the New York State Office in Washington. (The Scheduling Office and the Office of Executive Services handle internal Chamber activities and are not considered here.)

Who does what within the Chamber depends a great deal on the Governor's philosophy and style of governing. As one Cuomo staff member remarked, "This is not a hierarchical office—the Governor will call us directly if he needs a question answered that falls within our area of expertise." Governor Carey's administration, in contrast, was more hierarchical and provided few points of access to the chief executive.

The Lieutenant Governor in New York State has limited constitutional and statutory duties and therefore is available to take on responsibilities as the Governor assigns them. Constitutionally, the Lieutenant Governor assumes the position of Governor if the latter dies, resigns, is impeached, convicted and removed from office, is absent from the State, or is disabled (NYS Constitution, Art. IV, Sec. 5). The constitution also designates the Lieutenant Governor as the President of the Senate. As such, he or she may cast a vote in case of a tie—but only when the vote concerns legislative procedure. Additionally, as President of the Senate, the Lieutenant Governor has the authority to convene a joint session of the Legislature to elect members of the Board of Regents if both houses cannot agree (Education Law, Sec. 202). Other laws provide for the Lieutenant Governor's membership on specified committees, councils, and the like.

Historically, the Lieutenant Governor and the Governor have not always had a close working relationship, in part because the gubernatorial candidate does not necessarily select a running mate. Rather, the nominee for Lieutenant Governor may be selected by a primary election before running on a joint ballot with the nominee for Governor. The joint election of Governor and Lieutenant Governor ensures that the two are of the same party, but it does not guarantee either political or personal compatibility. As former Lieutenant Governor (under Nelson Rockefeller) and Governor, Malcolm Wilson expressed it, a "feeling of total trust and confidence . . . is required to make the Lieutenant Governor an effective day to day working partner of the Governor" (Legislative Committee on Economy and Efficiency in Government, *Annual Report, 1984–85*, p. 286).

When the Governor and Lieutenant Governor work well together as a team, the latter may serve as a valued adviser and participant in activities concerning the Executive Budget and the Governor's legislative program. The Lieutenant Governor's office can also serve as an important communication link between the administration,

19

interest groups, and localities. Depending on the incumbent's particular experience and interests, he or she may take an active role in a particular area (or a number of them). An incumbent with a strong legislative background may assist in developing and shaping the administration's legislative proposals; one with local government experience may take on responsibilities in shaping state-local relations.

In short, the particular role of the Lieutenant Governor is largely fashioned by the Governor and the working relationship established between the two is therefore subject to change with each set of incumbents.

Perhaps the most influential nonelected position in the Chamber is that of Secretary to the Governor, who coordinates the activities of all of the Chamber offices and plays an important role in policy development and executive relations with the Legislature. The Secretary also serves as "gatekeeper" to the Governor, helping to avoid situations where the Governor is overwhelmed by dozens of concerns that might have been handled at a lower level. The particular nature of the Secretary's interaction with the Governor is largely a function of the personalities holding each position.

The Program and Counsel's Offices

The Program Office, under the direction of the Director of State Operations and Policy Management, acts as liaison between the agencies and the Chamber. The Office is organized into units that include Education, the Arts and Local Government, Health and Human Services, and Energy and the Environment. In some areas, one person is responsible for both the agency and policy recommendations to the Governor (Economic Development, Housing, and Criminal Justice). The larger units are headed by deputy secretaries or assistant secretaries, and the smaller ones by program associates. Unit heads act as staff advisers to the Governor, and year round provide ideas and collect materials for the Governor's program. Many proposals arise from agency contacts and interest groups; others may be developed because of personal interest in a particular topic.

Generally, program associates report to the assistant secretaries and are assigned to maintain continual contact with particular agencies. One associate described the job as having four major components:
  o agency work (keeping abreast of agency problems and issues);
  o transmission of the Governor's priorities to the agencies;

○ negotiation with the Division of the Budget (DOB) in the concurrent development of the Governor's program and the Executive Budget;

○ special assignments involving single issues.

The Director of State Operations and Policy Management also coordinates the activities of the various subcabinet groups (discussed below) and of a variety of consultative groups and task forces. Under Governor Cuomo, the Director of State Operations plays a key role in developing the Governor's program and the State-of-the-State message and in presenting broad programmatic ideas for the Governor's consideration.

The Counsel's Office is responsible for handling all legislation (including the drafting of the Governor's program bills) and for advising DOB about appropriation bills. This office also responds to legal questions posed by the Governor, reviews all bills passed by the Legislature before the Governor signs them into law (or decides not to sign), assists agency counsels, and handles clemencies and extraditions. It is a central point for coordinating legal opinions. Within the Office, eight assistant counsels are responsible for different subject areas.

The staff in the Counsel's Office work closely with other offices in the Chamber on policy decisions. For example, the Office circulates agency bill proposals for comment, and it is then involved in evaluating the responses and making decisions. The Office often takes an active role in the development of the Governor's program.

The Press Office

The Press Office serves as an important link between the Executive Chamber and the public. "That office makes sure that our message gets out and that we're able to respond" (program associate). When reporters call the Press Office with questions on specific policies, programs or plans, the office often contacts the appropriate person elsewhere in the Chamber, and that person either may relay the answer through the Press Office or may return the reporter's call directly. In addition, the Press Office is responsible for casting the administration's activities so as to maximize public support; it is also concerned with timing of the release of stories.

Contact between the Agencies and the Chamber

There are two formal processes that facilitate communication between the agencies and the Chamber. These are the development of annual agency legislative packages and the submittal of agency monthly reports. To initiate the first of these processes, a letter is sent from the Chamber stating when a complete list of departmental proposals is to be submitted to the Chamber. In 1987, the date fell in mid-October. In early November, drafts of legislative proposals and supplementary memoranda were to be submitted, and by mid-December, introductory drafts of all departmental bills were due. During this period (October-December), the Chamber is involved in analyzing, collecting opinions on, and giving feedback to the agencies about their proposals. As part of this process, the Counsel's Office circulates the proposals to any agency that might have an interest in them for consideration or comment. In this way, bills are cross-reviewed and examined by officials with different interests and backgrounds; it is hoped that any potential problems with the bill are noted at this stage. "The purpose is for the agencies to voice their concerns at this stage—we let them know that it is OK to be critical," said one source in the Chamber.

During this process, many program ideas are eliminated and the remaining ones are negotiated and changed so that there is no duplication or crossing of tracks. "When agencies are formulating bills, we have to make sure that these bills support, or at least don't work counter to the Governor's priorities," said one source. Through this system, consensus can be reached so that when the agencies submit their departmental bills to the Legislature, the Executive Branch speaks with one voice. "Ultimately it comes back to the Governor to sign anyway. We try to iron out the problems at this early stage."

The Program Office also gets involved in crisis management in agencies when issues "blow up." Clearly, as Chief Executive, the Governor is concerned and implicated in the press when crises occur. "We do on occasion get involved in internal matters" said one Program Office source, "but only to track events and gather information, or to help resolve an issue. After all, the Governor is the boss, and he needs to know what's going on."

Another formal, structured contact that agencies have with the Chamber comes in the form of agency monthly reports, a management system that Governor Cuomo initiated. Each week, one quarter of the agencies submit monthly reports to the Chamber. These reports are read in full by the program associates, and then condensed for review by the Governor. This process is one of the ways that program associates keep up on what is occurring in the various program areas and stay in touch with agency goals and objectives.

"If I have questions about an agency's report, I'll go in and ask them about it," said one program assistant. If the Governor has any questions on the summary, he will go to the specialists in that area who should know the answer, or know how to get an answer quickly.

One commissioner described these reports as beneficial to the agency as well as to the Governor. Monthly, they force the agency to step back and identify the activities most important to it at that point in time. Besides keeping the Governor updated on agency priorities, the reports may alert the Governor to potential problems.

Agency contact with the Chamber usually involves the top level of agency personnel, most often commissioners and their deputies. Aside from the monthly report, agency heads are in contact with Program Office personnel regarding problems and issues, as well as generally educating them on agency activities. "When action occurs, for example, a newspaper story, I know the Governor is going to call me on it—I want to know that the commissioner is on top of it and what he or she is doing about it," said one source. "There is a constant demand on the agencies to let us know what's going on even if we won't like it," said another representative from the Program Office.

The formal monthly reports and continual contact whether regarding proposed agency bills or publicized agency activities are important because they ensure a communication link between the agencies and the Chamber.

To facilitate communication within the Chamber, Governor Cuomo holds a weekly meeting with 20 senior staff members. These meetings provide a forum for open debate on the most critical issues facing the State and how they might best be handled.

The Appointments Office

The Appointments Office is responsible for appointing qualified individuals to agency positions that are exempt from civil service classification, as well as to paid and volunteer boards and commissions throughout the state. The Office receives applications from a variety of sources. Under Governor Cuomo, particular attention has been given to working toward the administration's affirmative action goals. Extensive outreach is done to implement the Governor's Executive Order No. 6 for both jobs and membership on boards and commissions.

Agencies are asked to notify the Appointments Office when exempt positions become available. The skills and qualifications of applicants are then matched with those required for particular positions in the agencies that need to be filled. The Office refers candidates to the agencies for consideration. Agencies then contact the applicants for an interview and follow up with the Appointments Office regarding the outcome of the interview process.

Under Civil Service Law the State Education Department, Office of the State Comptroller and the Department of Law also have

PAYNE

exempt positions. However, since the heads of these agencies are not appointed by the Governor, the Appointments Office does not make referrals to them.

Office of Contract Compliance and Minority- and Women-Owned Business Enterprises

To further the current administration's affirmative action goals, this office was established in 1983 to encourage agencies to increase contracting with qualified minority- and women-owned businesses in construction and procurement, within the State's overall contracting procedures guidelines. As such, the Office works closely with offices established for similar purposes in the Office of General Services and the Department of Economic Development. (Additional detail will be found in the chapter on purchasing and contracting.)

The Office of Hispanic Affairs

Created by Executive Order in 1986, the Office serves as a liaison between the Executive Branch of State government and the Hispanic community in the State. It advises on issues that directly affect the Hispanic community, including education, social services, immigration, and recruitment into the State's workforce.

Advisory Committee for Black Affairs

This Committee researches the needs of New York's black population and advises the Governor on issues, proposed policies and programs, and services provided by state agencies for the black community. It also develops awareness programs to assist the black community in identifying and participating in State-sponsored programs.

The Office of Management and Productivity

Private sector organizations have a strong incentive to manage as efficiently as possible; if one firm manages better than others in the same business, it will profit at the others' expense. Because government does not have the same kind of competition, other mechanisms must be created to keep the cost of governing as low as possible while ensuring high-quality services. In 1983, Governor Cuomo established the Office of Management and Productivity (OMP) within the Executive Chamber with this as its mission.

The Office differs from other State organizations charged with increasing efficiency in that it serves as a consulting organization, working with agency staff on both agency- and Office-initiated projects. The Governor's Advisory Council on Management and Productivity, a group of private sector and academic executives, has input into the projects. The Director of the Budget and Director of State Operations and Policy Management also review the projects. With State agency cooperation, OMP has saved State government $270 million over the past three years.

One focus of the Office is on agency support services, including paperwork management, printing, mailing, transportation and supply operations. For example, in conjunction with the Office of Business Permits and Regulatory Assistance, the Office has thus far eliminated 3,568 forms and simplified 622 others as part of the Governor's Forms Simplification/Reduction Project (1986 OMP Annual Report). Other recent projects include:

- coordination of the Governor's Productivity Awards Program;
- development of improved management controls over the Office of General Services' fleet of 6200 passenger vehicles (in cooperation with OGS and DOB);
- improvement of agency mailing operations, including applications of technologies such as electronic mail;
- refinancing of 120 State leases (together with DOB), which resulted in lower interest costs;

25

o improvement of statewide agency internal control systems, through an educational effort and guidance in developing an organized approach to control; and

o implementation of the Improved Printing Management Project.

The Office has also helped develop major improvements in management practices, service provision, and technology applications within State agencies. The brief descriptions of many statewide improvements, found in its Annual Reports, provide a refreshing change from the governmental inefficiencies that are more often publicized.

The Division for Women

Created by Executive Order, the Division advises the Governor on all matters relating to women and is charged with reviewing and monitoring proposed legislation, State policies, procedures, practices, and programs regarding their impact on women. Its major responsibility is to bring women's concerns and needs to the attention of State government. The Division also serves to inform women of State programs that are of direct interest to them.

New York State Office in Washington

The NYS Office in Washington provides a key link between the State and federal governments. Its staff (currently nine full-time employees in addition to the Director, who is appointed by the Governor) is divided by subject area, and works as an advocate for the State's interests, both by lobbying Congress and by interpreting Congressional actions to the Executive Chamber and to the agencies. The staff frequently correspond on policy issues through memos and phone calls to the Program and Counsel's Offices, as well as directly to executive agencies. Further discussion of this office is found in the chapter, "State Government in an Intergovernmental Setting."

DOB's Relationship to the Chamber

Although not officially part of the Chamber, DOB, through its responsibility for developing the Executive Budget, plays a significant role in policy development. The extent to which the process of development of the Executive Budget and the Governor's program are integrated depends on the administration, although there has been a trend since the Rockefeller governorship (when the two processes were quite isolated) to bring the two processes closer together. Robert Morgado, Secretary to Governor Carey, stated in the recently published *Making Experience Count,*

> . . . I brought the first floor up to the second floor. That was difficult. I made the Budget Division part of the central policy process, a participant in the executive process. I forced them to understand the political judgments as well as the financial judgments in ways that they were not previously prepared to do.

Although the two offices have worked more closely in recent administrations, due to the backgrounds of the respective staffs and the nature of the two offices, DOB and the Program Office often don't see eye to eye. There is a built-in healthy tension due to the differing responsibilities of the two offices.

Although DOB and the Program Office are both directly accountable to and work within the framework of the Governor's priorities, when the same idea is filtered through the budget process and the Chamber, different conclusions can be reached. The strength of the system lies in the method of resolving such disagreements. "I have to ensure that there are enough resources available to properly execute the Governor's program," said one source. "I may go and fight over a point for one of my agencies [with people at DOB]." Part of the dilemma lies in the fact that both organizations see themselves as representing the Governor but, due to the nature of their roles, they necessarily approach issues differently. When disagreements occur, staff from the two offices meet and negotiate to try to reconcile their different positions on issues. The mixing of the ideas from both offices provides a much broader examination of the issues than either could provide alone. Through this exchange, many of the initial disagreements are solved at the staff level. Problems that remain may then be discussed at higher levels, and the final level of review is a meeting with the Governor. DOB also develops programmatic ideas of its own, and introduces these to the Chamber.

DOB works with the Counsel's Office on occasion in drafting the appropriation bills to implement the Executive Budget, but the extent of contact varies depending on the nature of the issue. To the extent that the appropriation bills involve amending substantive legislation which the Chamber is interested in, DOB would work in conjunction with the Counsel's Office. In other words, if the particular appropriation bill is implementing something that is part of the Governor's program, or which arose through the Program Office or the subcabinet process, such as a new criminal justice initiative, DOB would work directly with the Chamber, whereas in routine matters that came about through the budget process, they may not.

Players From the Agencies

The extent to which agencies are brought into the policy process depends on the governor. Governor Cuomo has sought, through the subcabinet process (discussed below), to involve agencies more directly than did his immediate predecessors. In general, access to the Chamber depends to a considerable extent on personalities and political style, as well as establishing good working relationships with those within the Chamber.

The role the Commissioners play in policy formulation is a function of the structure of the particular administration. The Rockefeller administration, for example, had a very strong Program Office, and much policy development stemmed from that office rather than through the agencies. Under Carey, on the other hand, the Program Office had a more limited role, and the agencies played a larger role in policy development within their particular area of responsibility.

Clearly, the impact that commissioners and their agencies can have is dependent on the management style of the incumbent. However, due to the nature of their role as agency heads, commissioners in any administration may have substantial influence. They often have large constituencies, and can muster significant political support for particular programs. They may also have easy access to the press, and to the Legislature, ranging from the formal legislative hearings on programs to informal ties, typically with members of the appropriate standing committees. The skill of using these forces to the advantage of the particular agency, while still being seen as working within the Governor's priorities—as a "team player"—is a difficult line to walk. "Don't box in the Governor; leave him room to make decisions," urged one top-level source.

The Process of Policy Formation

It has been noted that what makes public sector management so hard—and so interesting—is that the players act simultaneously, with few clear lines of authority, constantly changing public mandates, and frequent turnover of people: not an easy environment in which to operate. Potentially, there are a multitude of ways to gain access to the decision-making process—the key lies in familiarity with the structure and people within the administration.

A direct and institutionalized manner of access to the Chamber occurs through the budget process. Of course, agencies can solicit ideas for programs from as broad a base as they see fit, and they can use the advice of constituency or advisory groups in their development. When placed in an agency's budget request, a new program is scrutinized and analyzed through the extensive budget review process. In this process, examiners make objective studies of the program, but policy decisions, such as the initiation of a program, are pushed up to be made by gubernatorial appointees within the Division or by Chamber staff. By including a new program in their budget request, agencies force policy choices either to proceed with the program in some form, or to cut it.

Very often, if agencies are proposing a major new initiative in their budget request, they will concurrently work through other links within the Chamber to foster support for the program. Commissioners often have different levels of concurrent communication. "Never rely solely on the monthly reports as a reporting mechanism," said one cabinet member. "It is important that you touch the right bases—you can't count on straight authority lines. Other levels under the Governor must be apprised so that when the Governor initiates discussion" his advisors will be familiar with your side of the story. Within the Chamber, these agency representatives may speak with anyone from program associate up to the Governor. "Many of the agency heads in my areas deal directly with me, while others have developed relationships with the Director of State Operations and Policy Management, or the Governor," said one program associate. This source noted that agency heads who deal with higher-level officials also keep him current on agency issues.

Another route of access is through political visibility. Whether through the press, lobbying activities, or constituency pressure, highly visible ideas will certainly attract the attention of the Program Office. If legislative support for such a program seems strong, the idea may be left to the Legislature rather than incorporated into the Governor's budget. Whether this is the case, or whether the Governor decides to incorporate the initiative into the budget or State-of-the-State message often depends on political considerations.

One important process leading to executive decisions is the system of subcabinets. (While the Governor does meet periodically with his cabinet, composed of all agency heads, this group is much too large to consider specific substantive issues frequently.) The subcabinet process, therefore, is one which is used in analyzing major, interdisciplinary issues, although the issues are generally not as broad in scope as those considered at senior staff meetings. One source said that he particularly values such "roundtable discussions" as a technique to refine complex ideas.

The four substantive areas of subcabinet groups under Cuomo are Criminal Justice, Economic Development, Energy and the Environment, and Health and Human services. These subcabinet groups consist of agency experts in the particular substantive area, as well as DOB staff. Many commissioners serve on more than one group. Subcabinet meetings are designed to elicit technical input from experts, and then weigh and discuss the alternatives in the light of political considerations. Top-level civil servants often take part in the meetings to provide additional subject matter expertise.

During the process, people with conflicting views are brought together and a forum is provided in which discussion on the differences can be addressed. This system "forces an interdisciplinary view," said one source. In getting adverse groups together, you may not reach agreement, but "the process lends itself to a greater sense of consensus," when the various groups taking part are obliged to see other sides of an issue. "It makes you step back and look at the larger perspective rather than just day-to-day crisis management," said one subcabinet member. Although commissioners may send representatives when the meetings are expected to be non-critical, the need to be present increases in the fall, as the subcabinet groups meet to consider major bills proposed in the agencies' legislative packages. Beginning in mid-October, the subcabinet groups meet about once a week.

In sum, although the centralized process of shaping the state's major policy initiatives occurs within the Chamber, the process does not take place in a vacuum. Through the need for political sensitivity, the day-to-day contact that the various offices within the Chamber have with the public and the agencies, and through the broad solicitation of opinions that occurs through the subcabinet system, there are many routes of access to the decision-making process. The key to using these routes of access is building and maintaining relationships of mutual trust with people internal to the Chamber, so that access is timed to coincide with the decision-making process. One senior staff member commented on the potential difficulties for an agency that deals with a diverse number of issues, but is not seen as the major agency in the particular area. "It is a challenge under these circumstances for them to get their views on the table at the point when the decision is being made."

Additionally, although major initiatives are often introduced through the Governor's program, agency submittal of departmental bills to the Legislature provides a much less centralized method of policy formation. "To some extent, the agencies are involved in policy formation, and the Chamber is involved in agency internal management issues, and so there is a mixing of roles," said one source in the Chamber.

The Chamber and The Legislature

Shortly after giving the State-of-the-State address, the Governor submits to the Legislature a package of programs. The course of budget and Governor's program negotiations vary greatly depending on the state of Executive/Legislative relations under the incumbent. Under Carey, for example, the two institutions tended to be adversaries, sometimes leading to missed April 1 deadlines, as well as overrides of gubernatorial vetoes. Under Governor Cuomo, a much better rapport has developed between the two bodies.

One source in the Chamber stated that in the process of developing the Governor's program, there is a factor of anticipated reaction: since the Governor's program can only become a reality if passed by the Legislature, probable legislative reaction to programs is considered throughout the process. "We are constantly reaching out and building grass roots support for program ideas," for the whole process hinges on a sensitivity as to what will fly in the Legislature.

Other sources in the Chamber stressed the informal processes of communication during the negotiation phase: "Communication is the lifeblood of the whole process: it's all part of broadening your information base to foster greater sensitivity [to legislative priorities]," said one Chamber source. "Hopefully, you know their values and priorities and you've laid the groundwork" by the time the Governor's program is introduced, said another source.

After the Governor's State-of-the-State message, the legislative leaders set out their own priorities for the coming year. During the course of the session, legislative fiscal committees analyze the proposed Executive Budget and the bills submitted to implement the Governor's program. In March, negotiations between the two parties over the Executive Budget begin in earnest as the April 1 deadline approaches. The Governor frequently seeks to have key people in the Legislature, such as leaders and committee chairpersons, sponsor the program bills.

Partisan politics does play a role when the budget and the Governor's programs are being considered. For example, Democratic Governor Cuomo is currently working with a Democratic controlled Assembly and a Republican controlled Senate (as did Governor Carey for most of his two terms). Under these circumstances, the Chamber may work more closely with the Assembly on certain issues, but ultimately all three agents must agree since all bills must be passed by both houses and approved by the Governor. Governor's program bills typically have a higher success rate in gaining legislative approval than do other bills. (These issues are discussed in greater detail in the chapter on agency-legislative relations.)

Chapter III

The Executive Budget Process

In the weeks before April first, the beginning of the new fiscal year, the budget process becomes a headline item, with stories of legislative squabbles and tense compromises splashed throughout the media. But this is only a glimpse of the budget process. In New York State, budgeting is an ongoing process, rather than one with distinct starting and ending points, and budget development and execution occur simultaneously. There is a flurry of activity during the period between mid-September, when agencies submit their budget requests to the Division of the Budget (DOB), and the passage of the budget in early April, but this is only part of the cycle. Year round, the agency and DOB are executing the current budget and are concerned about future spending. Taken as a whole, the budget process is an institutionalized mechanism for making priority decisions regarding resource allocations statewide.

The budget process begins with the State's financial plan, which is the premise for the whole state budget.

Financial planning occurs throughout the year, but there are a few key events in the annual development of the financial plan. By the end of October, the expenditure estimation and control section of DOB's fiscal planning unit has prepared a base level budget that reflects the cost of projecting the current year's programs into the next year. This includes accounting for inflation, probable salary increases, annualizing new programs, and cutting out single-time expenditures for these new programs. Actual budget examiner participation in this process occurs during October.

Simultaneously, the revenue estimation and tax policy section of the unit is working on revenue projections for the next year to estimate the available resources. At this early stage, information about federal resources to be disbursed to the State and about revenues that are sensitive to economic conditions (such as sales tax receipts) cannot be calculated accurately; these factors are figured in as estimates and revised as updated information becomes available.

These two projections, the estimated disbursements and available revenues, form the basis of the financial plan that is used in the development of the preparation of the Executive Budget. The plan is developed assuming enactment of the appropriation bills drafted to implement the Executive Budget.

When the Executive Budget is submitted to the Legislature, both the budget items, and the financial plan itself are subject to negotiation. Most often, the Legislature argues that the Division's revenue projections are too low. This pattern is understandable for two reasons. First, the Governor has a constitutional responsibility to submit a balanced budget, and so the Division (which prepares the Executive Budget with the Governor's participation and approval) must be cautious and guard against an overestimation of revenues. Second, it is to the Legislature's advantage to find additional revenues, because they can be used to add programs.

Although the Legislature and the Governor do not agree on exact figures, they negotiate the plan until the estimates are not too far afield, and each side considers the other's projection reasonable. The Comptroller has been involved in reviewing the financial plan since 1976, but it is only in the last several years that the Governor has requested the Comptroller to report publicly on the plan. A stamp of approval by the Comptroller lends credibility to the Governor's estimates. In 1986, for example, the Comptroller reported that the revenues were underestimated by one percent, a small amount in percentage terms, but a rather large one when translated into dollars.

The financial plan is formally updated in April, and another update in July is statutorily required. By that point, much more accurate information on Federal grants and the overall economic climate is available.

Budget Formulation—The Agencies

Once the financial plan estimates have been formulated, the process of centralized planning of expenditures can begin; however, decentralized budget planning in the agencies may begin long before this plan is completed. In the formulation phase of the Governor's budget, attention is focused on the final steps that involve decisions made by DOB and the Governor. Much of the substance of budget formulation is done at the agency level.

In developing budget requests, agencies must attempt to reconcile many conflicting program interests with the reality of limited resources. Conflicting demands of constituent and public groups are weighed against internal agency and gubernatorial priorities. Commissioners, on the one hand, are appointees, and as such, they must support and work within the Governor's framework. At the same time, they have responsibility for carrying out their agency's statutory mandates and for serving the agency's constituencies. Developing an agency budget request involves considering these several aspects, as well as the dynamics of the budgeting and program development processes themselves.

Agencies are fundamentally oriented toward expenditure. As experts in their particular areas, agency officials are acutely aware of the needs in their field. However, the budget process, to some extent, is driven by revenues. The Executive Budget process forces the agencies to be aware of both sides of the coin.

By the early summer issuance of the DOB call letter, many agencies are already well into the budget development process. This letter sets out the guidelines for agency requests based on the financial plan, the overall economic climate of the State, and gubernatorial expectations. On this basis, agencies begin to finalize their requests. The call letter also sets the date when agency requests are due at DOB; in recent years that date has been in mid-September.

For the past several years, call letters have asked for maintenance of base level spending (adjusted for salary increases and inflation); proposed new spending was to be offset by a cut elsewhere in the agency's activities or by revenue increases. Agency budget requests often ask for more than is specified in the call letter "but not more than we need in order to meet statutory mandates," stated one agency manager.

Each agency has its own system for drawing out and evaluating ideas for programmatic initiatives. Some agencies solicit input from a broad base of agency personnel; others limit involvement in the process to the managerial level. In either case, there are bound to be differing opinions about priorities, so that the matter of choosing among these within the agency can be stormy. Once the proponents of the programs have had a chance to defend their ideas, a top management team headed by the Commissioner makes the final decisions as to what to include in the requests.

Form of Agency Requests

The Division of the Budget issues a Budget Request Manual, as well as forms to be filled out by agencies in preparing budget requests. The forms solicit statistical tabulations and projections, narrative statements on policy objectives, and a listing, in priority order, of new projects. The agency is also asked to provide a separate listing of projects that could be cut to offset the costs of new ones and to specify the cash receipts for each fund, any changes in fees charged, and any projected changes in the number of clients.

The objective of this extensive financial and statistical reporting is to provide DOB with an overall picture of the agency's financial needs so that it can, in the context of developing a balanced budget, support the funding necessary for the agency to carry out its mission.

One budget examiner noted that agencies are sometimes reluctant to adhere to the request guidelines. They often hesitate to set out agency priorities explicitly for fear of inadvertently supplying a "hit list" of projects for DOB to cut. Also, the agency may not want to lay out its priorities because of internal disagreements. "If they know DOB will cut a program request anyway, why would commissioners want to take the heat?" asked one examiner.

After agency submission of requests, some agencies provide a full briefing for the examiners on issues, priorities and choices, discussing the inherent trade-offs. After this, budget examiners are often in daily contact with "their" agencies, checking numbers in the budget and clarifying program needs. Agency personnel should be prepared to respond promptly to DOB inquiries; competent and timely response fosters an agency's image of credibility. When it receives the requests, DOB must cut and shape them so that the aggregate expenditures can be covered by the State's revenues.

Before considering specifically how the final Executive Budget is developed, a word about the general nature of the process is in order. The budget itself is much more than simply a fiscal document. Far from being formulated in a bureaucratic environment, the budget evolves in a political arena and reflects the influence of diverse groups of players. Even before negotiation and compromise with the Legislature begins, the Governor must weigh against his own priorities the (often conflicting) advice of his program and counsel offices, other key advisers, the agencies themselves, and DOB.

From the agency perspective, fiscal restrictions often seem to hinder the agency's ability to carry out mandates, but these restrictions are not imposed frivolously. Agencies are concerned with specific program areas, whereas the Governor is concerned more broadly with proposing a budget that balances agency expenditures and state revenues (mainly taxes) in a politically acceptable way. The fact that the agencies are held accountable to a popularly elected official ensures at least indirect agency accountability to the people of the State.

In sum, the Division limits agency freedom to spend. However, within these restrictions, agency managers have a good deal of discretion and flexibility. They have the opportunity to develop programs creatively, to play a role in policy formulation and to support program implementation actively. The many checks that administrators face, then, are not merely red tape or bureaucratic creations. They are also the key to ensuring executive branch accountability to the people.

Agencies are the source of program expertise within the system. An agency that is doing its job performs the bulk of the work in designing programs within a particular area, as this is not one of DOB's primary roles. The interaction between Budget and an agency evolves as the two organizations work together. The Division may play an almost insignificant role in shaping policy direction in an agency that has strong and effective leadership, but step further into the process in another agency that has proven to be less effective. Budget examiners respect achievers. "They may be willing to give you a little more money in this very finite world when they know the job will get done," declared one manager.

Budget Formulation: DOB's Role

At the heart of the executive budget system is the Governor's constitutional responsibility to submit to the Legislature a balanced plan of disbursements and anticipated receipts and to prepare appropriation bills to carry these into effect. As part of its legal responsibilities, the Division reviews all executive agency requests for expenditures and prepares the budget document and appropriation bills for legislative approval. "It all boils down to choices among worthwhile alternatives," said one examiner. "We tell the Governor the implications of these choices." The Legislature and Judiciary each prepare its own budget and these are added to the Governor's budget untouched, although the Governor may comment on them.

Although the processes of budget development and the development of the Governor's program were quite separate in former years, within the past decade the two have become more meshed. While open discussions involving all three entities—DOB, Governor's Program Office, and agency—do not take place, each communicates with the other two. For example, an agency head might work simultaneously with the Division and with the Program Office. The Program Office and DOB might also discuss the initiative between themselves. In general, the tone and frequency of communications between the players is set by the Governor.

The exhaustive review and justification of all requests forced by the executive budget process is not meant to screen out the good ideas, but occasionally this is unavoidable because of the balanced

3.1 Division of the Budget

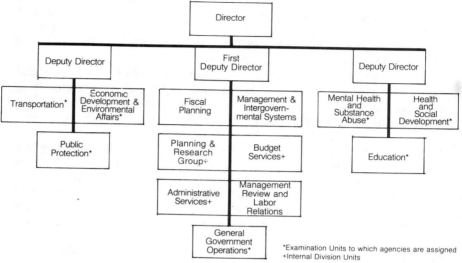

*Examination Units to which agencies are assigned
+Internal Division Units

budget requirement. Intensive review before a program is added to an agency budget is necessary because once entered in the budget, the program usually remains part of the base budget in subsequent years and is continued with much less scrutiny by DOB than that given new programs. The effectiveness of individual agency internal program evaluation operations varies widely. In some agencies, the program evaluation units are quite independent and influence the budget development process considerably; in others, "program evaluation" calls may be dictated largely by political considerations. In theory, cutting back on programs of low effectiveness could free up funds for departmental initiatives. However, there is no comprehensive system in the State for evaluating programs. Also, client groups' expectations of certain services make them politically difficult to eliminate. The tension between the demands of the agencies to meet their perceived program needs on the one hand and the Division's responsibility to balance state expenditures and revenues on the other, mandates creativity, compromise, and cooperation.

The Division of the Budget is organized in units to which related clusters of agencies are assigned (see Chart 3.1). For example, the Health and Social Development Unit is responsible for the Departments of Social Services, Health, and Labor, the Division for Youth, the Office for the Aging, the Council on Children and Families, and the Division of Human Rights.

Of the approximately 250 professionals who work in DOB, eight to ten are exempt employees, who serve at the pleasure of the Governor. These are the director, whose appointment is not subject to senatorial confirmation, three or four deputy directors, and their secretaries. The remaining staff are civil servants selected and promoted through the examination process.

A look at the distinction between the roles of civil servants and those of exempt employees sheds some light on the various roles that the Division itself plays. In simplified terms, civil servants can be described as the objective information gatherers and analysts, examining agency requests from the standpoint of need and efficiency; exempt employees are the decisionmakers, evaluating the basic information supplied by the examination units and making priority decisions. However, such a brief description does not provide the whole picture. DOB functions as a single unit, and in the course of day to day interaction, the roles of the two types of employees become less distinct. High-ranking civil servants, valued for their long years of experience, may be trusted advisers to the appointees and thus play a substantial role in policy making. Additionally, these high level civil servants act as a link between the two groups and work to sensitize the examiners to the policies and priorities of the Governor. This may affect the examiners' perceptions of their roles. In short, the policy-making/policy-implementation dichotomy is not clear cut.

In dealing with the Division, managers need to have some feeling for DOB's sense of itself. The organizational climate of the Division is quite different from that of other agencies. Traditionally, Budget has had a reputation as an elite organization within state government. Many high-level state managers began their career as civil servants in the Division—in a sense, it is seen as the training ground for developing a mind set about responsible fiscal management and high standards of professionalism. The civil servants, or "career professionals," and the long-standing systems for budget analysis are highly respected within the Division itself. Some high level managers in other agencies, realizing this, consider their relationships with high ranking civil servants in DOB as important as relationships with (exempt) appointees.

Another important characteristic of DOB is its particular relationship to the Governor. Although it is not specifically within the Executive Chamber, the Division plays an important role in shaping State policy. DOB's expertise in the State's fiscal position gives it a unique perspective in working with the Governor's Office in the policy making process.

One of the first steps in the development of the Executive Budget is the decision made by the Governor and the Director of the Division of the Budget as to which of the agencies should have a formal hearing. In recent years, only twenty or fewer of the largest agencies or those with unusual problems have had formal hearings scheduled. At these hearings, the commissioners make presentations to the assembled representatives of Division of the Budget, the Governor's Office (program associates and members of the Governor's Counsel's Office), as well as the secretary and chair and staff personnel of the two legislative fiscal committees. Both major political parties are represented. During the past two decades these formal hearings have come to provide mainly an informational overview. One budget examiner described them as "marketing sessions."

The nuts and bolts of the budget review process in fact begins with the examiners. They start with two basic tools, the guidelines that grew out of the financial plan and a base level estimate. The latter is a projection of cost for the department to run the same programs in the upcoming year. For example, it may reflect projected increases or decreases in the number of clients in a particular program, or the program may be affected disproportionately by inflation—as was the Home Energy Assistance Program (HEAP) during the years of increasing oil prices—or the revenues from particular agency fees may be expected to change.

On the basis of these two estimates, the examiner gains a sense of the resources available to cover the necessary expenditures. If there is either a surplus of money or a deficit due to decreased revenues or increased costs, this sets the tone for the review process.

Shortly after agency submission of requests to DOB, the budget examiner or examiners for that agency meet informally and privately with agency fiscal and program officers to discuss the requests. Examiners look at such issues as:

- Is there really a need for the proposed new program?
- If so, would it be best handled in that particular department or in another one?
- Is the suggested organizational structure the best option?
- Are the workload indicators (estimating the amount of staff needed) realistic?
- Are the stated goals likely to be reached?

In looking at these and other questions, the examiner's role is to make objective, well-supported judgments that can be satisfactorily explained to the top-level decision makers at DOB. The examiner does not have the authority to decide, for example, to cut a program. Rather, the examiner studies the issues and makes recommendations at internal meetings. Generally, an examiner's

3.2 Executive Budget Process
Phase I — Agency Budget Preparation

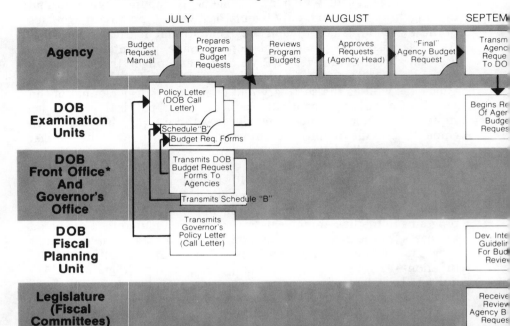

NOTE: Legislative special/supplementary sessions that consider budget bills and budget management after the budget has become law have not been included here.

*DOB Front Office includes the Director, First Deputy and Deputy Directors of the Division

☐ Action Step
☐ Document

recommendation is given substantial weight when the decisions are being made.

"Budget making" sessions behind closed doors follow the hearings. These are the decision-making sessions at which examiners are expected to explain, justify, and defend their budget recommendations to the unit head, deputy director, and director. In one sense, the examiners have a vested interest in being good advocates for their agencies, for to some extent they are evaluated by their agencies' success. Examiners like to look good, too, and there is some intertwining of the perceived credibility of the agency and the examiner. Over time, examiners become specialists in each of their agency's issues, but they are not expected to have a mastery of the State's entire financial position or of the Governor's confi-

Phase II — Division of Budget Review

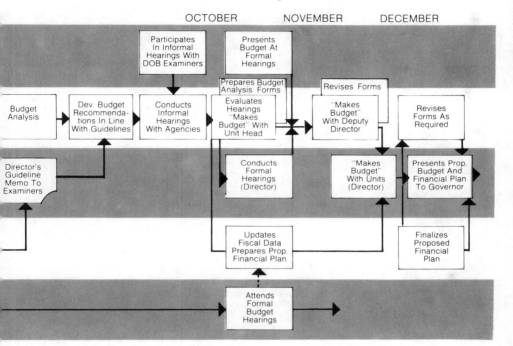

dential priorities planned for the upcoming year. At the end of the DOB process, the director makes recommendations to the Governor. "At each level, a different perspective is put on programs. By the time it gets to the Governor, the product is a very refined, sophisticated thing that reflects gubernatorial priorities," said one DOB examiner.

The course of broad policy decisions, directed by the Governor, is developed simultaneously with the budget. In recent administrations, communication between staff members working on the Governor's legislative program and those working on the budget is continuous until the two processes fall into lock step by the time of the Governor's State-of-the-State message in early January.

Each unit at DOB knows the guidelines that apply to "its" agencies and, assuming there has been stability in staff, it also

Phase III — Governor's Decision

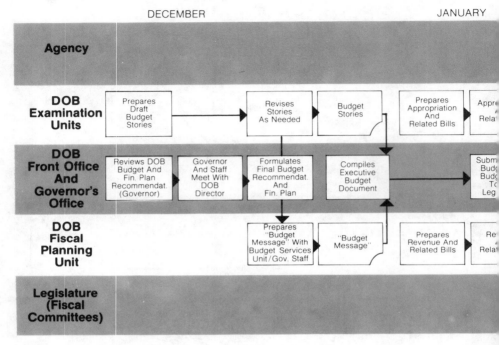

knows the agency and its track record in budget requests. The agency's history of budget requests—whether it is known for writing a tight set of requests or for extravagance—is one factor taken into account by the budget examiner. There is a "Catch 22" here as pointed out by Aaron Wildavsky in his *The Politics of the Budgetary Process*: "Whether it is disposed to pad or not, the agency finds that it must take into account the prospect of cuts, and the cycle begins again as these prophesies confirm themselves." One examiner recalls an exception to this pattern, a former Department of Transportation (DOT) Commissioner who had come in with a budget that followed the call letter guidelines very closely. His requests did include some increases, but these were justified extensively and were offset by other cuts. Some DOT managers felt that submitting a budget which followed the guidelines was a tactical error—that, rather, the more requested, the better. During the review process, it became evident that the budget was sound, and DOT got everything it asked for. "I pointed out to the director that it was worthwhile for him to support it (DOT's budget request) because it adhered so closely to

Phase IV — Legislative Action

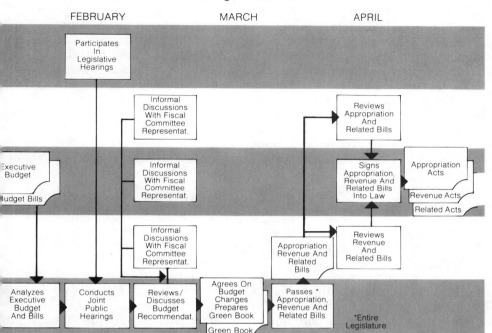

the guidelines," stated the examiner. The latter went on to say that although there may have been a time back in Governor Rockefeller's day when more money was available, and one could make requests above and beyond the call letter's guidelines, "now it just causes resentment at DOB because money is tight and there is no room for phoney justifications."

Continual agency contact with DOB throughout the year is vital to the budget process. In order to "hit the ground running" when the requests come in, examiners have to have a working knowledge of agency issues. To make a good case within DOB for an agency program, the examiner must understand program needs thoroughly, and the prudent agency continually strives to educate examiners on current and upcoming issues. Later in the process, the examiner may be asked to suggest cuts from a particular agency's budget. The better educated and attuned the examiners are, the better the agency's needs will be served. During the hearings between the agency and its budget team, the examiner plays the role of an adversary, scrutinizing all requests and looking for ways to cut the requests so that they conform to the guidelines. Later in the process, however, the examiner becomes an advocate for the agency, representing it and justifying its requests in DOB internal discussions.

Budget examiners have authority to recommend approval of agency requests to spend beyond call letter guidelines, but the burden of proof is on the examiner. Guidelines are drafted according to the limits of State funds. If extra expenditures are granted in a year when the call letter asks for maintenance of base level spending, the additional funding has to come from somewhere—either from another agency the examiner works with or from equally deserving agencies assigned to other examining units.

The agency process for developing requests is effective when the need for a program is foreseen and plans are developed over a period of time, but there are many situations in which planned program development is impossible. Emergencies may require unforeseen expenditures of an agency. For example, Environmental Conservation may have to deal with an unexpected environmental disaster, or the Department of Health may have a fast breaking problem, such as the AIDS epidemic was, initially.

There are many ways for an agency to fund unforeseen expenditures. The Division of the Budget may approve transfers of money from other programs (within specified statutory limits) or the Legislature may appropriate additional money. If the Legislature has appropriated money for a special emergency fund, it may be allocated to other funds subject to the conditions of Section 53 of the State Finance Law, but this money may not be used for activities the Legislature has determined should not be performed. Depending upon the fund receiving the money, the allocation may be subject to approval by certain legislative leaders. "If the Governor asks you to do something, do it, and worry about the finances later," advised one agency manager.

With the budget proposal that goes to the Governor for his consideration in late December goes a list of significant items that have not been recommended by the Division of the Budget. The Governor may choose to reinstate some of these items before approving the budget for submission to the Legislature. The final document as produced is known as the Governor's Budget or, more formally, the New York State Executive Budget, for it is, in fact, the Governor who ultimately decides on every item in the Executive Budget.

A Case Study In Budgeting

When all else fails, old fashioned determination is sometimes the best route for managers working in the budgeting process. When new programs are proposed, it may take several years to sell them to the extent needed to obtain funding.

One manager from the Department of Labor was successful in using a different tactic to obtain funding for a program. As a result of a 1981 study of the working conditions in the garment industry, the Labor Department wanted to establish positions for inspectors to enforce the laws dealing with sweatshops. The Department believed such a program would be very effective in eliminating or reducing sweatshops in the New York City area. The mere existence of a "strike force" would be a deterrent to such establishments. Because, at the time, there were no inspectors available for this purpose, sweatshop operators had no fear of being caught. The proposal for new inspectors was supported by the unions, so it was a politically feasible issue. For three consecutive years the Department requested funds for the program, but each year the request was deleted from the Governor's budget due to "hold the line" budget requirements coupled with other priorities of the Governor.

Included in the Governor's budget, however, were thirteen positions under the Occupational Safety and Health Program for which State funds were no longer required since the Department had secured federal funds to support a larger public safety program and federal dollars to support these thirteen positions. Shortly after the Governor presented his budget, the Department was approached by the Division of the Budget as to the Department's priorities for these positions. The Department placed highest priority on the use of eight of these positions to staff a Garment Industry Enforcement Unit. The Division of the Budget approved the Department's plan for allocating the positions for that purpose. The Legislature concurred and funding for the unit was continued in FY 1986–87. Four of the other five positions were allocated to other program areas.

Through close cooperation between the Department of Labor and the Division of the Budget, the Department finally received funding for the Enforcement Unit as well as for several other positions. All thirteen positions could have been eliminated by the Division of the Budget before the Governor submitted the budget. Rather than eliminate these dollars, the Division of the Budget saw fit to redirect them to identified areas of concern to the Department.

Passing the Budget: The Legislative Role

The Governor has a constitutional responsibility to submit the Executive Budget, including recommended appropriation bills to the Legislature on or before the second Tuesday following the first day of the annual meeting of the Legislature, or before the first of February in the year following gubernatorial elections. The Legislature may not consider any other appropriation bills until it has reviewed all the Governor's bills, unless the Governor issues a statement of necessity. The Governor can amend or add to any of the appropriation bills within thirty days of submitting the budget to the Legislature as long as budget balance is maintained, or with the consent of the Legislature any time thereafter. Such amendments by the Governor (with the requisite trade-offs demanded by the Legislature), may be contained in a supplemental budget.

Several months before submission of the Governor's budget, DOB sends the Senate Finance Committee and the Assembly Ways and Means Committee (the two fiscal committees) copies of the original agency budget requests. Staff members from these two committees attend the formal hearings that DOB conducts with selected agencies, and they carry out their own analyses of agency requests. The Legislature cannot act on agency requests, however, but must await submission of the Governor's budget. The budget consideration period in New York is shorter than in any other state or the federal government. The Legislature has from eight to ten weeks to analyze and vote on all items in the Executive Budget, including gubernatorial initiatives which are first unveiled to the Legislature at the State-of-the-State message.

Aside from acting on bills submitted by the Governor, legislative leaders announce their own priorities after the Governor's message and seek to have these programs included in the budget. Also, the Legislature includes some "member items," programs that are geographically and/or recipient specific, and that are identified as helpful to particular legislators.

Informal discussions between the Executive Chamber and the Legislature take place throughout the year so that each is aware of the other's priorities, at least in a broad way. For example, in working with DOB in the development of the Executive Budget, the Chamber may choose not to include a particular program it sees as important but not of top priority. This may occur if it has a sense that the issue is a legislative priority, and will be added by the Legislature anyway. On the other hand, in the case of particularly noteworthy new program ideas that may attract the public's attention and become political assets to their creators, both the Chamber and the Legislature sometimes keep major initiatives secret prior to public announcement.

Constitutionally, the Legislature has the power to eliminate or reduce any line (with budget items and amounts) of the Executive Budget. It can also add lines to the budget. However, any amount of money added by the Legislature for a program included in the Governor's budget and any new program added must be inserted in a separate line each with a single object or purpose. Each addition (but not eliminations or reductions) is subject to a gubernatorial veto. Vetoes can be overridden only by a two-thirds vote of both houses.

The Governor and the Legislature often have very different priorities but, due to the Governor's veto power and the Legislature's power to eliminate items from the Governor's proposed budget, the two have an interest in working together to facilitate the budget process. Of course, with each post-election Legislature and administration, the flavor of legislative-executive relations can change dramatically, with important consequences for the task of budget passage.

By law, the budget must be passed by April 1, the beginning of the fiscal year (although this deadline is sometimes missed). Theoretically, no money can be spent after March 31 until the budget is passed unless it was allocated and encumbered during the preceding fiscal year. But there is a practical deadline for passing the budget: Spring borrowing must be undertaken so that school aid payments can be made by June—the end of the school fiscal year. Although informal communication between DOB and the Legislature occurs throughout the year, March is generally the most active month for interactions between the two organizations. Occasionally, agreement on some issues is worked out before March, but as one source said, "People are hesitant to go forward with one piece of the puzzle without knowing how the other pieces will fit together—you can lose leverage that way." Within each house of the Legislature, a consensus building process is used to establish the will of the majority. The majority leaders have substantial influence in the process, but because the leaders themselves are elected by the members every two years, they must be responsive to members' priorities. The two houses of the Legislature usually come to some agreement before starting budget negotiations with the Governor.

As time grows short and compromises are necessary in order to get the budget through both houses, the Governor and the majority leader of each house get together and fashion the broad policy directions. After broad agreement is reached, the Director of DOB (working as the Governor's representative), the Secretary of the Assembly Ways and Means Committee (acting as the Assembly speaker's representative) and the Secretary of the Senate Finance Committee (acting as the Senate majority leader's representative) meet to work out the specifics. Party dynamics can also affect budget negotiations. For example, a Democratic governor may deal differently with a Democratic-controlled Assembly than with a Republican-controlled Senate.

Constitutionally, the budget that the Governor proposes to the Legislature must be balanced on a cash basis, but nowhere in the

PAYNE

Constitution is it explicitly stated that the budget passed by the Legislature or executed by DOB and the agencies must be balanced. As a practical matter, however, the Legislature generally stays close to a balanced budget in the interest of maintaining the State's credit rating.

In April, the Governor's item vetoes of legislative add-ons are released. No action by the Governor is required for the budget bills that he submitted earlier to become law, if there have been no changes, but customarily the Governor does sign such bills.

At this point, attention shifts back to the Division of the Budget. The appropriation amounts approved by the Legislature represent the maximum that can be spent for the stated purpose. The state finance law specifies that "The several amounts appropriated in any act shall be deemed to be only for so much thereof as shall be sufficient to accomplish in full the purposes designated by the appropriations . . ." (Article 4, Section 42). Of course, the question of what is needed to live up to legislative intent can be a controversial one.

The Division of the Budget is responsible for monitoring budget execution and insuring that the monies are spent in accord with legislative intent. None of the appropriated money except for line item appropriations can be spent until DOB allocates it, unless an appropriation is expressed in terms of a formula. Through this mechanism, the Division maintains control over agency spending.

Budget Execution

Shortly after passage of the budget, DOB requests a spending plan from each agency outlining how it plans to operate within its budget. The purpose of vesting this authority in DOB is to insure that agency execution of programs is in line with legislative intent. In this examination of the spending plan, DOB must work within restrictions established in the State Finance Law regarding agency spending. For example, money cannot be taken from the program to which it was allocated and spent on another program without the approval of the Director of DOB, who must follow legal guidelines.

In most cases, DOB's review of the spending plan and issuance of certificates is routine. For well-managed agencies with predictable spending patterns, review of the spending plan is an opportunity to keep DOB up to date on agency fiscal planning. In instances where agencies spend erratically from year to year depending on the problems they need to address, or if their revenues are provided by sources other than state money (such as, fees or federal funding), problems may arise after the budget is passed. For example, if an agency expected to receive $5 million in federal money for a particular program and only receives $2.5 million, it may have to work closely with Budget to plan adjustments so that it can continue to conduct the underfunded program.

In addition to the main budget, supplemental and deficiency budgets may be passed later in the fiscal year. Deficiency appropriations can be provided for programs that are running short of funds due to unforeseen developments, but they are not designed to provide another opportunity for the agencies to make a pitch for more money. One DOB examiner stated that, on occasion, agencies have come to the Division just a few months after the budget was passed, looking for substantial deficiency appropriations. "There is a difference between a legitimate need for a deficiency appropriation, and a fundamental lack of respect for the laws, the Legislature, and the Governor."

The amount of detail about implementation and legislative intent provided in any particular bill varies. As appropriation bills are drafted, legislative fiscal committees also put together a summary of the proposed legislation. This compilation, generally referred to as "The Green Book," is an additional resource used to clarify legislative intent. DOB is legally bound by the appropriation bill rather than the Green Book, but the latter is considered an important source nonetheless.

Upon DOB approval of agency spending plans, the Division issues certificates of approval that allocate money to the agencies and to other entities named in the appropriation bills. These certificates confirm that funds are available for the specific purpose stated; copies are sent to the Office of the State Comptroller for spending authorization and to Legislative fiscal committees. These certificates are an important control mechanism because no money for state operations can be disbursed without them.

The Division of the Budget develops various systems for monitoring agencies as they go about the business of executing the budget. For example, DOB may initially allocate one-fourth of the money that the Legislature appropriated to one agency, while initially allocating all the money that the Legislature appropriated to another agency. The former would then have to go back to Budget after the first quarter for another allocation, since the Comptroller cannot disburse any money without a certificate. In exercising this authority, Budget is playing a key role in insuring accountability. However, the fewer sign-offs an agency needs from Budget, the more expediently it can administer programs. The extent of control that Budget exercises over an agency is, to some extent, a reflection of the Division's perception of the agency's capabilities.

Although DOB does have the authority to allocate less for certain programs than was appropriated, this power is limited and was recently tested in the case, County of Oneida vs. Berle [398 NY Supp 2d. 600, 91 Misc 2d. 694; 411 NY Supp 2d. 884; 427 NY Supp 2d. 407, 49 NY 2d. 515]. In this instance, the Court of Appeals ruled that the Governor cannot refuse to make an expenditure mandated by law in an effort to maintain a balanced financial plan. Mandated expenditures include local assistance appropriations (see Chapter IX), which are allocated according to statutorily established formulas. The Division of the Budget cannot touch the legislative or judicial budget, nor can it refuse to allocate money for debt service or construction in progress. Since over sixty percent of the state budget is used for assistance to local governments, when legislative, judicial, capital and debt-service appropriations are taken into account, DOB's flexibility is substantially restricted. Cuts necessary to maintain a balanced budget fall upon the operating (State Purposes) budget, magnifying the impact on state agencies.

One DOB examiner stated that, in recent years, the practice of allocating an amount less than appropriated has become less common. The Legislature and DOB have to work together each year in the budget process. If Budget were routinely to allocate less than the amount appropriated, this would create unnecessary tensions between it and the Legislature, making everyone's job more difficult. The flexibility that results from the power to allocate less than the full appropriation enables the Division to keep the books balanced even in instances where revenue projections were too high. The basic purpose of the full appropriation must be achieved, however.

Another circumstance in which DOB may not allocate all the appropriated funds shortly after the passage of the budget is when an agency has received a "Maintenance Undistributed" appropriation. In New York State's budgeting system, all money for state purposes that is to be drawn from the General Fund falls into one of three categories: Personal Service (salaries, benefits), Non-Personal Service (contract services, equipment, supplies), and Maintenance Undistributed. Maintenance Undistributed funds are appropriated when the needs of a particular program are unclear and it is not certain whether the money will be needed for personal service or for nonpersonal service. The money appropriated for Maintenance Undistributed cannot be made available until defined under one of the other two categories through the allocation/segregation process. Agencies sometimes request the Maintenance Undistributed device to facilitate the start-up of a new program within their budget requests.

Other DOB delays may occur when the Legislature adds programs. Funds for these add-ons frequently take longer to allocate, in part because the Division must start anew in developing the expenditure plan and in part because the add-ons are often poorly defined.

The GAAP Accounting System

In 1981, the State changed its accounting system and adopted Generally Accepted Accounting Principles (GAAP), which have been incorporated into the State Finance Law. Under GAAP, accounting is done on an accrual rather than a cash basis. Before the implementation of this system, receipts and disbursements could be pushed forward or back into other accounting periods so that the State's nominal financial position was frequently misleading. For example, the State could delay issuing tax refund checks until after April 1 so that the money would still be in its treasury at the beginning of the new fiscal year, making its financial position look deceptively strong. Governor Hugh Carey referred to this in his so-called "wine and roses" State-of-the-State speech in 1975:

> The last budget of the previous administration was balanced only in the most technical sense: by deferring into the first budget of this administration, hundreds of millions of dollars of expenditures that have been made, but not paid for.

Under the new system, expenditures and revenues are accounted for as incurred, so that the figures provide a more accurate picture of the State's current financial position.

The GAAP system also changed the way the budget is reported. The new fund structure set up under GAAP provides more detail about how money is spent, permitting greater accountability than was previously possible. (For a summary of the GAAP fund structure, see Appendix I at the end of this chapter.)

The projected revenues shown in the annual budget take into account all monies that will flow into the State's coffers during the entire fiscal year. However, New York pays many of its obligations near the start of the fiscal year. For example, it expends a substantial amount of money to school districts between April and June (which is the end of the school fiscal year). Recent changes in the payment plan for pensions allow a reduction in the amount of money the State must borrow in the spring. In the 1985–86 fiscal year, twenty-three percent of the State's receipts were collected during the April–June period, while forty-one percent of its disbursements were made during the same period.

State Oversight of Nonstate Funds

All monies that are paid from the State's coffers must be appropriated by the Legislature, regardless of source. Thus, agencies that receive most of their funds from the federal government, or from fees to service users, are subject to the same oversight by the Division of the Budget as those agencies that receive only tax revenues. Thus, the State Energy Office (which raises every cent of its budget through user fees) and the Department of Labor (which receives most of its money from the federal government) are held as accountable to the Division of the Budget as are other agencies.

Capital Budgeting—State Finance

Requests for capital projects, which may include building construction, rehabilitation of facilities, or major purchase items such as an agency-wide computer system are written directly in the agency's budget proposal. The examination unit reviews the project from a programmatic perspective, but once it is decided that a project should be undertaken and financed, the particulars are handled by the capital planning and finance unit at DOB.

The theory behind financing is that future generations of taxpayers will reap the benefits of the project, so there is no reason to meet all the costs in a single year. Several general types of bonds (see Appendix II to this chapter for additional information) are used to finance these projects, including:

1. **General Obligation Bonds.** These are backed by the full faith and credit of the State. The Comptroller can disburse money for debt service on these bonds with the first revenues received by the State, without a legislative appropriation. In other words, the bond pledges the taxing powers of the State, and thus is a safe investment, allowing the State to borrow money at a relatively low interest rate. Before a general obligation bond can be issued, an authorization bill must be passed by the Legislature, and then a statewide referendum held. Constitutionally, no general obligation bond can be issued without being approved by a majority vote of the electorate. Due to the difficulties of getting a referendum passed, general obligation bonds are used only occasionally.

2. **Revenue Bonds.** There are many types of revenue bonds, but all share some common characteristics. When sellers go to the market with bonds, prospective buyers naturally are interested in knowing the revenue source to be used for debt service. There is not the insured revenue stream of tax dollars behind revenue bonds that backs general obligation bonds; instead, money from an identified revenue stream is pledged, and bond holders have rights to that money. For example, the State Dormitory Authority pledged dormitory room rent revenues for debt service, while the State Thruway Authority pledged toll revenues. In this way, payment is tied directly to usage.

The state itself cannot issue revenue bonds without a referendum. Public authorities such as the Dormitory Authority, the Thruway Authority, and the Housing Finance Authority can issue bonds if they have legislative authorization to do so.

The Dynamics of Dealing with DOB

"Dealing with DOB is more of an art than a science" (senior agency official).

Although some managers feel mystified and frustrated by certain aspects of the budget process, most agree that there are useful tactics for reaching a better working relationship with the Division. Managers stress that dealing with the Division in an honest and straightforward manner is crucial. As one budget examiner put it, "Nothing angers control agencies more than an agency trying to slip something by them." Gamesmanship doesn't work in the long run because credibility inevitably suffers. Managers who have a reputation for successfully overcoming obstacles and achieving stated program goals are more likely to be taken seriously by Budget than those who do not.

The success of the budget request process is partially a function of relationships between the agency and the budget examiners. The agency must rely on the examiners to explain and represent its interests within the Division. When one side isn't listening or responding, or has a hidden agenda, the relationship suffers.

One source of frustration for many people working in the system arises from the perception that budget examiners have extensive (or even excessive) influence over the final budget document. Meyer S. (Sandy) Frucher, former director of the Governor's Office of Employee Relations, expressed this frustration in an interview for *Making Experience Count* (p. 154): "This is the DOB. You think you're the commissioner. Wrong! The budget examiners are the commissioners."

Another manager expressed similar frustration: "If someone is there [at DOB], they are important. They may not be able to help you, but they can hurt you. They can kill a program with a wave of their head or some body language."

Although these statements do not characterize the typical role of examiners, there are cases where the latter do lose objectivity and act beyond their scope of responsibilities. In general, the examiner's role is much more that of an information gatherer and objective analyst than a judge. Also, examiners in different units go about their jobs differently, depending on the unit director.

Technically, an agency need not be informed about how its requests are faring in the review process but, in practice, agencies often have at least some sense of where projects stand. For example, an agency can gauge an examiner's support for a project by the questions asked at informal hearings. A program's survival chances are probably better if the examiner requests information to substantiate it ("give me something to work with"), rather than questioning the program itself.

Contact between the Division and the agency can occur on many different levels. Agency fiscal officers and program personnel may work with examiners while commissioners or their deputies may concurrently be conferring with their counterparts at the Division. The most effective point of contact may also differ depending on the nature of the issue. Agency commissioners and staff alike must be sensitive to the organizational operations of DOB when trying to determine the best approach. In all cases, managers stress that examiners be kept aware of any other contact the agency has with the Division so they do not get the sense that the agency is trying to bypass them.

Although other points of contact within DOB are important, working with the examiner often proves to be the most effective method. While examiners do not have the final say in budget decisions, their support will help as agency budget requests move through the process. Several agency managers suggested that it can be more productive to take the time to work with the examiner to win support instead of seeking to convince someone higher up in the DOB hierarchy. First, over a period of time of working with a particular agency, the examiner gains a familiarity with the subject area, becomes somewhat of an expert, and, therefore, may be the agency's best advocate within DOB. Further, if the agency has developed and maintained good rapport with its examiners, some problems may be handled informally.

Sometimes, though, agencies are not able to convince DOB that funding for a particular program should remain intact. When Governor Cuomo first took office, for instance, his budget included a substantial cut in funding for park rangers. Since the budget process does not force as much review and justification of programs that are dropped or reduced in size as of those that are added, the ranger program was cut and not considered again until the news media seized upon it when the Executive Budget was submitted to the Legislature. The Governor eventually chose to use the thirty day amendment period to restore funding for the rangers, at least in part because of the public outcry. "Everywhere I went that month, I think I was introduced to a forest ranger or a ranger's family," recalled Cuomo. In this case, ultimately the program was not cut, but the story illustrates the possible fate of a program that lacks an internal advocate (and is not subsequently publicized by the media).

One manager noted that in developing budget requests and working with examiners, it is important to state trade-offs explicitly. In other words, provide evidence to DOB that if a particular program is not implemented, some situation will still exist, and the State will need to deal with it in other ways. "Sometimes DOB is hesitant to spend money to save money. Your job is to explain what will happen if the program is not implemented."

From the agency perspective, one of the most frustrating aspects of the budget process is its secrecy and the fact that at the time when crucial decisions are being made, the agency is isolated from the process. As the date for submission of the Executive Budget and the State-of-the-State message draws closer, the Division is continually receiving updated revenue and expenditure estimates and information about the State's fiscal needs for the upcoming year. In light of the continually changing outlook, quick decisions must be made to keep the Governor's budget in balance, sometimes by making last minute cuts. This is where the examiner's insight into agency priorities and politics becomes crucial. If, during the last minute crunch, an examiner is informed that an agency budget must be reduced, he or she often has no time to involve the agency in discussions to determine which cuts will hurt the least. Rather, this decision is made within DOB. One agency manager stated that if included in the process at the crucial decision-making points, "most commissioners would be able to handle that trust without going to the press or fighting. They have the informal process of appeal to the Governor open to them, but generally they understand that sometimes you have to take cuts."

Agency contact with the Division and with the examiner should not end with budget season. Agencies should keep their examiners knowledgeable about activities, plans, and potential problems year round. In an effort to do this, some agencies make a point of involving examiners in their activities. For example, recently the Public Service Commission (PSC) took budget staff to Niagara Mohawk's Nine Mile Two nuclear power plant construction site when there was a question of mismanagement, and the PSC also invited budget staff to sit through a Niagara Mohawk rate-setting session. This can be useful because, in subsequent internal DOB discussions, the examiner can say, "We've seen this—these problems really do exist."

Issues that are brought to public attention by the press through constituencies or public action may provide instances for a commissioner to take an issue to the Governor. "If I didn't have an identified constituency, I'd have to create one," one commissioner was quoted as saying. The commissioner can use constituency pressure to tell the Governor that the agency is on the firing line, and that politically it would be wise to initiate a particular program. Alternatively, constituency and public priorities are sometimes different from agency ones, and these pressures can make life difficult for managers.

Another tactic that agencies use quietly is that of going directly to the Legislature to obtain funding for a program. In approaching the Legislature, agency managers often deal with staffers on those standing committees that interact with their agency. As noted earlier, the Legislature has the power to add lines to the Governor's appropriation bills (although these add-ons are subject to the Governor's veto). Here again, the agency's relationship with the Governor is important. Agencies with a close relationship to the Governor's Office do sometimes use this tactic, but "if we do, we're careful not to leave any footprints," said one manager. The more independent agencies may use this tactic more overtly.

In any event, it is crucial to keep the legislative staff members educated and informed on agency issues and problems. If this has been done effectively, the Legislature may approach the agency about a program between January and April, and the agency's role may turn into the much less controversial one of supplying technical information.

Finally, several managers mentioned the general utility of recruiting agency employees from the control agencies and from DOB in particular. The perspective of someone who knows DOB "from the inside" can be useful in budget preparation.

When the Governor's budget has been submitted to the Legislature, agencies are expected to fall in line and support the document. Even if some of their requests were slashed, appeals to the Legislature at this stage can be interpreted as treasonous. "After all, we're all in the Executive Branch together," stated one manager. However, in recent decades the Legislature has been more assertive in exercising its power to add lines to the Governor's appropriation bills. Legislators may be interested in certain programs for a variety of reasons: They may be trying to satisfy a particular constituency, or they may be interested in supporting a program that gives them greater visibility in their home districts. Whatever the motivation, legislators' programmatic goals are often at odds with the Governor's goals and DOB's priorities, and agencies have been known to use this fact to their advantage.

On the other hand, the Legislature may create programs that are not at all in line with agency priorities. In the last minute crush of passing the budget, the Legislature may pass programs that the agency didn't even know about until they had become law. "Sometimes these little programs pop up like mushrooms overnight—you never knew they would appear."

In such instances, keeping a broad perspective on the system can be useful. Legislators are elected representatives and, in responding to constituent demands, they may be filling gaps in areas where agencies are not meeting particular needs.

As one agency manager put it, "When the curtain is closed, be sure you have given it your best shot, but then fall in line. There's no sense in blaming the institutions."

APPENDIX I

Accounting Terms Related To Generally Accepted Accounting Principles (GAAP)

Generally Accepted Accounting Principles (GAAP) set forth uniform minimum standards and guidelines for financial accounting and reporting as promulgated by authoritative national standard-setting bodies, primarily the National Council on Governmental Accounting (NCGA), its successor, the Governmental Accounting Standards Board (GASB), and the American Institute of Certified Public Accountants (AICAP).

Accounting is the process of discovering, recording, classifying, and summarizing financial information to produce financial reports and provide internal controls. A governmental accounting system should make it possible to (a) present fairly and with full disclosure the financial positions and results of operations of the funds and account groups of the governmental unit; and (b) determine and demonstrate compliance with finance-related legal and contractual provisions.

Generally Accepted Accounting Principles require that government resources be accounted for in separate subentities, called funds, based upon the purposes for which they are to be spent and the means by which spending activities are controlled. GAAP emphasize reporting by fund type, rather than consolidated reporting for the government as a whole.

GAAP FUND STRUCTURE

Under GAAP, the State's money must be accounted for as either governmental, proprietary, or fiduciary funds.

Governmental funds class includes
The General Fund
   —state operations
   —local assistance
   —capital projects
Special Revenue Funds
Capital Projects Funds
Debt Service Funds

Proprietary Funds:
Enterprise Funds account for operations that are financed and conducted much like corresponding private enterprises (for example, the commissary in the Department of Correctional Services).

Internal Service Funds account for the financing of goods or services provided by one department or agency to another on a cost-reimbursable basis.

Fiduciary Funds account for money over which the State maintains custody, for example, the Common Retirement Fund.

In New York State an appropriation (from any State fund) must be classified into one of the following categories:

State Operations: This category relates to appropriations for the operation of State agencies regardless of fund source.

Aid to Localities: This category includes all appropriations for aid to localities, regardless of fund source.

Capital Projects: When used as a category, "Capital Projects" includes all appropriations for capital construction projects, regardless of fund source.

Debt Service: This category includes all appropriations for tax-financed State debt service on long-term debt, contractual obligation and lease purchase arrangements.

APPENDIX II

Budgeting Terminology

(Source: 1985–86 Executive Budget, but each annual Executive Budget document includes a useful glossary)

BUDGETS

Executive Budget: This term refers broadly to the structure and process of the constitutional system of budgeting in New York State, which vests most authority and responsibility for budget formation and execution in the Governor. More specifically, the term refers to the Governor's constitutionally mandated annual submission to the Legislature containing his recommended program, expressed in dollar terms, for the forthcoming fiscal year.

The annual submission is an overall plan of recommended appropriations, expenditures, and cash disbursements necessary to carry out the program, together with estimates of revenues and cash receipts expected to be available to support these expenditures and disbursements.

Amendments to the Budget: Under the constitution, the Governor may amend or supplement the Executive Budget within thirty calendar days after its submission or, with the consent of the legislature, at any time before the close of the session.

Supplemental Budget: Following negotiations between the Governor and legislative leaders, a legislative supplemental budget bill may be introduced that reflects, in part, the Governor's recommendations. As a multiple appropriation measure, it is subject to an **item veto** by the Governor.

Other Appropriation Measures: An appropriation bill may also be submitted throughout the regular legislative process. However, the Legislature must act upon the Governor's constitutionally mandated appropriation bills, also called budget bills unless the Governor certifies the need for immediate passage for another appropriation bill, pursuant to his constitutional authority to issue a "Message of Necessity." These appropriation measures are subject to veto by the Governor.

FINANCIAL PLAN

The Director of the Budget is statutorily mandated to act on behalf of the Governor in the exercise of certain of the Governor's constitutionally prescribed responsibilities. For each fiscal year the Division of the Budget prepares a financial plan that sets forth the Governor's projections of State revenues and expenditures, and of receipts and disbursements that would result from legislative adoption of the Executive Budget recommendations. Chapter 405, Laws of 1981, requires submission of a revised financial plan as soon as practicable after the Executive Budget is enacted. The plan is the basis for DOB's administration of the State's finances. Chapter 405 requires updates of the plan.

Until Fiscal Year 1981–82, the financial plan reflected only State General Fund activity. Under the fund reclassification initiated by Chapter 405, it has reflected the receipts and disbursements of all government funds. In 1984–85, the plan prepared in accordance with **Generally Accepted Accounting Principles** (see above) also became an official plan of the State.

MAIN BUDGET FUNDS (This section has been adapted from the Executive Budget, 1987–1988, pp. A 107–108).

General Fund: This is the major operating fund of the State. It receives all State income not earmarked for support of a particular program or activity and not specified by law to be deposited in another fund.

Local Assistance Account: This fund finances all the following:
- ○ State grants to, or State expenditures on behalf of, counties, cities, towns, villages, school districts, and other local entities;
- ○ certain contractual payments to localities;
- ○ certain advances for reimbursable costs (see **advances,** below); and
- ○ certain financial assistance to individuals and nonprofit organizations.

State Purposes Account: The State Purposes Account finances such items as:
- ○ salaries and nonwage compensation for most State employees;
- ○ other operating costs of State agencies, the Legislature and the Judiciary;
- ○ certain contractual payments (including some contractual payments to localities);
- ○ interest payments on tax and revenue anticipation notes (TRANs), bond anticipation notes (BANs), and BANs issued in the form of commercial paper.

The **General Fund** also includes revenues and expenditures of funds budgeted as internal service and enterprise funds and certain special revenue funds.

APPROPRIATIONS

Appropriations are authorizations, rather than mandates, to spend. Expenditures and disbursements from an appropriation need not—and generally do not—equal the amount of the appropriations since less than the full amount of the appropriation is usually spent within the fiscal year to which it pertains (see **carry-over,** below). An appropriation represents maximum spending authority unless a lower maximum has been set by an expenditure ceiling (see below).

In New York, all appropriations are classified as one of the four following types:
- ○ **State Operations,** which includes all appropriations for the operation of State agencies, regardless of fund source.
- ○ **Aid to Localities,** all appropriations for aid to localities, regardless of fund source.
- ○ **Capital Projects,** all appropriations for capital construction projects, regardless of fund source. It should not be confused with "Capital Projects" as a fund type, or with the Capital Projects Fund.

○ **Debt Service,** all appropriations for tax-financed State debt service on long-term debt, contractual obligation and lease purchase arrangements with several public authorities and municipalities, and lease-purchase payments for State University, health and mental hygiene facilities, and for highway construction, reconstruction, reconditioning, and preservation projects under contractual agreements with public authorities.

A **deficiency appropriation** is used to meet actual or anticipated obligations not foreseen when the annual and supplemental budgets were enacted and for which the costs would exceed available spending authorizations.

A **special emergency appropriation** may be allocated by the Governor to various funds. Allocations to the General Fund, the Capital Projects Fund, and funds receiving federal monies are subject to legislative approval.

An **advance** is a payment by the State on behalf of an agency, authority, fund, public benefit corporation, or the federal government that must be reimbursed by such entity.

A **lump-sum appropriation** is one made for personal services, for nonpersonal services, or as maintenance undistributed for all State agencies or to a designated agency for a stated purpose, without specifying the maximum amount that may be spent by such agency for specific activities or individual objects of expenditure.

CAPITAL FINANCING TERMS

Lease-purchase bonds are secured by a lease-purchase agreement between the State and a public authority or other governmental entity. These bonds have been used by the State Dormitory Authority and the City University of New York, for example, to finance dormitory construction. In such a case, the university makes periodic "rental" payments to the Authority, which owns the property from the time the bonds are issued until the debt is paid off. At that point, the university officially acquires the property.

Moral obligation bonds are secured by a statutory provision in the specific authority's enabling act that obligates the Governor to request the Legislature to restore any deficiencies in the fund supporting the bonds.

State contractual obligation bonds are those for which the State contracts with a public authority to make payments that can be used for authority debt service. State taxes are the source of funds used to pay the debt.

Certificates of participation (COPs) represent shares of lease-purchase payments for property made by agencies. These COPs, sold publicly or privately to investors, are a new financing instrument that became available in 1986.

OTHER USEFUL TERMS

A **carry-over** is the amount of an appropriation that is encumbered but not spent (and not repealed or reappropriated) at the close of the fiscal year for which it was appropriated. Expenditures may be made against such a balance only through the following September 15, to liquidate any outstanding obligation or commitment incurred against that appropriation during the preceding fiscal year.

An **encumbrance** provides a mechanism for reserving all or a portion of an appropriation for future expenditure. Entering into a contract generally requires an encumbrance, although the funds will be expended or disbursed over a period of several months. Encumbrance accounting provides management control to prevent spending in excess of authorized appropriations.

A **lapsed appropriation** is an appropriation that has expired and against which obligations can no longer be incurred.

An **obligation** is a commitment (such as a contract or purchase order) to spend against a given appropriation.

BUDGET EXECUTION AND CONTROL

Certificates are documents issued by the Director of the Budget that authorize various fiscal actions, depending upon the type of certificate. Copies of all certificates must, by law, be sent to the State Comptroller and the chairpersons of the two legislative fiscal committees.

A **certificate of approval** is an instrument issued by the Director of the Budget to indicate approval and authorization to an agency to make certain financial transactions.

An **expenditure ceiling** is a limitation placed on an agency by the Director of the Budget to indicate the maximum dollar amount of **expenditures** that the agency may make against its current-year appropriations from a given fund, subfund, or account.

Chapter IV

Human Resources Management

The Personnel System

In the United States, public service positions were filled by the spoils system prior to the Pendleton Act of 1883. Although the idea of a merit based civil service system had existed at least since the Han Dynasty in China, not until the assassination of President James A. Garfield by a political supporter who had not received a job after the elections did serious civil service reform occur in the U.S.

New York State followed the federal example and established its own merit personnel selection system later the same year with the adoption of Article 5 Section 6 of the New York State Constitution:

> Appointments and promotions in the civil service of the state and all civil divisions thereof, including cities and villages, shall be made according to merit and fitness to be ascertained, as far as practicable, by examination which, as far as practicable, shall be competitive.

Subsequently, a provision for additional credits in competitive exams to be assigned to veterans was included in the section. The vast majority of state service positions are now part of the civil service system.

In addition to the constitutional provisions, there are many laws that pertain to New York's civil service system. Most of the governing provisions are contained in the Civil Service Law. The Rules and Regulations of the State Civil Service Commission, Regulations of the President (of the Commission), Rules for the Classified Service, and an extensive body of court decisions implement the civil service law and provide procedures and other details for carrying out the principles expressed in the constitution and relevant laws.

Department of Civil Service

The Department of Civil Service recruits and tests applicants for the state workforce and examines candidates for promotion within state service. The Department is also the lead agency for affirmative action in state government, and approves and monitors affirmative action plans for all state agencies. The constitution specifies that the principles underlying the civil service system also apply to local governments. Accordingly, the Department provides examination, classification, and other services to the State's municipal civil service agencies. However, before a position can be filled, it must be both classified and allocated, which is the job of the Division of Classification and Compensation.

Division of Classification and Compensation

The Division of Classification and Compensation (C & C), part of the Department of Civil Service, is specifically provided for in the Civil Service Law. The Division is responsible for examining the duties and responsibilities of all positions in the State's *classified service* (see Appendix I to this Chapter for definitions) and for allocating all permanent competitive and noncompetitive class positions to one of the salary grades set forth in the salary schedules. Classification and Compensation also reviews positions. At the request of a state agency or an individual, C & C may classify and allocate a new position or reclassify and reallocate an existing one to a different title and/or salary grade. When an agency requests a classification or allocation action it should provide a complete and detailed description of the duties to be performed, including the proposed bargaining unit for the position, in the format prescribed in the State Personnel Management Manual. The personnel office of every agency has a current copy of this manual which gives specifics on all classification, reclassification, allocation, and reallocation procedures as well as instructions. It also includes copies of all forms needed in any of the procedures.

Position classification is the process of grouping similar jobs in order to implement the statutory provision of equal pay for equal work. The guiding principle is that jobs with "substantially similar" levels of responsibility, qualifications, and job duties should carry the same descriptive title and the same pay grade. This principle, which is applied across agencies and across the varied population of the classified workforce, limits managerial flexibility, because entry level salaries are specifically established, so that managers generally cannot offer extra incentives to attract particular people. There are mechanisms built into the law, though, which provide some leeway, including provisions that allow for offering salary incentives when there are recruitment difficulties, or when candidates with extraordinary qualifications present themselves.

In addition to the determination of proper title and salary, a new or reclassified position must also be assigned to one of the four jurisdictional classes: competitive, noncompetitive, labor, or exempt. Chart 4.1 illustrates this process. Note that each new or reclassified position is put into the competitive class unless a request is made to the Civil Service Commission to place it in one of the other three classes. The C & C determination must be approved by the Director of the Division of the Budget and the funding provided before the position can be filled.

One of the results of the practice of having new titles created continuously was that the number of titles in the civil service system grew to an unmanageable size. By 1986, there were over seven thousand titles in the classified civil service. Such a profusion of titles served to restrict employee mobility and made the system cumbersome to administer. Consequently, the Department is implementing a reduction in the number of titles through creation of more broadly descriptive ones.

The Civil Service Commission

The Civil Service Commission is the rule-making, investigative, and appellate arm of the civil service system. It comprises three gubernatorial appointees, of whom no more than two can be members of the same political party. Each serves a six-year term, the term of one member expiring every two years. The president, who is chosen by and serves at the pleasure of the governor, is also head of the Department of Civil Service. The Commission hears cases on such issues as:

- appeals regarding classification and allocation action of the Division of Classification and Compensation;
- appeals on jurisdictional classification issues;
- appeals from exam ratings; and
- appeals about administrative decisions made by the Department of Civil Service.

Interviews with agency managers seemed to indicate a general belief that classification matters take an inordinate amount of time to be processed through the civil service system. A recently conducted independent classification and compensation study reported

4.1 CIVIL SERVICE

All offices and positions in the Service of
the State except certain positions in the
Division of Military & Naval Affairs

Unclassified Service

- elected officials
- legislative officers & employees
- gubernatorial appointees
- officers, members & employees of the board of elections
- teachers & professors in public schools, certain community colleges & the State University & supervisory personnel

Classified Service

Jurisdictional Classification Process putting positions into one of the four categories based on the extent to which an exam is practicable.

Competitive Class
- all new positions are placed in this class unless appealed to the Civil Service Commission
- 80% of the state's classified jobs fall into this category

Non-Competitive Class
- positions for which it is practicable to examine applicants as to qualifications but not practicable to hold competitive exams
- mostly skilled trades
- up to 900 of these positions held for handicapped
- appointer has freedom as long as applicant has minimum qualifications.

Labor Class
- unskilled labor
- qualifying tests may be required

Exempt Class
- one secretary from each department & temporary state commission, certain people authorized to act in place of the principals, & certain court clerks
- appointer has complete freedom

that the Division of Classification and Compensation processes at least one-fourth of all transaction requests (other than short form and decentralized program transactions) on the date received, and more than 60 percent within ten days. Some requests do take considerable time to process because of the nature of the request or the interagency dynamics among the three control agencies that may be involved (the Division of the Budget, the Governor's Office of Employee Relations, and the Department of Civil Service).

Part of the impression of delay may be because agency managers are sometimes unfamiliar with what the Division of Classification and Compensation can and cannot do under the Civil Service Law. Managers often come to Classification and Compensation with requests for actions that are prohibited or severely proscribed by law. Continuous communication is important: managers need to know why requests are rejected or delayed.

Intertwined Roles of Agencies in the Classification Process

When new programs are being developed, the agency's staffing plan or "workload indicators" are scrutinized from many angles. The first level of review is undertaken at the Division of the Budget. In analyzing requests, DOB first evaluates the basic need for, and soundness of, the program and its proposed organizational structure; it may also look at the current staffing pattern to determine whether employees can be transferred from other divisions within the agency or whether new personnel are needed.

Once the Executive Budget is complete, the legislative fiscal committees examine each item thoroughly. During this process, they too scrutinize the proposed staffing pattern looking for flaws, adding a different perspective and political slant.

It is only after this initial process that Classification and Compensation is requested to classify the positions for the new program. In actions other than the initiation of a new program, there is much less input from the other control agencies. For example, in reclassification and reallocation actions, Classification and Compensation acts much more independently. But, in any action that has fiscal implications, even the approval of a single new position, DOB has the final say. (See Chart 4.2).

Examinations and Staffing

The Division of Examinations and Staffing Services of the Department of Civil Service is responsible for creating and maintaining lists of people qualified for appointments to state positions. To do this, the Division establishes minimum qualifications for each position and devises tests to identify qualified people for particular positions. The Division also oversees agency personnel practices to ensure that they are in compliance with Civil Service Law, rules and regulations.

In the state classification system, a common title may stretch across a wide number of agencies, even though the incumbents are doing somewhat different tasks, depending upon the needs of their agency. Examinations must therefore test for the title, not for the specific job or position. Since an examination must be fair for all positions in a title, it cannot test for all the knowledge or skills required of any single position. For example, there may be only 30 percent of a Department of Health Program Research Specialist position that is common to the title Program Research Specialist statewide; the remaining 70 percent of the position is determined by the needs of the Health Department itself. Thus, the Program Research Specialist examination can properly test only for the common 30 percent that, in theory, captures the essence of the position.

In order to develop a fair examination, the Division needs much more detailed information about the nature of the title and the various positions that fall within it than is collected by the Division of Classification and Compensation. The Division therefore, does its own investigation, typically seeking assistance from agency program managers and experts in the particular field when designing the examination. Examinations take many forms. They may be written, oral, practical, or a combination of several forms. They may also include training and experience ratings such as educational credentials and prior work experience.

To grade the examinations, the Division often calls in subject matter experts. In all cases, there must be a reviewable record of the examination in case the grade is challenged or appealed. When a score is challenged, an established administrative appeals procedure is followed; the last step is an appeal to the Civil Service Commission. When all administrative appeal channels have been exhausted, a case may be taken to court. Although the courts have been reluctant to overrule the Commission, they have sometimes decided in favor of the plaintiff. The courts also hear cases challenging decisions about who qualifies to take an examination.

Appointment Procedures

Once the examinations are scored, the Division develops a list of eligible candidates for the position. In New York State, there is a rule of three: agencies consider only the three highest scoring

Determination by
Agency of new position
need for new or re-
directed program

Agency request
to budget for new
position funds

Agency request for new positic
to Classification
and Compensation

Budget approval of
program including
new position funds

Analyze position description—classify position
- Compare With Classification Standards, Occupationally Related State Positic
  Private Industry And Other Government Jurisdictions
- Obtain Clarifying Information From Agency Program And Personnel Office S
- Assign Appropriate Title And Grade
- Establish Requirements For Minimum Qualifications
- Forward Decisions To Division Of The Budget

Issuance of
Governor's Program
Budget

Legislative approval
of Governor's
Budget

**Approval by
Division
of the Budget**

Update Dept. Information System
- Input Into Civil Service Automated Position/
  Personnel System (APPS)
- Reaffirm Determinations Between Agency
  And Civil Service Department Records

Establish Position
- Issue Budget Certification Including
  Authorization For Position By Division
  Of The Budget

Jurisdictional Classification
- Determine Whether Position Should Be In Competitive, Non-
  Competitive, Exempt, Or Labor Jurisdictional Class

Examination Planning
- Identify Need For Examination
- Define Nature, Extent, And Level Of Abilities Required For Successful Jo
  Performance
- Determine Minimum Qualifications For Taking Exam
- Determine Test(s) Most Appropriate For Selection To The Job
- Determine If Sufficient Numbers Of Current State Employees Are Qualifie
  To Participate In Promotion Exam Or If An Open Competitive Examinatic
  Is Appropriate
- Order Preparation Of Exam Material

**Examination
Development and
Preparation**
- Prepare Subtests
  Meeting Professional
  Standards Of Job Re-
  latedness And Reliability
- Prepare Exams For
  Duplication
- Duplicate Sufficient
  Quantities For No. Of
  Applicants
- Arrange For Test Centers
  And Monitors Through-
  out State
- Distribute Test Material
  To Each Center

Recruitment
- In Consultation With Agencies, Prepare And Issue Exam Announcement
- Review Applications To Determine Qualification Of Applicants
- Provide Information On Numbers Of Applicants Qualified To Take Exam
  Each Test Center
- Notify Candidates To Appear For Exam

Exam Administration
At More Than 30 Test Centers Throughout State

Certification for Payment of Salary
- Certify To The Department Of Audit And Control That Each Transaction Is Made In Accordance With Appropriate Law (Civil Service Law §100)
- Authorize Drawing Of Salary Check

Note:

This flow chart is intended to show only the basic steps in the creation and filling of a position in the Executive Branch of the State government, from the conception of the need for an additional position(s) right to the point where the position is filled and the incumbent receives a salary check. This is a "bare bones" chart—it is not and is not intended to be a comprehensive picture of the process. There are a number of subsidiary and collateral processes omitted.

Employee Transactions
- Review All Appointments, Promotions And Reinstatements For Compliance With Civil Service Law and Rules (Civil Service Law §61, 71, 72, 80)

Certification of Preferred Lists
- Establish, Maintain And Certify All Preferred Lists (Civil Service Law§81)
- Ensure Use Of Preferred Lists For Reinstatement In Compliance With Civil Service Law

Certification for Appointment
- Maintain Roster Of Fully Qualified People Currently Interested In Employment In State Positions
- Certify Rosters To Agencies For Filling Vacancies (Civil Service Law §460)
- Place Qualified People Who Are Physically Handicapped Or Laid Off Into Proper Available State Positions

List Establishment
- In Consultation With Agencies And Based On Projected Needs For Personnel In The Job, Determine How Raw Scores Will Be Converted Into Final Scores
- Determine Final Scores For Each Candidate (This is the first time that individual candidates are identified against their exam results)
- Establish List Of Qualified Candidates For Appointment

Commission Review of Appeals
- Determine Appropriateness And Necessity Of Making Changes In Tentative Answer Key

Exam Scoring
- Conduct "Pre-Rating Review" For Candidates
- Analyze Preliminary Results Of Tests To Determine The Relative Utility Of Each Item And Each Subtest
- Determine Validity Of Objections Raised By Candidates To Specific Test Items
- Develop The Final Answer Key
- Score All Answer Papers And Develop A Raw Score Distribution

applicants willing to accept the position, regardless of how many names are on the eligible list. The public employee unions have argued that there should be a rule of one, so that the highest scorer is offered the job, but the rule of three allows some managerial flexibility in hiring while still selecting from among the most qualified applicants. (See Chart 4.2).

If the Division cannot produce for the agency a list of at least three people interested in taking the position, a provisional employee may be hired to fill that position until a list is developed. The provisional appointee must meet minimum qualifications for the position and is allowed to hold it only until the examination system produces a list of qualified candidates. Many provisionals remain in their positions well beyond the nine month limit set in civil service law, but they can be appointed permanently only if they take the exam and are "reachable" (within the top three scorers); otherwise, they must be replaced by someone from the eligible list. In the past several years, there has been a sustained effort to reduce the number of provisionals in the system. In the 1982-1985 contracts signed by the State and the largest public employee unions, funds were provided specifically to seek effective ways of reducing the number of provisional appointments. Contract funds supported additional staff within the Department of Civil Service to develop appropriate tests and create eligible lists so that positions could be filled permanently, rather than provisionally. As a result of these efforts, the number of provisionals was reduced by more than seven thousand between April 1982 and April 1985.

Promotion

Competitive class positions above entry level are usually filled by promotion of an employee from within the agency on the basis of a promotion examination. However, the Department of Civil Service has the authority to expand the number of people eligible to take the test if it is determined that limiting the group is impracticable or contrary to the public interest. Eligibility to take the exam may be extended to other agencies within the State or to a wider range of titles, or the Department may decide to conduct open examinations, for which prior state service is not mandatory. These determinations can be made on the Civil Service Department's initiative or at the request and explanation of an agency appointing officer.

Affirmative Action

Executive Order No. 6 (1983) assigns to the Department of Civil Service the responsibility for insuring equal employment opportunity to members of protected classes including minorities, women, disabled persons, and Vietnam era veterans.* Under this executive order, the Civil Service Commission issues guidelines for agencies to follow in preparing annual affirmative action plans. These agency plans are submitted to the Civil Service Commission in consultation with the Governor's Executive Committee for Affirmative Action, which can revise or amend them. The Commission also monitors the implementation of agency plans and reports to the Governor on progress. If an agency fails to meet the Commission's guidelines, the latter can notify the agency, which then has thirty days to submit a remedial plan. In an extreme case, the President of the Commission can step in and assume responsibility for plan implementation.

As the watchdog of the State's Affirmative Action plan, the Civil Service Commission also prepares an annual report of the composition of each state agency's workforce by sex and ethnic identity for all categories, salary grades, and civil service classifications, and works to resolve problems of under-utilization of any of the protected classes.

From the agency's perspective, this report serves as a snapshot of its workforce composition, which can be compared with the goals and timetables for the workforce. Timetables are established on the basis of projected personnel turnover.

Executive Order No. 6 also established the Executive Committee for Affirmative Action as an advisory group to the Governor and the President of the Civil Service Commission on affirmative action issues. This group is composed of:

o the President of the Civil Service Commission
o the Commissioner of the Division of Human Rights
o the Secretary to the Governor
o the Appointments Officer to the Governor
o the Secretary of State
o the Director of DOB
o the Commissioner of Labor
o the Director of the Governor's Office of Employee Relations
o the Director of the Division for Women
o the Advocate for the Disabled
o the Director of Veterans' Affairs.

---

* Executive Order No. 28 (1983) prohibits employment discrimination based on sexual orientation. Executive Order No. 96 (1987) calls for equal opportunity employment regardless of age.

The order also mandates that each agency have a full-time Affirmative Action Officer and support staff as necessary. These officers make up the Affirmative Action Advisory Council, which advises the President of the Civil Service Commission on existing and proposed affirmative action policies and procedures. The Council also examines the causes for one group's seeming to dominate a position and works to eliminate barriers to mobility.

Occasionally a particular civil service examination proves to have an adverse impact on minorities. When this occurs, the selection process can be subjected to official review. For example, if one exam produces an eligible list of white males only, it could be challenged in court; the burden of proving the test to be valid and job-related falls on the its designers.

Comparable Worth/Pay Equity

Funding for a comparable worth/pay equity study to be conducted by an external consultant was provided in the 1982-85 contract between the State of New York and the Civil Service Employees Association (CSEA), the largest state employee union. The purpose of the study was to determine what weighting the State should place on various job components (such as supervision, responsibility, interpersonal communications) and to develop a pay model that eliminates or substantially reduces inequities in salary among different job titles in the classified civil service.

In late 1985, two major external studies of New York's Classification and Compensation system were released, both of which documented deficiencies in the system resulting in pay inequities. One study was conducted by the Center for Women in Government, SUNY at Albany, funded through the CSEA-State contract; Arthur Young and Company, Certified Public Accountants, directed the other one, funded through the Public Employees Federation (PEF)-State contract. Both found that people working in jobs that are traditionally female dominated, as well as in some male-dominated titles, were paid less than those in other jobs of equal value to New York.

As a result of regular meetings among CSEA, PEF, and state officials, an agreement on how the system should be established was worked out. The Division of Classification and Compensation has developed a new pay model, based on job content components. The model is designed to adjust salary grades so that all employees receive similar salaries for comparable work. Previously, job classes (titles) were grouped by occupation and ranked within their occupational group; salary grades were assigned to each group independently of the others.

Performance Evaluation

The performance evaluation program was first included as a negotiated agreement in the 1979 union-management contracts. The program was expanded in both the 1982 and 1985 series of contracts. The Governor's Office of Employee Relations, representing the Governor, administers the program in accord with guidelines agreed to by the State and the public sector unions. The system has the following stated goals:

- to serve as a motivational, rather than a disciplinary, tool;
- to ensure that supervisors and employees communicate on a regular basis to discuss employee performance and that they continue communication throughout the year;
- to assist in employee personal development so that job performance can be improved where needed; and
- to provide incentives based on employee performance through increased pay and recognition.

All annual salaried, probationary, part-time, and temporary employees are eligible for performance appraisal and rating on an annual basis.

Code of Ethics

Sections 73 through 78 of the Public Officers Law describe the State Code of Ethics for all State employees, which is administered by the Department of State. All executive branch employees are required to file a statement with the Secretary of State within two weeks of initial employment that they have read and will abide by the provisions of the code. Included in the provisions are specific limitations on employees' activities. For example, an employee may not receive compensation from outside sources if his or her agency is in a position to take action favorable to the source offering compensation. The employee may not accept gifts valued at $25 or more, nor accept profits from a firm of which he or she is a member that does business with State agencies. Further, a former employee must wait two years after ending State service before starting work with persons or firms directly related to activities in which the employee was engaged while in State service. Employees may not have direct or indirect interests, financial or otherwise, in activities that conflict with the proper discharge of their duties.

Additionally, employees are proscribed from disclosing confidential information related to public service responsibilities or from seeking privileges because of their official position. They may not sell goods or services to any person or organization that is directly regulated by the State agency at which they are employed.

Depending upon grade level and job responsibilities, managers who are exempt employees may be required to file a financial disclosure statement annually with the Governor's Office to verify that they are not involved in conflicts between public service responsibilities and private or personal interests. Any conflicts that are identified must be resolved promptly.

PUBLIC EMPLOYEES' FAIR EMPLOYMENT ACT

In 1967, the State's human resources management system changed dramatically with the passage of the Public Employees' Fair Employment Act (Article 14 of the Civil Service Law). Previously, labor relations were carried out in the context of the 1947 Condon-Wadlin Law, which prohibited strikes and did not allow workers any direct input into such basic issues as salary and leave schedules. Further, to insure that sympathy for illegal strikers did not lead to concessions, the law also stated that any negotiations subsequent to a strike would not be honored by the State as employer.

In this volatile labor relations environment, there were several public employee strikes, including two crippling actions by the New York City Transit Authority workers against the city. In both cases, the state legislature voted to exonerate the strikers and give them a raise as demanded, rather than deal with the difficulties inherent in replacing them.

During this period there was a growing realization that the existing statutes did not ensure a smooth continuity of state services. In 1966, Governor Rockefeller established the New York Committee on Public Employee Relations, whose mission was to propose legislation that, if enacted, would protect the public against the disruption of vital public services by illegal strikes, while at the same time protecting the rights of public employees. The chairman of this commission was George W. Taylor, Professor of Law at the University of Pennsylvania, and the Public Employees' Fair Employment Act of 1967, which resulted from the commission's work, is commonly called the Taylor Law. This law recognized the legality of public sector employee unions and mandated that the State and executive branch employee organizations negotiate collectively, in good faith, all issues dealing with the terms and conditions of employment and the administration of grievances that might result. (For a summary of the Taylor Law, see Appendix II at the end of this Chapter.)

Two years after passage of the Taylor Law, the Governor's Office of Employee Relations (GOER) was established by Chapter 491 of the Laws of 1969 to promote a cooperative relationship between the State's Executive Branch and its employees and to protect the public by insuring the orderly and uninterrupted operation of state government.

By the mid-1980's, GOER's major responsibilities (see Chart 4.3) included:

○ representation of the Executive Branch at contract negotiations with state employee unions;

○ contract administration, including contract interpretation and advice on employee relations, personnel policy matters and continuous contact with the unions to ensure smooth working relationships;

○ grievance review, including determination on behalf of the State of all contract grievances, and administration of the Grievance Appeals Board;

○ Employee Training and Development Programs, providing, jointly with the unions, a variety of educational opportunities to state employees for enhancement of skills and job effectiveness;

○ compensation, training and development, and other benefit programs for management/confidential (non-unionized) employees.

Creation of the Office of Employee Relations changed the nature of the Department of Civil Service's responsibilities and has resulted in the transfer of some issues formerly determined by management alone onto the negotiation table.

The Taylor Law created a structure that mandates the State and the public employee unions to negotiate the terms and conditions of employment for the State's executive departments. The law guarantees employees in designated units the right to join the union of their choice, or to refrain from joining any union at all. Employees who have been designated managerial or confidential are prohibited from unionizing. In practice, most State employees who are eligible to join a union do so, because membership provides them a voice in what the union will do: members have the right to vote for union officials and on contract approval as well as to participate in a variety of union-sponsored activities. The law also states that once union representation is established, the State is required to negotiate with that union in good faith. The law prohibits strikes, and sets up procedures to be followed if an impasse arises in the negotiation process.

The Taylor Law also created the Public Employment Relations Board (PERB). The Board is composed of a full-time chair and two part-time members, all appointed by the Governor. It has respon-

4.3 Governor's Office of Employee Relations, 1987

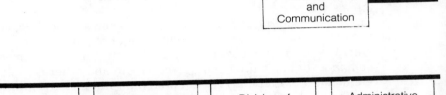

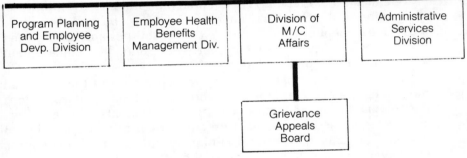

sibility for defining the statewide bargaining units in such a way that there will be "a community of interest among the unit employees," and has jurisdiction throughout the State for improper practice cases.

In large population areas such as Suffolk and Nassau Counties, "Mini-PERBS" have been established to consider issues of representation and other local level issues. In New York City, the Board

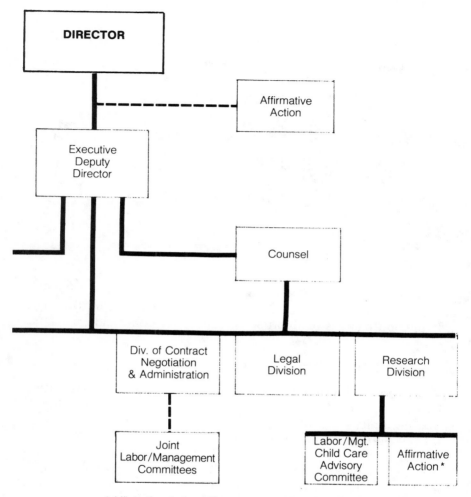

* Affirmative Action officer reports to the *Deputy Director for Research* on a daily basis, but has direct access to the Director of GOER in affirmative action issues, in accord with the Executive Order establishing an Affirmative Action Officer in every executive agency.

of Collective Bargaining performs these functions. (New York City elementary and secondary school and transit employees, however, are under PERB's jurisdiction.) PERB retains the right of limited appellate review over the Board of Collective Bargaining.

The Public Employment Relations Board settles questions of union representation, analyzes issues relating to conditions of public sector employment, establishes panels of mediators, arbitrators or

PAYNE

members of fact finding boards to aid in the resolution of disputes, and rules on charges of improper practices on either side.

Unions and Negotiating Units

The State's unionized workforce is divided into twelve bargaining units as shown on Chart 4.4. Six separate unions represent these bargaining units:

- Civil Service Employees Association (CSEA)
- Council 82
- Public Employees Federation (PEF)
- United University Professions (UUP)
- Police Benevolent Association (PBA)
- District Council 37.

A brief description of each union is found in Appendix III at the end of this Chapter. Because of their large membership, New York's public sector unions have frequently played a leading role nationwide in establishing standards for public employment. As one union official put it, "What we [unions] do or don't do is important nationally as well as locally. Other public jurisdictions pay attention to what New York does in the area of labor-management relations." The unions have played, and continue to play, an important role in helping to shape the State's human resources policies.

4.4 New York State Employees Bargaining Units
(1986 data)

Unit	# of Employees	Typical Positions	Union
Administrative Services (ASU)	32,000	office support staff, administrative personnel	CSEA
Institutional Services (ISU)	40,000	therapeutic, custodial care workers in State institutions	CSEA
Operational Services (OSU)	21,000	craft and machine workers, maintenance and repair personnel	CSEA
Professional, Scientific, & Technical (PS & T)	53,000	professionally trained personnel such as engineers, nurses, accountants	PEF
Rent Regulation Services (RRSU)	600	rent controlled/stabilized housing employees	DC 37, AFSCME
Security Services (SSU)	17,000	correctional officers, institutional safety and security personnel	Council 82
State Police Investigators (BCI)	700	investigators	PBA
State Police Troopers	2,300	troopers	PBA
State Police Comm. & Non-comm. Officers	600	officers	PBA
State University Professional Services	17,000	faculty, non-teaching professional staff, SUNY	UUP
Division of Military & Naval Affairs (DMNA)	800	DMNA civilian employees	CSEA
Security Supervisors	500	supervisors	Council 82

Preparations for Contract Negotiations

The Taylor Law was designed to establish structure and foster an environment in which negotiations could be carried out in good faith. Virtually from the day a contract goes into effect, managers and union members alike begin to gain an understanding of problems that stem from the contract and collect documentation about them. Evaluation of the current contract and identification of needed changes is a continuous process: representatives of the State and each of the unions meet periodically either formally or informally to review problems that arise during the life of the contract and to consider whether contract provisions are working out in practice as anticipated. By the time they arrive at the negotiating table, each side has in hand a list of needs that have developed and been articulated in the work place.

Development of Union Proposals

"Who can better tell you how to fix a problem than the person in the job?" (Union Representative)

In developing their proposals the unions try to address the most pressing problems that affect the largest number of members. Typically, problems with the contract are discussed at local meetings and the opinions expressed are passed on to union leadership. As one union official explained it, the leadership strives to remain in continual contact with members, through newspapers, fliers, and personal meetings. "It is important for us to know what members believe their union should be doing," he declared. Unions periodically survey their members as well as local labor-management committee participants to ascertain what problems employees have encountered and how the union can best address these issues. On the basis of comments received and grievances filed during the life of the current contract, each union establishes its list of proposals.

In developing its salary and major benefit positions, each union's research department compares salaries and benefits of its members with those of employees throughout the country in both the private and public sectors in equivalent positions.

Development of State Proposals

The Governor's Office of Employee Relations (GOER) is responsible for establishing the State's list of proposals in preparation for upcoming negotiations. In formulating its proposals, GOER seeks the advice of the agencies, because it is at this level that day-to-day use of the agreement as a working document occurs. During the past decade, GOER has sought to increase agency involvement in the entire negotiation process.

Since the creation of GOER, many communication links, both formal and informal, have developed between that Office and the agencies. Each negotiator in GOER's contract administration unit serves as liaison with a number of specified agencies so that all agencies are part of the process. Further, the Employee Relations Advisory Council (ERAC) was established in 1982 by Executive Order to incorporate agency input into the daily process of employee relations. This group, composed of eight agency Human Resources Management directors each serving a three-year term, advises GOER on agency issues and perspectives and provides continuous two-way communication.

Some agencies put more emphasis on continuous informal communication with GOER than others, but GOER's agency liaison system is designed to encourage communication with all agencies, regardless of size. In preparation for negotiations, the Office requests agency input on a variety of issues. Each agency is invited to meet with GOER to discuss the issues and possible resolution of identified problems. Agency viewpoints are incorporated into the list of proposals that GOER ultimately takes to the negotiating table.

Along with the trend of increasing agency involvement, many agencies have sought ways of involving more people within the agency itself in the development of recommendations. The method devised by the Office of Mental Retardation and Developmental Disabilities (OMRDD) is instructive in its broad involvement of agency personnel. Central office solicits written recommendations about current contract problems from each of its facilities. The small book compiled from the recommendations is used as the basis for discussion at several regional meetings. After the meetings, the central office develops a final list for submission to GOER.

According to an official at GOER, one of the major goals of the State team at the negotiating table is to create a structure that will allow managers to manage in the most effective way. The Office has a perspective on statewide problems as identified throughout all the agencies. It is also able to gauge the statewide impact that an agency proposal would have if it were incorporated into the contract. If GOER is aware of a problem but cannot follow through on an agency's recommendations for resolution, it can often develop alternate solutions or at least seek to reduce the impact of the problem.

The Negotiations

All State public employee unions (except UUP) are currently on an April 1 to March 31 three-year contract cycle. (The UUP cycle is July 1 through June 30, coinciding more nearly with the academic calendar.) Contract negotiations begin in November or December for agreements that expire on March 31. The unions have usually established their formal demands by October.

The composition of the union negotiating teams varies widely, depending on the size and structure of the union. Only CSEA assigns different negotiating units to consider particular categories of proposals; later the units merge for coalition bargaining. The other unions prefer to create teams that negotiate the entire contract. Typically, the teams include representatives from the agencies in which the union is heavily represented and from job titles in which union members predominate. State teams are composed of the chief negotiator (the Director of GOER), other GOER negotiators, team members from a number of agencies, and representatives from DOB and the Department of Civil Service. The Division of the Budget is involved both in the planning stages and at the table because of the heavy financial implications of many of the negotiated items. It works closely with GOER in studying the fiscal effects of the union's demands.

While the negotiating teams have the power to bind the parties on the basis of what they agree collectively, the clauses of the contract dealing with issues requiring an appropriation or change in law require legislative approval before they can be implemented. Generally, such approval of the contracts is routine, but there have been cases in which some clauses did not become part of the law. The Taylor Law mandates that the two parties negotiate some issues (such as salaries and working conditions), and permits the parties to discuss other issues (such as staffing), but prohibits consideration of certain issues (such as retirement). The Public Employment Relations Board maintains lists of mandatory, permissible and prohibited subjects.

The March 31 expiration date of most contracts coincides with the last day of the State's fiscal year and, as is often the case when parties with conflicting interests are talking, the two sides are frequently unable to reach agreement until the pressures of impending deadlines are upon them. Thus, the Governor and the Legislature may have to plan the State's budget for the upcoming fiscal year without knowing precisely what costs incurred by the contract will be. The Governor builds cost projections (such as likely salary increases, training and education, health, and safety program costs) into the budget. In so doing, the Division of the Budget works with

GOER to establish projections based on revenue and expenditure forecasts, the general economic outlook, and knowledge of what other employers are doing.

Some Major Agreement Issues

One of the issues discussed at the bargaining sessions is the set of procedures that managers must follow in disciplining employees. Sections 75 and 76 of the Civil Service Law set forth disciplinary procedures, but these have subsequently been modified or replaced through collective agreements, and therefore now serve only for management/confidential employees and any other employees not covered under the Taylor Law. In the landmark case *Antinore v. State* (371 NYS 2d 213, 49 AD 2d 6) (1975), the Court of Appeals decided that unions could negotiate different procedures from those set forth in the law as long as the same due process considerations are maintained (see Chapter VIII of this *Guide*). Under the Civil Service Law the agency head had the final determination in reviewing disciplinary actions; under current negotiated agreements an independent third party (an arbitrator) has the final say.

Handling grievances through established procedures is another important issue. If the grievance concerns an item specifically covered in the contract for the employee's bargaining unit, there is an established procedure for resolving the dispute. First, a decision is made by a facility or division/bureau head. If the grievant is dissatisfied, the decision can be appealed to the agency head or designated representative. The next step is an appeal to GOER for a review of the record and, if the grievance remains unresolved, the last step is binding arbitration.

There are other types of grievances as well, such as disciplinary grievances, non-contract grievances (where an employee grieves a matter not specifically covered by the agreement), and out-of-title grievances (where an employee grieves work assignments believed inappropriate to the job title).

Management rights is another major issue in the agreement. The contract lists in various provisions what management may not do. Otherwise, within the limits of good judgment, each contract states that management retains "all of the authority, rights and responsibilities possessed by the State."

Over the life of each agreement, the union and the Office of Employee Relations are immersed in the business of interpreting and administering the document. In the event of interpretation differences between the two parties, established procedures work toward an interpretation that is agreeable to both sides.

Joint Labor-Management Committees

Joint Labor-Management Committees were created through the collective bargaining process with their membership, funding, and purposes defined in each agreement. These committees are most effective when both parties have an interest in looking at a complex issue and want to resolve it in a mutually satisfactory way. The prevailing philosophy underlying the committees is that for some issues there are "win-win" solutions that improve the situation for both sides, with each side recognizing that it must work at reaching accommodation. As Tom Hartnett noted when he was Director of GOER, "We want the best thinking in the State on a particular issue, regardless of whether it's a union or a management idea."

There was some initial skepticism about the committees on the part of the unions. "The jury is still out on them [the committees], but each year I get more convinced," declared one union official.

New York State first ventured into a formal labor-management committee arrangement at the state level in 1976 with the creation of a Continuity of Employment Committee. In 1979, contract negotiations led to the creation of joint labor-management committees with the State's two largest employee unions, CSEA and PEF. The Committee on the Work Environment and Productivity (CWEP) was formed with CSEA, and Professional Development and Quality of Working Life Committee (PDQ) was formed with PEF. Late in 1980, a joint labor-management committee, the Quality of Working Life Committee (QWL) was formed with Council 82. All three were continued in the 1982-85 and 1985-88 contracts, and the fourth and fifth joint labor-management committees were set up with the PBA for State Police investigators and senior investigators, and with the State University system's UUP, respectively.

Labor-management committees allow both sides to address issues of mutual interest, particularly those broadly defined as directly related to quality of working life which is now, according to one union official, as important to the unions and their members as are economic rewards and general conditions of employment such as working hours or sick leave. The committees have initiated literally hundreds of projects. In many instances, committees representing each of the unions as well as the State have banded together to fund projects of mutual concern. For example, all of the committees have contributed start-up funds to provide on-site day care centers for all State employees. A number of day care centers are in operation at State work sites and more are in the planning stage. These centers constitute the first systemwide effort in the U.S. to provide day care for children of public sector employees. The Statewide Employee

Assistance Program is another program funded jointly by all the unions and the State.

Employee Training and Development

The unions and the State recognize employee training and development as important both to employees themselves and to the organizations in which they work. Funding for these programs is negotiated as part of the contracts with each of the unions. Programs are designed to:

- develop competent supervisors, managers, and leaders;
- support individual growth and achievement;
- address organizational needs;
- strengthen job skills; and
- assist employees to adapt to new technologies.

The unions, individual agencies, and GOER, together with employees' own assessment of training needs design courses and programs in conjunction with colleges, universities, or private consultants. For example, the Public Service Training Program (PSTP) was first funded in 1982 by negotiated agreement between the State and the Public Employees Federation (PEF), representing 53,000 employees in the professional, scientific, and technical bargaining unit. The Program was funded again through the 1985 agreement. A national model, PSTP operates as a cooperative, systematic approach to professional development by the union and its membership, the State, and more than seventy institutions of higher education in New York.

The Department of Civil Service is responsible for implementing the Clerical and Secretarial Employee Advancement Program (CSEAP) that permits secretaries to make the transition into administrative and managerial positions. It also handles training for Council 82 employees.

All state employees are eligible for tuition reimbursement, which permits them to enroll in courses offered by local colleges and universities at greatly reduced tuition costs if eligibility requirements (relevance to job responsibilities) are satisfied. In 1985, employees were eligible for reimbursement due to enrollment in more than 10,000 courses.

Changing Workforce

It is instructive to look at the context in which collective negotiations occur. The composition of New York State's workforce is changing, and many of the issues that concern the unions are related to these changes. Statistics from the Governor's Office of Employee

Relations state that nearly half the State's employees today are women. The average age is 42. Further, an increasing number of female employees are single parents, heads of households, and sole breadwinners for families that often consist of young school-age children.

These workforce characteristics help to shape union demands. In response to the needs of state employees, several programs that permit attendance flexibility and seek to accommodate differing lifestyles were developed. Examples of these programs include the voluntary furlough program (currently available to M/C and PS & T employees), flextime, maternity/paternity leave, and part-time/ shared jobs.

Recent studies indicate that aging of the State's population will be a major demographic trend in the remainder of this century and beyond. The resultant changes such as employees remaining longer in the workforce and having fewer children (and hence less concern about maternity/paternity leave or daycare and more concern about elder care), could have a substantial impact on future union demands.

Division of Management/Confidential Affairs

The Division of Management/Confidential Affairs was created by Governor Hugh Carey in 1979, ten years after passage of the Taylor Law. Throughout the first decade of the Taylor Law, unions gradually gained substantial benefits for their members and the collective agreements began to provide funding for programs beyond those of basic health insurance, training, and quality of worklife.

Traditionally, Management/Confidential employees received salary increases similar to those negotiated by the unions for their members, but prior to the establishment of the Division of M/C Affairs, there was no institutionalized system to insure that the needs of M/C employees (approximately 15,000 people) in these areas were met. Members of the management/confidential group hold a variety of diverse positions, from commissioner to clerk, so it can be a difficult task to serve the interests of all of them simultaneously. However, in a broad sense they share many concerns.

In 1982, and again in 1985, the Legislature explicitly established a salary schedule for M/C employees and provided funding for their employee benefits. The funding provided by both laws was to be used for additional benefits, for creation and implementation of management and confidential training and development programs, and for quality of working life programs.

New York State government with an executive branch workforce of some 200,000 employees, is among the largest employers (public or private) in the United States. Its human resources management system is necessarily varied and complex and its personnel system is highly stratified, although some simplification is expected to result from full implementation of measures developed in response to the classification and compensation/pay equity studies' assessments.

New York's strong public employee union system has a substantial impact on State personnel policies. In adapting to the system of collectively negotiating, management has been obliged to define its own rights and prerogatives more clearly. In recent years, both sides have focused on more than compensation and benefit issues, discipline and grievances. Employee development, working conditions, and quality of working life issues have assumed an importance they did not have a decade ago.

APPENDIX I
Glossary*

Allocate. To assign a class to a particular grade in the salary schedule based on an evaluation of its relative worth. To **reallocate** is to change the existing allocation of a class to a different salary grade in the schedule.

Application. A request to the Director of Classification and Compensation filed by an employee or appointing officer asking a change in title and/or salary.

Base Salary. Standard salary before the addition of inconvenience pay, geographic differential pay, or other similar adjustments.

Class or Class of Positions. One or more positions sufficiently similar in duties and responsibilities that the same title may be used to designate every position in the group, the same salary may be equitably applied, the same qualifications required, and the same examination used to select qualified employees.

Classification Standard. An administrative document promulgated by the Division of Classification and Compensation that describes in detail duties and responsibilities of a class. Standards are primarily concerned with the accurate and efficient classification of positions.

Classified Service. That portion of the state's civil service under the direct jurisdiction of the Department of Civil Service, composed of all offices and positions except for those filled by election or gubernatorial appointment. The classified service is divided into four jurisdictional classes: competitive, non-competitive, exempt, and labor (See Section 40 of the Civil Service Law).

Classify. To group positions according to their duties and responsibilities and assign a class title; to establish a new position with a proper and descriptive title.

Competitive Class. That jurisdictional class composed of positions for which it is practicable to determine the merit and fitness of applicants by competitive examination. A new position is automatically assigned to the competitive class unless the Civil Service Commission specifically places it in a different class (See Section 44 of the Civil Service Law).

Desk Audit or Job Audit. A review and discussion of the duties and responsibilities of a position made at an employee's desk or other regular place of work.

Decentralized Project. A project under which classification determinations for standard titles are decentralized to individual agencies. The titles included are those on the CC-1A listing and all titles for which there is a

---

* Definitions from the *Department of Civil Service State Personnel Management Manual.*

tentative or final classification standard. The agency keeps on file a description of job duties and any physical ability required to perform them. In some cases, an added qualification, such as possession of a valid driver's license, may be required.

Exempt Class. Among others, this class consists of one secretary from each department and deputies authorized by law to act generally for and in place of their principals. Any other subordinate position for which competitive and non-competitive grouping are found not to be practicable can be placed in the exempt class.

Minimum Qualifications or "Quals." Education, training, and/or experience requirements denoting the minimum standards that all candidates must possess to give reasonable assurance that they can perform satisfactorily.

Noncompetitive Class. The jurisdictional classification that includes positions which are not in the exempt or labor classes and for which it is found by the Civil Service Commission to be not practicable to test by competitive examination. An agency may fill this position by appointing a person who meets the minimum established qualifications of training and experience (See Section 42 of the Civil Service Law).

NS (Non-Statutory). A position, of which the salary is not fixed by statute but is established by the Director of the Division of the Budget.

OS (Other Statute). A position, the salary of which is established by a statute other than the Civil Service Law.

"Office Title." A title that differs from the classified title assigned to a job and that is used to describe a particular position for other than payroll, budget, or official purposes. For example, a Head Clerk position might have an "office" title of Office Supervisor.

"Out-of-Title" Work. Duties performed by the incumbent of a position which are not appropriate to the class to which the position has been assigned.

Parenthetic. A descriptive designation in parenthesis following a common base title, to distinguish a specialty within a given field, as a Senior Clerk (Library) and Senior Clerk (Purchase).

Position. An assigned group of duties and responsibilities, temporary or permanent, that can be performed by one person. A position may be occupied or vacant.

APPENDIX II

Some High Points of the Taylor Law

Units. The law states that the State's entire workforce (other than those designated management/confidential) shall be broken down into units established by the Public Employment Relations Board or PERB. Each unit is composed of job titles that are grouped together because of similarities and a common interest among the employees. Currently there are twelve units.

Unit Representation. Unit members select the union they want to represent them at collective bargaining negotiations.

Recognition and Certification of Employee Organizations. Once it is ascertained which union the unit wishes to have represent it, the State is required to negotiate collectively with that union in determining the terms and conditions of employment.

Good Faith Negotiation. The law states that there is a "mutual obligation" of the two parties to "meet at reasonable times and confer in good faith with respect to wages, hours, and other terms and conditions of employment."

Resolution of Disputes. The law lays out a sequence of steps to be followed in the event of an impasse at the negotiations. The last resort procedure is submission of recommendations to the Legislature by the Governor and the employee organization. The Legislature takes action as it sees fit.

Employer Improper Practices. These include interference with an employee's right to join or refrain from joining a union, domination or interference with an employee organization with the purpose of depriving employees of the right to organize, discrimination against employees on the basis of union membership, and refusal to negotiate in good faith.

Employee Organization Improper Practices. These include trying to restrain or coerce employees in the exercise of their right to join a union or to refrain from doing so, and refusal to negotiate in good faith.

Changing Union Representation. Eight months before the expiration of a contract between the State and a union, another union can challenge that union currently representing a unit for representation status (the right to represent that unit), if 30 percent of the unit's members sign a petition. An election is held to establish which union the unit wishes to have represent it. However, some unions add to these restrictions. For example, no AFL-CIO affiliated unit may challenge another.

Management/Confidential (M/C) Employees. In 1969, PERB made an initial determination regarding those jobs that would be classified as management/confidential. Employees in the M/C unit are prohibited from joining a union and bargaining collectively. PERB has the authority to change a position from M/C to a bargaining unit, or vice versa, upon petition.

APPENDIX III

Public Employee Unions Representing State Employees

Civil Service Employees Association, Inc. (CSEA). The largest public employee union in New York, CSEA represents employees in the administrative services, institutional services, operational services, and military and naval affairs units. These units include employees in clerical, secretarial, trades, maintenance, and mental hygiene patient care titles.

Council 82, AFSCME, AFL–CIO. Council 82 represents employees in the security supervisors and security services units. The largest single title is that of correction officer in the Department of Correctional Services.

District Council 37 (DC 37). DC 37 represents employees in the rent regulation services unit. Until 1983, employees in this unit were not State personnel. The union represents the majority of New York City employees.

Police Benevolent Association of the New York State Troopers, Inc. (PBA). PBA represents employees in the commissioned and non-commissioned officers (supervisors), investigators and senior investigators (BCI), and state troopers units. The organization is affiliated with the Police Conference of New York, Inc. and the National Troopers Coalition.

Public Employees Federation (PEF). The largest public employee union for employees trained in traditional professions, PEF represents medical doctors, nurses, lawyers, engineers, scientists, and technicians. The union represents personnel in the professional, scientific, and technical services unit.

United University Professions (UUP). UUP represents employees in the State University professional services unit, which includes both faculty and non-teaching professionals in such titles as student union director, financial aid advisor, technical assistant and technical specialist.

APPENDIX IV

The Workers' Compensation Process
in NEW YORK STATE

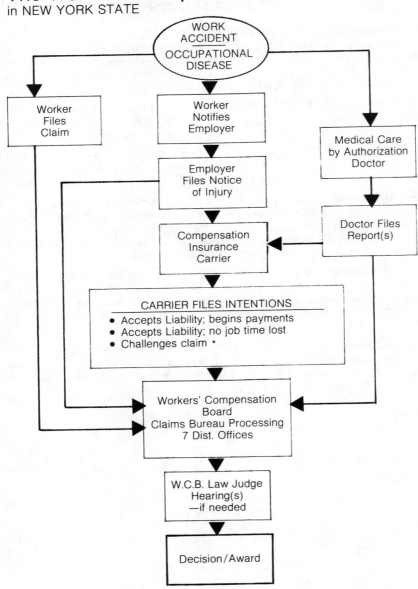

*The Claimant may be eligible to receive Disability Benefits payments, subject to reimbursement to the D.B. carrier from the Workers' Compensation Award, if any.

Chapter V

Agency—Legislative Relations and the Legislature

Developing a packet of proposed bills to be sent first to the Governor's office and possibly later to the Legislature is a prime order of business for every agency. Either in meetings or by a memo inviting suggestions, each agency gathers ideas for new legislation as well as information about problems with current law. Although this information gathering is an organized effort only once a year, agency–legislative liaisons, personnel responsible for their agency's relations with the Legislature, are receptive to ideas for bills at any time. Often, their list of possibilities is lengthy even before the formal gathering effort begins.

The commissioner and/or the legislative liaison must consider the following questions as they relate to each potential bill:

o Can the problem be handled by the agency in another way (for example, through regulation)?

o Is the idea likely to be a popular one that would have a chance of passage, or has its time perhaps not yet come?

The cost of the prospective legislation must also be evaluated. One agency, for example, asks that when submitting a suggestion for a new program or revision in the law, the employee who proposes it also suggest how it should be financed. Often, the liaisons are involved mainly in program aspects, while agency finance personnel are concerned with fiscal considerations and may play an important role in deciding which bills the agency should submit. Agency counsels generally draft the bills, translating ideas into proper legal format. In some agencies, especially those in which a separate legislative liaison position has not been established, counsels may play a much larger role, performing some or all of the functions ascribed to legislative liaisons.

Agency proposals are sent to the Governor's Counsel, who reviews them and passes them to the Division of the Budget. At this point, the agency is asked to suggest a way to fund the proposal from within its budget; there has been a clear understanding since the Carey governorship that agency expansion is not a part of the State's plan.

In early fall, the Governor sends out a letter to each agency head giving a schedule for the submission of bills to the Governor's Office. That office then has the task of deciding which bills to select as Governor's Program bills, which to approve for submission as "departmental" bills, and which to reject outright. Although agencies have sometimes gone to the Legislature quietly with bills that had been so rejected, this is a dangerous strategy and detracts from the cohesiveness of the executive branch. Throughout the fall the agencies work with DOB and the Governor's Counsel's Office on proposed bills so that when the Legislature arrives, the final drafts of the bills are ready for sponsorship.

The Division of the Budget studies, and may comment on, all bills submitted to the Governor, no matter what their fiscal impact. It screens for consistency, program implications, and administrative problems as well as for financial effect. The Governor's Counsel's Office also examines all bills, as noted earlier, and plays a role in determining which of them will be incorporated into the Governor's program. One impact of the Governor's Counsel's Office and DOB review is to screen out those bills which, although they may be good from a program standpoint, have prohibitive fiscal or legal consequences.

The number of bills submitted varies substantially by agency. Some agencies may submit only a few bills while others may submit thirty to forty, depending on the size and scope of the agency and the opportunities for program expansion. Most of the bills submitted are not proposals for new programs, but rather are technical, addressing problems with the implementation of laws already on the books. These technical bills are not normally made part of the Governor's Program. Some agencies have no bill selected for the Governor's Program in a given year but, by all agency accounts, selection is the most desirable fate for a bill. Forty of the 147 Governor's Program bills introduced were passed in the 1986 legislative session, for example, in contrast to a much lower rate for other bills.

To be considered in the Legislature, every bill except the Governor's Budget must have a sponsor or group of sponsors (in which case one or more is designated "prime sponsor"). Important bills are often sponsored by committee chairs, by a legislator who has taken a special interest, or by one recommended by the Counsel's

Office in each house. In some instances, no sponsor can be found and the bill is not introduced into that legislative session.

The Governor's Program and departmental bills begin to be introduced following the Governor's State-of-the-State message in January. The period provided for bill submission is limited. In the Senate, departmental bills can be submitted only prior to March 1; Governor's Program bills can be submitted until the first Tuesday in April. Once an agency's bill is introduced, the agency must work to promote passage of that bill, lobbying against the multitude of other bills threatening to affect it, and responding to legislative requests for information.

Promoting the Passage of Agency-Initiated Bills

Some agency legislative liaisons argue that the term "lobbying," generally used to describe efforts to influence the fate of a bill, does not really describe their activities because their work differs from that of non-governmental lobbyists in important ways. Liaisons see their role primarily as promoting the interests of the people of the State, not just of one or another political interest group. Although this is correct in a broad sense, each agency does have identified constituencies whose interests are particularly important to them. Secondly, of course, they do not contribute to legislators' electoral campaigns or spend money in hopes of gaining influence, as lobbyists often do.

However, agency liaisons are advocates, as are lobbyists. Like lobbyists, they recognize the importance of informal relationships. How these relationships are maintained, of course, is heavily dependent on the personalities of the individuals involved. One agency liaison agreed that informal but important contact with legislators or key staff frequently takes place on elevators and at restaurants, while another retorted, "We don't do that sort of thing in this agency," when asked the same question.

Whether contact is "social" or "informal," all agree that one key benefit of good relationships with legislative staff and legislators lies in access. The Legislature is such a busy place during March as the budget deadline approaches and toward the end of session in June that it is frequently impossible for a member or staff person who faces ten telephone messages to return more than two calls; chances are that those calls will be to respected friends, who will then have the chance to give input or get information at crucial times. One aim of legislative liaisons (and of lobbyists in general) is to gain and maintain this kind of access. Many agency liaisons are former legislative staff members, who have brought with them to the agency valuable friendships and knowledge of the legislative process.

Agency liaisons also recognize the importance of providing solid information in support of their position on a bill. Legislators and their staffs come to rely upon sources that provide accurate, concise, and timely material. Because an agency's constituencies can be of great service in providing information too, copies of agency bills approved for introduction in the Legislature are often sent to those constituencies that can be expected to lend support.

Persistence is another important component of the lobbying process, since bills are frequently not passed the first year they are introduced. In fact, one legislative liaison described the process as "evolutionary." As evidence, she related the following story. Although the population in Brooklyn is what administrators at the Office of Mental Health (OMH) term "high risk," there is no children's hospital separate from the psychiatric center, as there is in most other high risk communities. Recognizing the need for such a facility, for three years in a row OMH proposed a bill to construct a children's hospital. Community advocates lobbied for the bill, but to no avail. In 1985, although the bill still didn't pass, funds were appropriated in the budget to conduct a study that might demonstrate need. The study documented a huge need for the facility and the 1986 budget gave OMH money to find a site even before the bill authorizing the hospital had actually been passed. Thus it was continued pressure from advocacy groups and the department combined with a documented need for the hospital that finally moved the bill to passage.

Bills Initiated by the Legislature

More than 9,000 bills are introduced during each session in each house of the Legislature. Many bills not initiated by an agency will nevertheless potentially affect it. The Legislature receives ideas for bills from other sources besides the Governor's Office and executive agencies. Lobby groups may contribute ideas or even submit already drafted bills. Task forces, constituent groups, local governments, and legislators themselves are other important sources of legislation. The Legislative Bill Drafting Commission provides the legal expertise to draft most of the bills that originate in the Legislature.

The media play a very important role in influencing legislation. By focusing on an issue or following a particular bill, the press may pressure members of the Legislature to work out an acceptable compromise rather than postpone further consideration until the next session. The press also can generate public interest when broad interest group support is lacking. When the public is following a bill through the media, legislators are more likely to behave in ways that are responsive to their constituencies, rather than follow the party leadership. Thus, the press can influence the outcome of a bill both by increasing its general importance and by motivating constituents to make their preferences known. Agencies may, and often do, oppose bills that arise through other sources. The options an agency has for dealing with them depends on when it first becomes aware of them. Legislative staff contend that too many agencies do not follow bills actively enough throughout the legislative process and then complain when the bill is passed. One former legislative staff member recalled working for three years on a bill designed to give patients access to their medical records. In the last week of the 1985 session (when it otherwise might have passed), affected departments provided valid objections that caused the bill to fail. The story has a happy ending, for the following year the bill was amended and passed with the departments' support. A year's time had to pass, though, because of the timing of the agencies' comments. Limited agency attention is inevitable, however, because of the huge volume of bills introduced.

A legislative liaison for a large agency pointed out that, due to her small staff and the large number of potentially important bills introduced, the agency had to make decisions about which bills to focus on, based on an assessment of their chances of passage as well as their content. If a bill seems important, and there is time, the agency is likely to contact affected interest groups to determine their views before taking a firm stand, as well as to speak with legislative sponsors or relevant staff to become more knowledgeable about the measure.

When implementation problems are not considered as part of the proposed legislation, problems often crop up after passage. One agency liaison was able to provide a unique perspective: she had helped to draft a bill while working for the Legislature but subsequently joined the agency that had to implement it. She was quite surprised to find real difficulties with implementation. Periodic memos inviting managers' comments on bills that have the potential to affect their operations are now routine in her department in order to bring the managerial perspective into the lobbying process. Although potential problems with a bill's implementation should be brought to the attention of the bill's sponsor or supporters, legislators often do not seek out such information because their focus is on finding a politically acceptable solution, not necessarily one that can be implemented easily.

If an agency opposes a bill that is likely to pass, every effort is made to reach a compromise before passage. The legislative liaison may suggest that the same goal be achieved by an alteration in the way the agency implements an existing program. Although this may seem an attractive alternative, the liaison must be careful not to promise things that can't be delivered. Unkept promises influence an agency's chances of getting what it wants the next time around. Sometimes a compromise proves impossible, and the only option remaining for the agency is to ask the Governor to veto a bill. Before signing a bill into law (the Governor has ten days after it is received, with specific exceptions), the bill is sent for comment to those agencies on which it will have an impact. The agencies then have five days to respond in writing.

If the Governor does choose to veto the measure, the chances that two-thirds of the Legislature will override the veto are slim. If he signs it, the agency is forced to implement a law it opposes. Despite agency dissatisfaction, legislative staff claim that agencies need to realize that legislators, as elected representatives, rightfully hold the ultimate power to pass laws as they see fit, and that it is the agencies' responsibility to make the best of those laws they don't like. Furthermore, they argue, the law can be amended or even repealed in the future if the Legislature can be convinced that there are genuine problems with implementation.

Agencies, on the other hand, are understandably frustrated when a good bill is defeated or killed in committee because of a political power struggle (which may not be related to the issue at hand) or by the disproportionately large influence of a particularly effective interest group. At such times, disappointed agency staff may be found complaining about the unexpected lack of support in the Legislature, while frustrated legislators and staff at the Capitol are grumbling about an unresponsive bureaucracy.

Responding to Legislative Requests for Information

In 1970, agencies were practically the sole source of information for legislators. Although other resources are now available, legislative staff report they rely on agency information more than ever, particularly because often it is the only source of "dynamic data." The Legislature now has working as program staff, central staff and for commissions, professionals who conduct studies of specific areas and produce recommendations for action and reports. Members may also use their personal staff allotments to purchase external specialized services, but only the agencies, by monitoring day-to-day operations statewide and through long years of experience, can provide much of the how-to and how-much-will-it-cost and what-will-happen-if information that is needed continually by legislators and staff.

Coordination of the information flow between the Legislature and the agency is often important. Legislative sources stress the value of establishing one contact person in the Department, so that legislators unfamiliar with agency staff can call the contact who in turn will refer them to the appropriate employee or unit.

In most agencies, managers are asked to notify their counsel's office or legislative liaison of all legislative contact. Such policies are designed to keep agency positions coordinated and to ensure that the people who deal with the Legislature frequently (commissioners and deputies, counsels and/or a legislative liaison) know what has transpired. "You can't be caught not knowing what's going on in your own department" (agency liaison).

When responding to questions from a legislator or legislative staff person, both agency and legislative sources caution managers to be careful about expressing personal opinions. Instead, factual material should be provided to the Legislature and opinion provided to the agency liaison or higher management.

When asked for information for the Legislature, managers need to keep two rules in mind: BE STRAIGHTFORWARD and GET THE INFORMATION QUICKLY. The Legislature needs to be able to rely upon agencies for accurate information: an agency that proves consistently reliable will have a greater influence on legislation than one that does not. One agency liaison's comment on the consequences of once misleading a legislator or legislative staff: "You may as well go peddle pencils, because they'll never trust you again." Another stated, "I've seen lots of people's lives and careers ruined because a legislator stands up [on the floor of the Senate or Assembly] with incorrect information."

Managers who are asked to comment on a legislative idea also have a responsibility to inform the inquirer to the best of their knowledge about concerned constituencies' positions on the issue. This is important because getting support for a bill to pass requires successful coalition-building by those groups that favor the measure. For this reason, people who read constituencies well are valued by the Legislature, whereas withholding the known fact that a major constituency group opposes a measure that the agency supports may well be considered misleading.

Managers sometimes fail to understand why preparing information for the Legislature should take precedence over immediate program concerns. In fact, the Legislature's way of doing business sometimes appears unusual. Its schedule is such that it meets regularly two or three days a week for months, but then six or seven days a week under tremendous pressure before the budget is passed and again near the end of session. One reason for this is that bargaining is at the heart of the Legislative process. As the budget deadline approaches, legislators trade support for measures. Until the pressure becomes very intense, they tend to be unwilling to compromise much, hoping for a better deal. Certain issues must be dealt with each year, but normally it takes end-of-session pressure to force compromise. As one agency liaison noted, "The Legislature works on a crisis basis." During the most pressured times, a quick agency response to a cost or program question may mean the difference between the life and death of a bill.

In addition to bill-related questions, agencies are often asked to resolve constituency problems. The Department of Motor Vehicles, for example, occasionally faces cases like the following. An automobile owner returns from a winter in Florida to learn that he has been fined $4/day for not having current auto insurance. The required warnings and attempts to contact him were made, but he never knew about them. He calls his legislator, and the legislator calls the Department to ask for a special arrangement. Here the legislator's own words come back to haunt: the agency's role is to implement, not pass judgment on or distort the law that the Legislature has passed. Because the law is so specific, the man will have to pay the full amount of the fine, but perhaps a special payment schedule can be arranged. The legislator is then appreciative of a special effort the agency has made to handle the case in a manner satisfactory to all concerned.

In other instances, such as a long line problem at a local Motor Vehicles office, the agency has flexibility within the law; solving the problem frequently requires creativity and/or cutting some red tape. When such cases are handled with sensitivity and special effort, the agency's reputation in the Legislature can only benefit.

Legislative sources agree that those agencies with good reputations fare much better than others with their legislative programs. For the most part, good reputations are built three ways: by carrying out new programs and laws in good faith whether or not the agency wanted them; by providing the Legislature with prompt, accurate, and complete but concise information; and by solving local and constituency problems quickly and sensitively. Managers often play a role in each of these. Thus, in addition to providing critical feedback concerning old legislation and contributing ideas for new bills, they also influence agency-legislative relations by responding to legislative needs.

The Legislative Body

"What they do you have to deal with in year one, year two, year three, year four" (Former legislative staff member).

In order for an agency to be most influential on legislation that will affect it for years to come, its managers, as well as its commissioners, counsels, and liaisons must have a basic knowledge of the Legislature: how it is organized, what its priorities are, who holds the power, and how and why some bills triumph while others fail.

The Legislature is the law-making body of the State, organized into two houses: the Assembly, with 150 members, and the Senate, with 61 members. All are elected for two-year terms. Within each house is a system of committees and subcommittees—a few committees perform special functions, and so are discussed individually in the following sections. Each standing committee reviews bills relating to its subject area (e.g., energy, judiciary, education). Chart 5.1 outlines the progress of a bill through the Legislature. Most of

5.1 How a Bill becomes a Law

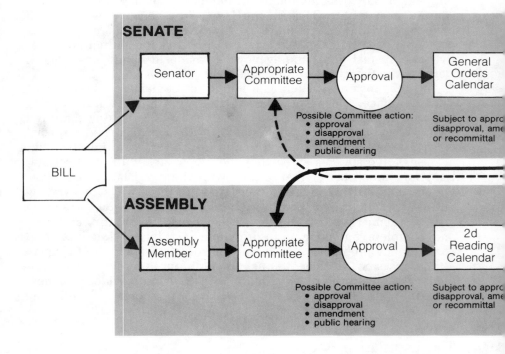

*In the Assembly there are two "dual reference" committees which must review certain bills approved by other standing committees: Codes reviews penalty provisions of any bill and Ways & Means reviews any measure with fiscal implications.
**If changed, originating house must concur before it goes to the Governor.
***Governor has 30 days to act on bills passed in session's last 10 days; bills sent to him earlier must be acted on within 10 days.

the bills that are introduced are never reported out of committee. Common reasons for this include cost—the bill, if enacted, would be too expensive or politically infeasible; or opposition by committee members on philosophical grounds. Others of the bills not reported out address the same problem as one that had been reported out, or are "study bills" introduced to raise an issue rather than actually to be passed. A committee may defeat a bill openly, with a majority vote, or it simply may hold the bill indefinitely. In the 1985-86 session, for example, only about 11 percent of the bills introduced survived the committee system and a floor vote to finally become law.

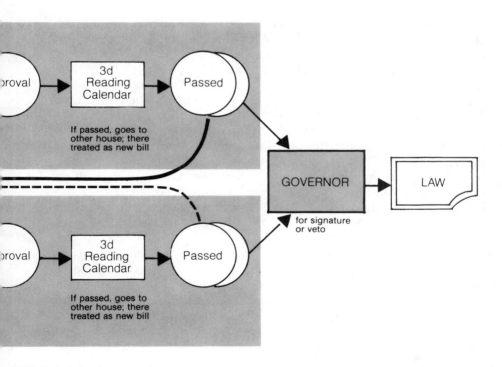

NOTE: Part of the above procedure may be bypassed or shortened by unanimous consent or if the bill is sent with a message of necessity from the Governor.

The Rules Committees

The Rules Committee in each house is chaired by the leader. Near the end of the session it becomes all-powerful as the committee determines the fate of a bill in the stacks waiting to be introduced. After a date set by the leadership, usually sometime in May, no bill may be introduced or reported to the floor by a committee without the approval of Rules. A former legislative staff member stated very simply the importance of the Rules Committee: "The Rules Committees in both houses control everything. They're the traffic cops, the flood gates of the Legislature—bills get to the floor or don't get to the floor, depending on them."

The Assembly Ways and Means and Senate Finance Committees

The Assembly Ways and Means and Senate Finance Committees and their staffs play a vital role in analyzing and altering the Executive Budget. As mentioned in Chapter II, the Legislature has only two months to analyze a budget that took essentially ten months to develop. Recently, staff members note that there has been even less time to work with a final Executive Budget, since Governor Cuomo has tended to use the thirty-day amendment period to make substantial changes. The month of March, then, finds staff and members of these committees working extremely long hours to meet the April 1 deadline. In addition to being involved in analysis of the budget, they are responsible for writing the "Green Book," which agencies and DOB look to for a more detailed explanation of the budget that is actually passed. Needless to say, when information is requested of an agency during this time, a quick response is of the utmost importance.

After April 1, the Assembly Ways and Means Committee continues to consider all bills with a fiscal impact. For example, a mental health bill that would require any kind of financing would be referred first to the Mental Health Committee and then to the Assembly Ways and Means Committee. Both committees are also concerned with oversight of the budget and focus especially on new programs or those programs whose budgets have been increased substantially.

Because the fiscal committees judge the feasibility of proposals on the basis of cost, they often take the blame for killing bills popular with interest groups. For example, every year a bill is proposed in the Assembly that, if passed, would require the State to assume total responsibility for Medicaid. This bill is routinely reported out of the standing committee with the members' full knowledge that it will not pass the Ways and Means Committee.

Leadership

Most power in the Legislature rests with its leadership. A party conference held on or before the Legislature convenes in January, after a general election, selects leaders for the two-year session. The Speaker holds the most powerful position in the Assembly, and the Majority Leader in the Senate holds the power there. Some power rests with other members of the majority (committee chairs, in particular), but very little is held by individual members of the minority party in each house.

How does the leadership exert its power? First, the Speaker and Majority Leader appoint all members to committees (in practice, the minority members are appointed to committees upon the Minority Leader's recommendation) as well as the chairperson of each committee. Because the leaders can appoint members who share their beliefs to chair committees, they have great influence over the kinds of legislation that is reported out of committee. Bills generally are not reported out without the support of the chair, since the latter is not likely to place a bill on the committee's agenda if he or she opposes it and does not want to risk its being reported out.

Second, as chair of the Rules' Committee, in their respective houses, each leader wields power in two other ways. Following the

PAYNE

111

date after which all bills must go through the Rules Committee—
a date set by the leaders—the chair of that committee determines
which bills will be considered on the floor. Before that date, the
chair has the power to refer bills to committees. Although there
are house rules about a committee's jurisdiction over bills in its
particular area, many important bills concern issues that can legit-
imately be considered by two or more committees. In these cases,
the leader has substantial flexibility in assigning the bill to the most
or least sympathetic committee.

The leadership also controls the amount of money each committee is allocated. Only the Finance Committee and the Ways and
Means Committee have separate lines in the legislative budget.

Lastly, in the Senate, the Majority Leader as well as the bill's
sponsor, has the power to "star" a bill. When a bill on the Senate
floor calendar is so starred, its progress through the legislative
process is halted until the Majority Leader removes the star. In
effect, a bill can be killed in this way. Although only the sponsor
has this power in the Assembly, bills are usually starred at the
request of the Speaker. Most often, bills are starred to allow time
for amendments to be made or to muster support for the bill before
a final vote.

Those are the formal sources of leadership power. The informal
sources are described succinctly by Alan Hevesi (*Legislative Politics
in New York State*, p. 60):

> A variety of techniques have been employed by dif-
> ferent leaders, such as the development of a club-like
> atmosphere, the exchange of amenities, assistance to
> lawmakers in their nonpolitical problems, and the
> building of personal relationships based on shared ex-
> periences. The most important techniques are, however,
> of a political character, such as assistance to members
> in legislative matters (such as passing local and private
> bills), giving members meaningful debate assignments,
> granting them extra lulus on staff allotments, interced-
> ing with the executive branch on behalf of members
> or their constituents, and so on.

Yet, in spite of the many formal and informal powers of the legislative leaders, "there's no tyranny. The maverick gets punished
by the loss of access, by losing his ability to get favors. The leader
will constantly adjust himself to his members' needs so that he can
call on their support when the time comes" (Senate Staff member
quoted in Hevesi, p. 31).

Although the fate of a bill is officially determined when it is
killed or passed on the floor of either house, the real decision is

often made in party conference. Party conferences are held according to need (weekly, except in late March and late June, when they convene at least once or twice a day) by each of the following groups: Senate Republicans, Assembly Republicans, Senate Democrats and Assembly Democrats. One legislative staff member described these closed strategy sessions as "dress rehearsals for floor debate," for the conference is used to determine the position each party will take on pending legislation. The secrecy of these conferences is protected under the Open Meetings Law. When a reporter prepared to challenge this in court in 1985, both houses requested and received a message of necessity from the Governor and immediately passed a bill clarifying the Open Meetings Law.

There may be initial disagreement among Assembly Democrats, for example, about the merits of a particular bill; the objective of the party conference is to provide a private forum for ironing out differences so that the party remains cohesive when the bill actually comes up for a vote on the floor. As followers of legislation well know, the goal of party cohesiveness is not always achieved.

When the "nose-count" taken during a party conference indicates that a bill favored by the leadership clearly has not attracted enough support to pass, then the leadership often arranges for the bill to remain in committee until sufficient support for passage is assured.

The Minority Party

The minority party members in each house have little power, formal or informal. The Minority Leader recommends the assignments of minority members to committees and allocates a lump sum of money for staff and office costs, but he or she does not have the same ability as the Majority Leader to grant favors to members, simply because the majority party can always outvote the minority. Minority party members often do cooperate with the majority in the other house, (i.e. with members of their own political party) although the relationship depends partly on the minority leader. The Assembly Ways and Means and Senate Finance committees are the only committees that have sizable staffs working specifically for minority party purposes, since committee staff allotments are distributed by the majority leaders and central staff report directly to those leaders.

The minority party is not completely powerless, however, as was demonstrated in 1983 in the Senate. Customarily, the Republican majority had passed many of the Democrats' local bills and special appropriations for programs in Democrats' districts. Following an organized attempt by the Democrats in the 1982 elections to win the majority, the Republicans retaliated by killing most local bills and special appropriations. The Democrats then responded by dragging out debate on every inconsequential issue raised over a period of several weeks. The Republicans soon made the concessions necessary for a return to normalcy [recounted by Hevesi in Peter Colby, ed. *New York State Today*, p. 159].

One agency liaison suggested that her agency's policy of interacting with minority party legislators and staff in the same way as with the majority was beneficial. When negotiations are taking place over a bill that is complex, the person who understands it best and is most articulate often influences its fate. That person might well be a minority party member, and the continuing working relationship that the agency has maintained with minority party staff will stand in good stead.

Sometimes the minority party may agree to vote as a bloc. If the majority party is less successful in voting together, the minority party plus a few majority votes may carry the bill, although this happens infrequently. The decision to vote as a bloc, or to offer amendments intended to kill a bill (another strategy often attempted) typically is made in party conference.

Hearings

Hearings are most often held by members of the standing committee considering a bill. Task forces or subcommittees may also hold meetings. Although these are ostensibly information-gathering devices, the Assembly Program and Committee Staff Guide to Public Hearings describes a variety of other purposes as well:

- o to seek advice and recommendations on committee initiatives and to judge the need to develop additional legislation on the subject under consideration;
- o to increase visibility and association with the subject;
- o to provide a "sounding board" or "release valve" for concerned citizens;
- o to give exposure to new ideas and proposals and to test public receptivity.

Although it is not infrequent for hearings to be held after the real decisions have already been made (in order to increase visibility, provide a release valve, or test receptivity), they are also often held with a genuine interest in gathering information and seeking advice. While hearings may be held for any bill, many do not undergo the process. Controversial bills with the potential for substantial impact almost always have at least one hearing, and sometimes a series of hearings statewide. When a hearing is set, it is announced on the weekly Senate-Assembly hearing calendar (available to the public), and hearing notices are sent to selected experts on the subject, and/ or to the committee's mailing list. Hearings are open to the public and may be held by the Senate or Assembly committee having jurisdiction, or by both together.

Hearings provide another opportunity for agencies to influence proposed legislation. At one time or another, every agency's commissioner is asked to testify at hearings that directly concern the agency's areas of responsibility; the extent to which this is necessary depends on the department. The Commissioner of Education, for example, testifies at about twenty hearings per session and sees them as important for the agency's agenda. Smaller agencies whose issues in a given year are not controversial may seldom testify, if at all.

Agencies also consider hearings opportunities to educate. Testimony becomes available to the public as soon as it is given. Further, as one commissioner commented, although committee members almost always know where they stand on an issue, other legislators may not. When the bill comes to a vote on the floor, every vote counts.

Constituencies and Lobbying

Reelection is a primary concern for every legislator—only by reelection can he or she continue to work for important substantive goals. For this reason, there is always some legislation (either controversial or locally important) that members support or oppose regardless of party or leadership sentiments simply because the residents in their district feel strongly about it. Since this is true for all legislators at one time or another, party leaders recognize and usually honor the practice. One legislative staff member notes that this excuse is "not like muscle (the more you use it, the better it gets), but rather like gunpowder (the more you use, the less there is)—and the smart ones don't use it a lot."

Legislative liaisons and commissioners are aware of legislators' need for reelection and the restraints this imposes upon their actions. Legislators must continually consider the political ramifications of their actions; they rely upon staff to gather and review the relevant data for each issue. Not surprisingly, then, it is the staff and agency people who most often interact on questions of fact, while legislators and commissioners (and liaisons) consider issues within the political context. Agencies can apply political pressure on legislators indirectly, by mobilizing their constituencies to support or oppose a bill.

Changes in the Legislature

The Legislature has changed dramatically since 1970. At that time it had virtually no staff to do research and analysis. Because of this, it almost always deferred to the expertise of the executive branch (a Governor's veto had not been overridden for many years prior to the Carey administration). Typically, the Governor's budget was changed only for political reasons, as the analytical capability to review it substantively simply did not exist.

Legislators themselves had a different attitude toward their jobs. Most often, being a legislator was a second job. Salaries were not high, and sessions typically ended in April, shortly after the budget was passed.

Today, staff resources are considerable. A base sum of money is allotted to each member for support staff ($22,000 in 1986 in the Assembly, for example, more for leaders and committee chairs). Additional money is allocated for district offices; staff is hired for committee use by the committee chair, and central staff, hired by the leadership, are assigned to committees.

In addition to staff resources, Legislative Commissions work directly for the members. They are created to research specific issue areas and to formulate legislative solutions when necessary. Although each has representation from both Senate and Assembly, all but two are partisan since a majority is always either from the Assembly or from the Senate and reflects the party in power there. The exceptions are the Legislative Bill Drafting Commission, which is co-chaired by an Assembly member and a Senator, and the Legislative Commission on Expenditure Review, in which the chair alternates annually. Since Commissions are re-funded each year, they can be eliminated if deemed no longer useful.

The Senate also has considerable staff involved in the Senate Research Service. This counterbalances some of the advantage the Assembly has by virtue of having more than twice the membership of the Senate and therefore considerably more staffers.

Despite all of these recently established resources, the Legislature still relies on agency information, for the legislative workload has at least kept pace with increases in staff and salary. As the number of State laws has increased, so have the number of opportunities to revise and repeal them (although many fewer are repealed than are added). Federal legislation frequently affects state behavior. For example, a bill raising the legal purchase age for alcoholic beverages to twenty-one originally was defeated by the State Legislature. Only after federal highway funding legislation included financial reductions for states with lower drinking ages, was the bill reconsidered and passed in 1985. A federal law, which was passed in the mid-70's requiring facilities for the handicapped in all public schools and subsequently expanded, produced a great deal of State spin-off legislation during the following several years.

Although the number of bills introduced and considered has risen sharply, there has not been a substantial increase in the number that are actually passed and signed by the Governor. (The Governor predictably signs about 90 percent of bills passed, with the result that some 6 to 11 percent of the bills introduced can be expected to become law.)

It is no longer unheard of for the Legislature to override a Governor's veto. Override is still a difficult feat, however, because in recent years at least one house has always been controlled by members of the Governor's party, and two-thirds of both houses are required to override.

The Legislature in the 1980's has had greater input in the budgeting arena than previously. More staff resources, more analysis, and a more independent role have resulted in more alterations to the Governor's budget each year. In addition, the 1981 court ruling in *Anderson v. Regan* [442 NYS 2d 404; 53 NY 2d 356; 425 NE 2d 792] held that Federal grants to agencies must be channeled through the Legislature, another boost to legislative power.

Finally, legislators themselves have a different attitude toward their role and responsibilities. Today, few have full-time second jobs. Salaries are substantial: in 1987, $43,000 per year plus additional stipends for majority and minority party leadership and committee leadership positions as well as provisions for reimbursing other expenses. (Toward the end of the regular 1987 legislative session, legislators voted themselves a substantial raise: as of January 1989, members of both the Senate and the Assembly will receive a salary of $57,500 annually.) Today legislative sessions last much longer than in past years, typically extending from early January through the end of June or early July. Members then return to their home districts, although most committee staff continue to work until the next session begins, holding hearings, researching issues, and planning an agenda for the next year. In recent years the Legislature has not formally adjourned, but rather "recessed." When in recess, it may reconvene to address a special situation at any time. If it has adjourned, it can only be reconvened by the Governor for a special session (where it may only consider bills relating to the Governor's agenda), or by petition of two-thirds of the members of each house. Frequently the Legislature has returned to Albany in December.

Legislative and Executive Powers

Since the Legislature rarely overrides a governor's veto, the mere threat of a veto is taken very seriously. When a bill is due for final vote, negotiations often take place between the Legislature and the Governor, as well as between both houses of the Legislature. On the other hand, if the Legislature knows a bill or an item (a line of the budget) will be vetoed, it may pass it and let the Governor take responsibility for disapproving it.

> Sometimes, as Governor Rockefeller once explained, legislators went along with bills to please individual members as a courtesy on local matters, only because they were confident that there would be a gubernatorial veto. 'I'll be the guy who vetoes the bill,' the governor said. This is all part of the act.
>
> (Gerald Benjamin in Colby, p. 134)

In the 1985-86 session, Governor Cuomo vetoed about seven percent of the bills passed by both houses. In order to avoid the veto, the sponsor of a bill sometimes recalls it from the Governor's desk. This allows the Legislature yet another chance to make corrections or alter the bill through substantive amendments in accordance with the Governor's suggestions.

New York has had, formally and traditionally, a strong executive. The discussion of the shift toward greater legislative assertiveness is not intended to understate the strength of the Governor, but rather to show the trend away from state government as it operated during the Rockefeller years, when the Governor's effective power was substantially greater due to the Legislature's more limited policy role.

The Governor has the statutory power to introduce Executive Budget bills without a legislative sponsor, which all other bills must have. The Legislature's power to alter this budget is limited. Requested money may be reduced, but never increased; additions must each be made on separate lines, which the Governor then has the opportunity to veto individually.

The Governor's program bills are almost always introduced as a courtesy to the Governor, usually by the chair of the standing committee that has primary jurisdiction or by the committee as a whole. If they are not introduced, it may be because a member is sponsoring a similar bill. In such cases, some type of compromise is likely to be arranged with the Governor. In the 1985 session, for example, the Governor submitted 108 program bills, of which eighteen were not introduced. Program bills are by no means rubber stamped by the Legislature. Like all bills, they are subject to change both in committee and on the floor. Although each agency hopes to have its bill selected as a Governor's Program Bill, selection does not guarantee passage; even so, the chances of passage are greater than for other bills mainly because of the extensive groundwork laid by the Executive Chamber as the Governor's program is developed.

Throughout the fall, the Governor's office and legislators talk informally about which issues are most important and what broad alternatives seem politically feasible. Before incorporation into the Governor's program, "each idea has to be tested, thought out, and reviewed," according to one member of the Governor's Program Office.

The character of legislative-gubernatorial relations, like legislative-agency relations, depends to a great extent on the political style of those in office as well as the political persuasions involved. As might be expected, the Governor often finds it easiest to deal with the house dominated by the same political party as he—in New York, since 1975, that has meant the Assembly. The fact that the Senate majority has been Republican during the same period, although sometimes frustrating to the Governor and Assembly, serves to provide some ideological balance. In a divided legislative arena, middle of the road issues are most likely to be addressed successfully. Negotiations sometimes take more time, because of more fundamental differences. And finally, "it keeps each house honest" because its positions are cross-examined very carefully in a body dominated by differing ones.

APPENDIX

Glossary

Bill. Specific legislative proposal, introduced, but not yet enacted into law.
   Companion bills are identical bills introduced separately into each house. **Uni bills** are introduced simultaneously in both houses, co-sponsored as long as identical amendments are approved by each house on the same day.

Budget bill. The bill introduced by the Governor to implement the annual Executive Budget; it may request appropriations or not.

Deficiency appropriation bill. A bill proposed by the Governor, to cover unanticipated expenditures from prior year.

Supplemental appropriation bill. A bill proposed by the Governor to cover additional expenditure requests for the current fiscal year.

Calendar. The list of bills and resolutions compiled daily for consideration by each house.

Conference. Closed sessions held by majority and minority party in each house to consider current legislative proposals. Usually held weekly; toward end of session, they may be held daily or even several times a day.

Engross. To prepare a bill with necessary accompanying materials for final passage.

Legislative Digest. A weekly publication identifying sponsor and providing summary of each bill's provisions and status.

Message of Necessity. From the Governor to the Legislature, calling for need for immediate vote on a bill, superseding mandatory time requirements; or need for special bill affecting local government.

Quorum. Majority of members elected to each house.

Three day rule. Bills awaiting passage by either house must sit for three legislative days before a final vote may be taken.

Chapter VI

Internal Control, Oversight and External Review

Some of the material in this chapter was provided expressly by the Office of Management and Productivity.

Internal Control

"Even small failures in control systems can tend to destroy the public perception of government" (Deputy Director within the Executive Chamber).

What exactly is internal control? The term is used differently by different organizations in state government. The Office of Management and Productivity (OMP), (established by executive order in 1983 and charged with, among other responsibilities, improving the State's executive branch internal controls system), defines internal control not as a separate and distinct system, but as *all* of the methods by which state agencies regulate their activities to accomplish defined purposes. There are more specific control systems as well: administrative controls are designed to ensure that organizational objectives and management decisions are being attended to, while accounting controls safeguard assets and reliability of fiscal records. Under the broad general definition, internal control may also include budget, data collection and maintenance, and equipment and inventory controls.

The Office of the State Comptroller (OSC), on the other hand, commonly uses the term more narrowly, to refer only to controls that safeguard assets and the reliability of fiscal records. The OSC's internal control review focuses on the operation of accounting controls. The Comptroller's office reviews administrative controls within the context of program audits (considered later in the chapter).

In August, 1987, the Governor signed into law the Governmental Accountability Audit and Internal Control Act. That Act states that "internal controls encompass the plan of organization and all of the coordinate methods and measures adopted within an organization to safeguard its assets, check the accuracy and reliability of its accounting data, promote operational efficiency and encourage adherence to prescribed managerial policies." Internal controls include both internal administrative and internal accounting controls.

The law directs every executive agency head to establish and maintain a system of written internal controls within the agency and designate an internal control officer to implement and review internal control responsibilities as outlined in the legislation.

The law also provides for the State Comptroller's Office to conduct periodic audits of executive agency internal control systems. Further, the Governor's Office, Division of the Budget, Department of Law, and Department of Audit and Control will be audited by an independent accounting firm at least once every two years, beginning in 1990. These audits are to be made public.

According to one Division of the Budget spokesman, the legislation is seen as a management technique: it establishes procedures to assist managers in avoiding overspending, operational failure, and violations of law.

Agencies routinely modify their control systems as new problem areas arise, or information and administrative needs change. For example, the Department of Correctional Services (DOCS) recently strengthened its internal control system by developing a self-assessment survey for all correctional facilities. The survey includes about three hundred questions compiled from previous audit reports relating to program and administrative concerns. Through their survey responses, facilities become aware whether they are in compliance with existing agency internal controls, and if not, what needs to be done.

Although auditors encourage surveys and other self-policing mechanisms, managers should be aware that any resulting information can subsequently be used in an audit. Auditors report "on an exception basis" and may use any information available to uncover exceptions. The results of the DOCS survey, for example, increased central office coordination of facilities and increased accountability of facility managers to the central office, both of which improved the efficiency and effectiveness of the agency. Whenever an agency initiates a survey or other reporting requirement, it presumably expects the benefits to outweigh any increase in short-term vulnerability that might result from the information collected.

Among the major objectives of an internal control system are:
- improving operational efficiency and effectiveness;
- safeguarding the resources of the State;
- assuring compliance with laws, regulations and policies; and

○ establishing and maintaining the reliability and integrity of all reports and data produced.

The Office of Management and Productivity suggests several essential elements of good management that will result when these objectives are made operational. An effective control system assures that the goals, purposes, and mission of the agency's various programs are succinctly stated and clearly enunciated so that each person in the organization understands what is to be done and how to accomplish particular assignments. It also makes certain that agency systems are in direct compliance with applicable laws, rules, regulations, and policies. Appropriate evaluation will show whether operations are being conducted in an economic and efficient manner and that maximum benefits are being realized from the resources utilized; and whether all revenues and resources applicable to agency operations are collected and/or accounted for. Lastly, the control system assures that accurate and reliable information is available and properly maintained. This last objective includes the timely collection of fiscal, personnel, and programmatic data, as well as the timely preparation and issuance of reports.

In order to keep internal controls abreast of programmatic, administrative, and technological changes, agencies may choose to perform some type of risk analysis to identify any areas of its operation susceptible to abuse or misuse, and to focus resources on control of the most vulnerable and important aspects of operations. In general, it makes little sense for an agency to establish complex and costly control systems for insignificant or incidental aspects of an operation.

Some common examples of accounting controls may be found in Appendix I to this chapter. More detailed guidelines relating to payroll, time and attendance, equipment control, materials and supplies, travel, and internal auditing may be found in the *New York State Accounting System User Procedure Manual, Vol. XI*, prepared by OSC.

An internal control system that is operating well provides a variety of benefits. Among them are:

○ increasing agency flexibility by reducing external control organizations' tendency to over-regulate those program areas that an agency does not appear to control satisfactorily;

○ facilitating the elimination of unneeded controls and paperwork;

○ enabling the agency to be more productive in day-to-day operations;

○ opening up formal feedback mechanisms through which organizations are better prepared to capitalize on employee ideas and proposals;

○ decreasing uncertainty, because management has greater confidence in the organization's ability to control itself;

○ reducing the management time needed to track resources;

○ enhancing a management information system through the inclusion of internal control evaluation results;

○ fostering communication within an agency; and

○ monitoring relationships among various program functions.

Functioning internal controls may also provide new and better ways of considering how resources should be used to accomplish identified goals and objectives.

EXTERNAL REVIEW

Auditing

"Auditing is a necessary practice that's beneficial for both the State and the agency" (Agency fiscal manager).

Auditing provides information feedback to the Legislature, the Governor, and the public about how well New York State's programs are meeting their objectives. Several managers note that audits test whether their system of internal controls is working properly. Because the Legislature appropriates billions of dollars every year for State programs, and because the public pays the taxes and elects the representatives who appropriate those billions, both parties have the right to objective information about the effectiveness and efficiency of state operations. Therefore, although auditing can be, in the words of one high-level manager "a royal pain in the neck," it is a necessary aspect of good government and is often considered part of the management review process.

Auditing is also beneficial to agencies. When asked if there were positive aspects to being audited, managers declared that audits almost always called attention to something they had lost sight of or let slide, due to other priorities. Sometimes an agency knows there is a problem but lacks the resources to improve the situation. An audit documenting the deficiency can provide justification for a budget request.

Occasionally, new managers request an audit to determine past activities within their areas of responsibility and offer some guidance as to what may need to be done promptly.

The Office of the State Comptroller and the Legislative Commission on Expenditure Review (see below) have the authority to audit any program or unit in any state agency at any time, in addition to the Comptroller's periodic audits mandated by the 1987 legislation. Although managers never know exactly when their programs will be audited, they do know for certain that audits will be scheduled eventually. The audit is similar to "a regular medical examination . . . [it] is valuable but difficult to measure in dollars." [Richard E. Brown and Ralph Craft, "Auditing and Public Administration: The Unrealized Partnership," *Public Administration Review*, Vol. 4 (3), May/June 1980].

Although auditing is recognized as both necessary and valuable, managers generally do not celebrate the arrival of auditors. Auditors report "on an exception basis"—they look for operations that are not in accord with stated goals and objectives. One manager's advice: "If you are running the operation well, you shouldn't be concerned— but you *will be criticized* no matter what."

The Office of the State Comptroller

The Office of the State Comptroller is the single state organization most involved with auditing executive agencies. Within the agency, the Division of Audits and Accounts audits all state agencies and authorities, while the Division of Municipal Affairs audits local governments. During the New York City fiscal crisis in the mid 1970's, an Office of the Special Deputy Comptroller for New York City was set up to assist in the overhaul of its financial system. Today, auditing of New York City agencies, authorities, and commissions is conducted from that office.

The Division of Audits and Accounts conducts both pre-audits and post-audits. Pre-audits are completed before the disbursement of money to ensure proper authorization, mathematical accuracy, and appropriateness of the expenditure. Pre-audits are conducted on all state agency payrolls, travel and merchandise vouchers, purchase orders, leases, local assistance vouchers, and property acquisition vouchers.

The Office of the State Comptroller is not the only prepayment reviewer of expenditures: before OSC ever sees a request for payment, a pre-audit occurs within the agency. This pre-audit includes both a clerical check for mathematical accuracy and a more rigorous audit to verify that the bill accurately reflects the service or product provided to the agency.

In the past, the Management Audit Group within the Division of Audits and Accounts audited each agency as a whole every few years. However, because of the expansion of agencies, it now tends to audit programs rather than entire agencies, and these audits do not strictly follow a cycle. In those agencies with facilities throughout the State, a program normally is examined in a sample of facilities rather than in all of them.

126

The Group's activities include financial as well as compliance audits, efficiency and economy audits, program results audits, and audits of most major contracts as well as some smaller ones. (For further explanation of terms, see the glossary in Appendix II of this chapter.) Often, routine pre-audits of expenditures, contracts, payroll, or state aid reveal a weak area. If so, the results are communicated to the Management Audit Group, which may follow up through a post-audit.

Many OSC audits involve only a routine check of accounts, accounting controls, and compliance with existing laws and regulations. These audits are quicker than program results audits, and in some cases may require little preparatory effort on the part of the manager responsible for the program. Prior to the 1960s, these were the only audits done. Then, following the trend established in the federal government, the Management Audit Group began conducting program audits intended to measure program effectiveness. The standards by which program effectiveness is measured are most often the agency's own objectives. If there are no stated objectives or if the agency's objectives seem out of line, objectives of similar programs elsewhere provide a yardstick by which to measure effectiveness.

The typical OSC audit takes about six months and involves an on-site team of three or four auditors. Financial audits tend to take less time; in-depth program audits may take longer. At any given time there may be 150 audits in process throughout the state. Upon completion, copies of the audit findings are sent to the agency head, legislative leaders, the DOB, the Governor's Office, and the Public Information Office at OSC. The reports are then available to any interested citizen through the Public Information Office.

Programs may be selected for audit for a number of reasons. Sometimes an audit is scheduled simply because the program has not been audited in recent years or because it carries a large budget. The interest of the Comptroller or of a legislator in a particular program may trigger an audit. Or results of previous audits may suggest a follow-up audit at some later time.

Audit directors refer audits that reveal serious conditions (and are otherwise appropriate) to a special unit for follow-up. These are conducted quickly and are not intended to be complete reexaminations.

Legislative Commission on Expenditure Review

The Legislative Commission on Expenditure Review (LCER) was created to assist the Legislature in determining whether executive agencies "have efficiently and effectively expended funds" as legislatively appropriated. The Commission's main responsibility is "to make a comprehensive and continuing study of the programs of and expenditures by State departments; local assistance programs; and federal and local government fiscal relationships and their fiscal implications" (Legislative Law, Article 5-A, Sec. 83).

The LCER, with a current staff of twenty-seven, is a much smaller organization than OSC's Management Audit Group of about three hundred. The Legislative Commission also serves to provide objective reports to the Legislature and the agencies and to assist in resolving issues and improving executive branch operations. Within a given year, the Commission typically publishes twelve to fifteen completed audit reports compared to the Comptroller's two hundred. However, the fact that key Assembly and Senate members are members of the Commission makes it an important component of New York's system of controls. Program budgets have been known to rise or fall based upon LCER audits, but elimination of an entire program following an audit is rare.

Established in 1969 as a permanent legislative agency, the Commission measures program achievement against legislative intent as stated in the law. For older programs whose purpose was not explicitly written into law, Commission staff try to ascertain the purpose from budget or agency sources. Since 1985, reports from LCER have contained staff recommendations. Just as with OSC's Management Audit Group, these are discussed with the audited agencies at the exit conferences that close the audit prior to being sent to the agency in a draft report. Thus, the agencies have a chance to comment and contribute before the draft reaches them. Reports issued by LCER are widely distributed: one thousand copies of each report are printed; they are sent to legislators and their staff, to the press, and to interested members of the public.

Audits by LCER originate as questions asked by Commission members or by the staff of the legislative fiscal committees. These proposals undergo a screening process that takes into account, among other things, whether the Comptroller's Office, another external auditor, or an internal auditor has visited the program. Once this screening is completed, the remainder of the audit is conducted according to the state audit process described later in the chapter.

Auditors Other Than State Governmental Organizations

As noted earlier, those agencies with independently elected heads are legislatively mandated to undergo an audit by an independent accounting firm at least once every two years. Further, the 1981 GAAP legislation requires that the State's financial statements be audited annually by an independent certified public accounting firm.

This is important because it provides a check external to government on those who do most of the checking internally. The Comptroller's Office and the Division of the Budget are both audited by an outside firm. In order to be certain that both agencies are performing their control functions properly, the outside auditor must also audit other agencies to confirm the accuracy of the control agencies' audits. Usually only the largest state programs are audited for this purpose, and not every agency is involved.

Additionally, because many programs administered by state agencies are funded through federal programs, the federal government may send its own auditors to review program activities and expenditures. To eliminate duplication, beginning in 1985, the federal government has required an annual single audit of all federal funds administered by the State. The single audit consists of three parts: an audit of the financial statements, a report on internal controls, and a report on compliance with existing laws and regulations.

In addition to the single audit, federal agencies continue to send their own auditors to review programs they help fund. For example, during the 1985-86 fiscal year, the Office of Mental Retardation and Developmental Disabilities (OMRDD) was the subject of 98 federal audits (by four different groups) in addition to 103 audits by state groups.

Agencies themselves may also hire private sector auditors (often from the "Big 8" accounting firms) to audit a program. Normally

they do this after accepting a grant that provides funding for an external auditor.

Other state agencies may be involved in auditing. Because OMRDD operates twenty developmental facilities that provide a variety of client services, the Department of Social Services, Department of Health, Department of Labor, and the Education Department all send their own auditors to review aspects of OMRDD programs that fall in their domains or for which they provide funding. While smaller, more centralized agencies are likely to be audited less intensely and by fewer groups, the OMRDD example illustrates that OSC and LCER, the two state agencies with *carte blanche* to audit, are not the only external groups that may request a review of agency programs or records. Other state groups that can make similar requests include the Commission of Correction, which is responsible for oversight of all state and local correctional facilities, and the Commission on Quality of Care for the Mentally Disabled (CQC), which is responsible for oversight and review of programs serving the mentally ill, mentally retarded, developmentally disabled, and alcohol and substance abusers.

In some cases, the line between oversight and audit is blurred. Do frequent, regular reviews of client case records by an external agency constitute an audit? Although in some senses similar, the routine nature of such reviews means that they are probably less formal than the audit process described below. The same is true of research studies conducted by various groups. The Commission to Revise Social Services Law studies various Department of Social Services programs with the intent of uncovering areas where new legislation may be warranted. An Assembly standing committee on Oversight, Analysis, and Investigation also conducts oversight reviews, although its staff is very small. Other legislative standing committees may conduct oversight reviews as well.

The State Audit Process

From the viewpoint of the agency, the audit process, whether conducted by the Office of the State Comptroller or by the Legislative Commission on Expenditure Review, has three basic parts:

- o initial contact between the agency and the external organization to define the area of review;
- o day-to-day contact between the staff of the reviewing body and agency personnel; and
- o agency responses to the draft and final copy of the document which sets forth the findings and recommendations of the review.

What follows is designed to give the reader a "feel" for the audit process and for the tensions that may arise, as well as to consider ways that agencies work to meet these challenges. (Managers preparing for audit may find it useful to refer to the U.S. General Accounting Office's *Standards for Audit of Governmental Organizations, Programs, Activities and Functions* (1981), commonly called the "yellow book." Although it was specifically designed for federal auditors, state auditors find it a useful guide and refer to it frequently.)

Opening Conference and Preparation for Audit

Except in very unusual circumstances, the audit begins with the auditor contacting the agency and arranging an opening conference to explain the purpose and scope of the audit. At the meeting, the subject matter of the inquiry is identified. It is a manager's prerogative to request this identification (which should serve to define the scope of the audit) and, as the audit progresses, to question deviations from it. Although managers have been known to resent auditors who "go fishing," OSC auditors do have the authority to broaden the scope or change the focus of the audit, should they stumble upon something unexpected or questionable.

To provide the necessary controls on external reviews and to establish effective communication procedures for tracking them, most agencies ask that any notice of review be communicated immediately to a designated high level staff member within the organization. Agencies are required to notify the Director of State Operations and Policy Management of each request by an external organization to audit.

Before the audit starts, managers may find themselves facing dilemmas about how best to prepare for it and uncertain about the auditor's expertise in the agency's subject area. Of course, this is not true in every situation: auditors performing strictly financial audits will for the most part be reviewing records. Aside from ensuring that the relevant data are available, no advance preparation should be necessary for program audits, either. Auditors emphasize that year-round effective, efficient management is the best preparation. At least one agency, as the following paragraph describes, has established specific, routine procedures to be followed to minimize problems with its facility audits.

When a letter notifying the agency of a facility audit arrives, a high-level fiscal manager from central office travels with one or two staff to the facility to be audited and meets with top management. Whenever possible, someone from another facility who is familiar with the auditors attends to offer helpful tips on what to expect.

131

Previous audits are reviewed to make sure that everything management agreed to do as a result of the last audit has been done before the auditors arrive.* After this meeting, all facility managers who might be involved in the audit are brought into the process.

Another agency is experimenting with an alternative to reviewing previous audit reports prior to audit. The agency's Coordinator of External Agency Audits maintains a record of the status of recommendations from previous audit reports listed by program. As recommendations are implemented, they are eliminated from the list. Thus, when the auditor arrives, each recommendation has been dealt with in one of three ways: it has been implemented; there is a plan for its implementation; or the agency has explicitly disagreed with the recommendation and stated its reasons for disagreement.

Good record keeping is important for many reasons, but it is absolutely essential to a favorable audit. Record keeping properly includes written documentation of all procedures, regardless of how routine they may be to those who use them. In the words of one manager who learned from experience, "You can't just say you had four aces before you threw the cards in; they want to see the aces!"

Another manager related the following about how a routine procedure was suddenly called into question. The agency being audited had a four-step procedure for reviewing the awarding of contracts. In the course of the audit, the auditor asked a nearby employee to describe the process. The employee, who was a trainee and had been with the agency for only a short time, was unfamiliar with the process and should have referred the auditor to a more knowledgeable source. Instead, the trainee answered (inaccurately) that the decision was simply taken without a clearly established procedure. Pressing onward without verifying the information, the auditor criticized the lack of procedure in the draft audit report. Fortunately, the agency had in its files a memo outlining the procedure, which supported the testimony of others involved in the process, and the situation was resolved to the satisfaction of both the agency and the auditors.

Lastly, awareness of the regulations and guidelines established by the Office of the State Comptroller and by the Office of Management and Productivity allows the concerned manager to anticipate to some degree an auditor's moves and findings.

---

* Although managers stress the importance of implementing at least those changes the agency agreed to make, caution must be exercised when making last-minute improvements; auditors are quite likely to discover the timing of the change and may assume that things will return to the *status quo ante* after their departure.

Day-to-Day Contact During the Audit

As a review proceeds, contact between the review organization and department or agency personnel usually follows a fairly standard format. Requests are made for manuals, files, and records; oral responses to various matters in the area being evaluated are also elicited; and auditors will visit the sites of agency operations and, perhaps, clientele groups. Instituting procedures to ensure that an auditor's questions or problems are quickly communicated to the appropriate level of management is useful.

Normally, the agency names a liaison at the opening conference with the auditors. Questions and problems can often be resolved at this level, but the agency may also benefit by establishing a second communication linkage on a higher level within the organization. Periodic meetings between the auditor and high-level management enable the latter to become familiar with both sides of the story if differences exist or develop. This is especially important when lower-level managers have a personal stake in maintaining the status quo.

The typically long lead time between initiation of a review and issuance of the final report may afford managers the opportunity to implement some changes before the final report is completed. Although the original finding may or may not still be included, an agency response indicating that appropriate action has been taken is obviously preferable to promises that it will be handled (assuming the agency agrees that a problem exists and needs to be addressed).

When there is frequent, comfortable communication between auditors and the agency managers responsible for the operation being audited, the agency is likely to answer questions and consider problems during the course of the audit from a positive rather than a defensive position. As a consequence, the draft audit report will contain no surprises and will be a summary of legitimate concerns rather than containing findings based on inaccurate or incomplete information.

Closing Conference and Agency Responses

At the completion of a study, the auditors hold a closing conference (also called exit interview or closeout) with management to discuss the findings. Differences may still be resolved at this stage.

One agency manager recalled that formerly closing conferences were attended only by the auditors and lower level staff involved. The latter were easily intimidated by the auditors and lacked the broad knowledge necessary to respond to some of the audit findings.

Now, with higher management in attendance, many more problems are resolved at the closing conference.

After the meeting, a draft report is prepared and, following reviews within the Comptroller's office or the Legislative Commission on Expenditure Review, copies are sent to the agency and to DOB. (If it is an LCER review, copies are also sent to the Commission members.) The agency then has thirty days to respond in writing and needs to clear its responses with DOB. The latter's responsibility is to provide the Governor with an early indication of possible problems, to assist agencies in correcting errors, and to help clarify and resolve important issues.

In agencies with facilities scattered across the State, a consistency check may prove beneficial. For example, a facility that has been audited may draft a response and send it to central office, where suggestions may be added or corrections made to ensure that the response is consistent with the department's statewide policies. One agency also found it useful to circulate a memo containing examples of recommendations and illustrating responses consistent or inconsistent with agency policy.

The draft audit report is then revised based on agency responses, and the revised findings and recommendations are incorporated into the final report along with the agency's comments. The agency has 90 days to respond to an OSC report to indicate how and when recommendations will be implemented or 180 days to respond to Legislative Commission findings.

Outcomes

Faced with a recommendation, the agency may either agree with the finding and agree to implement the recommendations, or it may disagree with the recommended action and refuse to adopt change. Less commonly, an agency may disagree that the recommended action should be a priority, but implements the change anyway in order to promote good will and avoid bad publicity.

Instances of genuine agreement between the agency and auditors on the recommended action are quite common. Even managers who were initially negative about the audit process have stated that nearly every audit brought something to their attention that they were unaware of, or forced a positive change that had not been implemented because of other priorities. One recalled having established a particular procedure several years earlier. He had assumed it was still being followed until told otherwise by the auditors. Yet, one by one, the original staff had been replaced, and only a very modified version of the procedure had been passed along to the newcomers.

Managers also reported being able to use a finding of weakness to substantiate a budget request. In one instance an agency used a finding of poorly trained food service supervisors to get approval for a title upgrade designed to attract better qualified employees.

From a broader agency perspective, an audit may sometimes be welcome when it provides an opportunity for staff to examine an issue of widespread interest to the department. On one occasion, the Legislative Commission on Expenditure Review, working in the Department of Social Services, pursued reasons for wide variation in administrative costs across counties. The Department had been interested in the variation as well, and was pleased when, after working with the auditors for six months, the final report confirmed the Department's hunches. The variation was due, in part, to productivity differences (measured by number of cases per worker), and this finding is being followed up within the Department through a work measurement study, which will result in the development of workload guidelines.

A second example of a welcome audit is evidenced by the following: "The LCER Audit has afforded MHIS [Mental Health Information Service] an opportunity to conduct an extensive internal review and assessment of the agency and to initiate the aforesaid enhanced methods and procedures with a view toward more efficient administration and operation" (Mental Health Information Service response to Legislative Commission Audit, 1984).

If the agency disagrees with a recommendation, the reason may be that it perceives the costs of change differently, or that it believes the auditors based the finding on incorrect or incomplete information. All sources (including OSC) agree that if an agency does disagree, it should state the reasons for objecting rather than implement a recommendation that it believes to be not in the best interest of the State, or agreeing to implement something when it has no intention of actually doing so. This is consistent with the primary objective of auditing, which is to promote more effective, efficient management.

Many disagreements occur because of the differing perspective of the auditor and manager on the pros and cons of change. One manager noted that although the Comptroller's guidelines state that internal controls should be instituted only when the benefits exceed the costs, it seemed to him that in fact auditors often did not adequately consider the costs of their recommendations for control improvements. While auditors tend to weigh the potential for fraud or waste heavily, many managers are more likely to be concerned with today's actual crises than with tomorrow's potential problems.

Another manager noted that his agency never disagrees with a recommendation because of "a lack of staff." They may disagree that the recommendation should be a priority and refuse to reallocate staff, or they may reallocate staff and make known their intention to request increased funding in their next budget request package. The Office of the State Comptroller agrees that agency responses are best framed in terms of priority issues rather than lack of needed resources.

A frequent agency response to audit recommendations is that the efficiency standards for an operation may not be relevant in view of other program considerations that auditors have failed to take into account. Food service practices in prisons, for example, have long been a subject of controversy. The Comptroller's office, in a recent audit of correctional facilities' food practices, cited as waste large amounts of food that were prepared but never eaten by prisoners. The Department, on the other hand, argued that if it cooked less food, prisoners would hear about it through the grapevine, show up for meals to demand more than was available, and use the resulting shortage as an issue to rally around. The Department felt the auditors considered one goal, reducing waste, but did not adequately consider the concurrent program goal of preventing possible violence.

The Power of the Press

Auditors do not control the press, but the latter does give them leverage because audit findings are "hot" news, and agencies do not appreciate having their dirty laundry hung in public. Bad press is unlikely to be the only consequence of a negative audit—obviously there can be repercussions from the agency's commissioner, from the DOB, and from the Legislature. Yet an article arousing public concern can create political pressures on each of these organizations to take stronger action than it might otherwise. Unfortunately, the press sometimes seizes on a minor finding and prints it out of context, thus greatly exaggerating its importance. The press has also, on occasion, reported findings that have already been corrected.

Making audit findings available to the press is viewed by the Comptroller's office as an important part of its mission. Managers who request that a finding be omitted from the final report provided they remedy the situation immediately are forgetting that the Comptroller's responsibilities include reporting to the public as well as exacting change within the agency. Are there advantages in implementing needed changes quickly, in terms of the agency's public reputation? At least one agency reported receiving positive introductions in its two most recent audit reports largely because it took immediate action during the course of the audit; if it did so partly to avoid bad press, the tactic succeeded.

Besides being part of the job, press coverage is useful to the Comptroller in demonstrating how well he is getting the job done. Newspaper headlines stating that x million dollars were found wasted indicate to the public that the Comptroller's office has been thorough in investigating State operations. One manager declared that such headlines seem to increase in frequency during election years. Of course, neither LCER nor the Public Information Office at OSC, both of which issue press releases on audit findings, can determine what the newspapers actually print or what the electronic media include in their news coverage.

Summary of Auditing

To assure a smooth audit process and avoid unnecessary problems, the following practices may be helpful:

All Year Round
○ Define the objectives; otherwise auditors may evaluate a program's effectiveness on the basis of goals created for a similar program elsewhere.
○ Document all procedures.
○ Make certain that accurate records are kept.
○ Perform spot checks whenever appropriate.
○ Be aware of the internal control guidelines set forth by the Comptroller's office.
○ Periodically evaluate operations in terms of compliance, efficiency, and effectiveness in order to discover and eliminate problems *before* an audit.

During an Audit
○ Make certain at the opening conference with the auditors that they describe the scope of the audit.
○ Request an explanation if they go beyond the planned scope.
○ Establish professional, frequent contact with the auditors; good communication pays off in fewer disagreements.
○ Create and maintain periodic contact between the auditors and management at the deputy commissioner or commissioner level if the audit is important for the agency (for example, a statewide program audit).

Concerning the Audit Results
○ Expect to see some criticism no matter how well run the agency is, for the "whole reason for auditing is to uncover things that need to be corrected."
○ Do not simply agree to implement changes regardless of agreement; rather, state any reasons for disagreement and the disadvantages that are likely to result from the proposed change.

Investigation

Unlike auditing, investigation is not a routine check on program outcomes or the management process. It is a review of people, operations, or programs that are suspected of wrongdoing. There is no formal process specified for an investigation; its objective is generally to discover and eliminate fraud, abuse, corruption, and waste. In spite of its different focus, investigation is considered here because, like auditing, it requires that managers respond to questions and requests for records by external organizations. In addition to the State investigative organizations described below, agencies may hear from federal investigators. The State Attorney General's Office may also investigate in connection with its main function, which is to provide legal defense to protect the interests of the State. Thus, its investigations of allegations of improper conduct or wrongdoing may involve State employees, but normally for a different purpose.

Office of the State Inspector General

The Office of the State Inspector General was established by Executive Order in late January of 1986. Its mission is the investigation of fraud, abuse, and corruption. Eight agencies were originally covered in the order, selected because of their large budgets and voluminous contractual arrangements: the Department of Environmental Conservation, Office of General Services, Division of Housing and Community Renewal, Department of Insurance, State Liquor Authority, Division of the Lottery, Department of Transportation, and Division for Youth. By the end of 1986, the order had been extended to include jurisdiction over all state agencies whose head is nominated or appointed by the Governor. The State Inspector General's Office operates through tips; every letter or call to its statewide hotline, whether anonymous or not, is investigated. If investigators find the allegation to be sound, the case may be referred to a prosecutor or may be presented to the agency's commissioner for appropriate disciplinary action. As an alternative solution, one recent case was referred to the Office of Management and Productivity for study. In some agencies, there are deputy inspector generals who both investigate reports of unethical or illegal activity and work to improve and maintain their respective agency's efficiency.

Temporary Commission of Investigation

Although originally envisioned by the Legislature as having a brief tenure, the Temporary Commission of Investigation has been in existence since 1958. It consists of six commissioners, two each chosen by the Governor, Senate Majority Leader, and the Speaker of the Assembly. Serving the Commission are twenty-three investigators and nine attorneys who investigate organized crime, corruption and waste in state government, as well as local problems (which consume about half of their time).

One key difference between the Temporary Commission and the State Inspector General's Office is the Commission's broader jurisdiction. The Commission is empowered to conduct investigations in both the public and private sectors. One recent topic investigated was the large increase in building construction costs, adequate explanations for which were found in both sectors. A second example was a recent examination of tax evasion. One aspect of the investigation concerned how people evade taxes; another sought to identify ways in which government allows evasion to occur.

Although only the Governor has the statutory power to request an investigation, in reality many investigations are self-initiated or originate in concerns of the public, the Legislature, or agency heads. Managers have been known to use the Commission to get the facts on a potential contractor's connections with organized crime.

Representatives of the Commission stress that the amount of money recovered due to an investigation is not as important as identifying reasons for a problem's existence, which could suggest statewide solutions. Although the Commission both holds public hearings and issues public reports, sometimes its reports are submitted confidentially only to the Governor.

Moreland Act Commissions

The Moreland Act, passed in 1907 (now Section 6 of the Executive Law), empowers the Governor to "examine and investigate the management and affairs of any department, board, bureau, or commission of the State." By 1965, there had been fifty-one "Moreland Commissions," varying in the scope and purpose of their investigations. Although early commissions were established to expose incompetence and corruption, since 1927 the focus has been on bringing a problem into the open and developing recommended legislation to eliminate it. (See Ernest Henry Brewer, *Moreland Act Investigation in New York: 1907-65*, State Education Department, 1965.)

APPENDIX I*

Examples of Internal Control

1. **Payroll.** A common example of the need for internal control is in the area of payroll, time, and attendance. The payroll procedure involves (1) authorization of payroll additions and changes, (2) maintenance of time-attendance and accrual records, (3) payroll preparation and (4) distribution of paychecks. Management control should be an element in every step of the payroll system. Such control includes staff competence and integrity, the independence of assigned functions, and understanding of documented procedures. Supervision should always be adequate to ensure that the routine recording of time and attendance is complete and accurate.

2. **Equipment.** It is also the inherent responsibility of management to maintain control over the assets in its possession, including the various items of equipment that are under the agency's control. The fundamental objectives of a system of equipment control are (1) to safeguard against loss, theft, and misuse; and (2) to facilitate effective utilization, including the determination of need and the identification of a surplus. To do this, a system of internal control would require that:

o all items of equipment to be brought under control be identified by a serial number affixed to each item;

o periodic inventories be taken of all items of equipment placed under control;

o some form of equipment utilization controls be maintained, whether they are in the form of daily usage records or simple periodic observations;

o no item of equipment be permitted to leave the premises without a pass signed by the proper authority;

o the unit supervisor be responsible for the equipment assigned to the unit and for ensuring that equipment assigned is not permanently transferred elsewhere without written approval.

3. **Material and Supplies.** Agency control over inventories of materials and supplies ensures that enough goods are on hand to meet anticipated needs while preventing an excessive build-up of stock from tying up needed funds. Management should be satisfied that inventories are safeguarded from loss by deterioration, obsolescence, and pilferage and that materials are being acquired in economic lots and maintained at the lowest cost with consideration to the risk of loss.

An agency's system of inventory control should incorporate certain basic standards. All materials and supplies received by an agency should be counted and inspected, and any discrepancies promptly reported. Issuances from inventory should be supported by signed requisitions, and periodic physical counts must be taken as an adjunct to the maintenance of perpetual inventory records. Storage areas should be secured to restrict unauthorized access and adequate to preserve the items satisfactorily until their use.

Payroll, time and attendance, equipment control and consumable inventories are three examples of internal control systems that are common

---

* Provided by the Office of Management and Productivity

to most management situations, but there are many others that may be of even greater importance. Among them are the administration of contracts, cash management practices, client eligibility for services, security of data processing systems, and grant administration. In all of these situations, internal controls are essential to achieve desired objectives, safeguard available resources, and ensure that the program is well managed.

APPENDIX II
Glossary

Compliance audit. An audit that evaluates adherence to laws, administrative regulations, and contract provisions, and determines whether past audit recommendations have been implemented; usually performed in conjunction with a financial audit.

Detective controls. Random review and checking processes intended to discover any undesirable events or activities that may have occurred.

Economy and efficiency audit. Term used by the Office of the State Comptroller for an audit that investigates how economically and efficiently a program is run.

Financial audit. Routine check to ensure the correctness of the accounts being audited, and to make certain that there exists an effective system of internal controls.

Internal audit. Audit conducted by a unit within the agency. Internal audits are an important component of an agency's internal control system.

Internal controls. Plan of organization and the methods and procedures used to safeguard assets and other resources, and to assure that those assets and resources are used as effectively and efficiently as possible (GAO and AICPA's definition).

Preventive controls. Controls that protect against unproductive, inefficient, ineffective, or aberrant events occurring.

Chapter VII

Contracting and Purchasing

Since the total dollar value of goods and services obtained annually by New York State through contracting and purchasing is more than one billion dollars, there must be mechanisms to ensure that the State gets the most for its tax dollar. Managers in immediate need of a service for which they must contract often find themselves confronted with a great deal of "red tape," procedures deliberately designed to obtain for the State the desired quality good or service at the lowest cost. The roles of the various organizations involved in contracting and purchasing are described briefly below, followed by highlights of the two processes. Although this chapter provides general information about the procedures and issues related to contracting and purchasing, many of the detailed requirements are not included. Managers who need to prepare contracts should contact the agency finance office concerning agency policies and refer to more detailed guidelines available from the Office of the State Comptroller and the Office of General Services.

Office of General Services (OGS)

The Standards and Purchase Group within the Office of General Services awards approximately five thousand contracts for about forty thousand different commodity items each year. Items purchased by OGS under contract include everything from ice skates to exit lights to scratch pads.

Centralized purchasing is advantageous for several reasons. First and foremost is lower price. Competition is likely to be greater for high volume purchases; a large State contract may be especially important for a firm to obtain, whereas a lower volume purchase might not evoke so much effort from a potential supplier. Secondly, OGS can sometimes obtain bids directly from manufacturers, thereby eliminating the cost associated with a dealer intermediary. Centralized purchasing also gives the State more power to enforce the contract terms or conditions; vendors may be more willing to meet the needs of the State when a million dollar contract is at stake.

Agency purchasing officers appreciate State contracts, because by using the competitive bidding process for a central contract, OGS relieves the individual agency of the need to compare prices or solicit bids for each and every item. Instead, a purchase order for a contract item may be sent directly to the contractor.

Legal Aspects: The Attorney General and Appendix A

The required approval of all contracts by the Attorney General's Office may appear to be just one more obstacle slowing down the contracting process, but it is important because the contract is understood to be binding on the State of New York, rather than merely on the agency involved. When the Attorney General's office rejects a contract, agency personnel recall that most often it is because Appendix A had not been attached.

Appendix A is a required part of all State contracts. It provides for the following:

- o the contract may not be transferred without the consent of the State;
- o the State accepts no liability beyond the extent of the money available to it to pay for the terms included in the contract;
- o fair labor practices (standard wage, appropriate hours) will be observed in provision of the goods or services;
- o the contract prohibits discrimination and specifies the consequences of violation of this condition; and
- o the contractor agrees there was no collusion or consultation in bidding.

Division of the Budget (DOB)

The Division of the Budget, which must approve all service and computer contracts, is generally most concerned with the need for each contract relative to other departmental needs. In order to plan contract expenses as fully as possible, DOB requires each agency, shortly after budget passage, to submit a list of contracts over $25,000 that it intends to let during the coming fiscal year. Justification for each contract, and for the proposed method of selecting a contractor, must be presented. DOB then determines whether to approve or disapprove each contract on the list. The list can be amended throughout the year as unexpected needs arise.

Department of Civil Service

The Department of Civil Service is involved in the contracting process because a personal service contract may be thought of as an "end run around the civil service system." Civil Service generally does not object to personal service contracts that provide the agency with a needed, otherwise unavailable service on a short-term basis. When the proposed contractual relationship becomes long-term, the contract's legal standing is less clear.

Although the Department of Civil Service suggests that all personal service contracts be approved by its legal unit, compliance is a matter of individual agency determination. Many agencies do obtain prior approval from Civil Service; others do not, and there is no penalty for choosing not to.

Office of the State Comptroller (OSC)

The role of OSC in agency expenditures depends on the dollar value of the purchase. For purchases of services less than $2,500, OSC requires only that the proper form for that type of purchase be submitted, that the appropriate signatures be on the form, and that there be no mathematical errors. The agency will need more extensive documentation for post-audit purposes.

When purchase amounts exceed $2,500, OSC looks at the documentation more carefully. In addition to checking for proper approvals, OSC determines whether the vendor was chosen through the appropriate selection method (i.e. sole-source or competitive bidder) and whether or not the price was reasonable. It does not attempt to second-guess the agency's need for the contract, but rather asks the question, "Given that this agency needs the identified service, is the price reasonable and was an acceptable method used to award this contract?" If OSC disapproves a contract, it sends an accompanying explanation. Rejected contracts may not be permanently unacceptable; they may just require some alteration or use of a different method of vendor selection.

Purchasing Goods

When a manager needs an item, he or she typically requests the agency purchasing office to order it (see Chart 7.1). Many agencies ordinarily require that these requests be in writing. The purchasing officer will first check the listings of "preferred sources." Items produced by these groups (currently Division of Correction Industries within the Department of Correctional Services, Industries for the Blind, and Industries for the Handicapped) are purchased even if the same item is available elsewhere at lower cost because the State is pursuing nonfinancial as well as financial goals. A source at OGS estimated that preferred sources did close to 100 million dollars in business with the State in 1986 and are expanding rapidly.

If an item is not available from a preferred source, the purchasing officer refers to the OGS "Index of Commodities" to determine whether it is on a State contract. If not, the agency may purchase it directly from the vendor of choice after determining that the price is reasonable by comparing prices of four other vendors unless the size of the purchase requires formal competitive bidding. A useful reference is the October 1986 booklet, "Agency Purchasing Guidelines," issued by the Standards and Purchase Group, OGS.

Competitive bidding is required when the purchase amount is greater than $5,000, or when it is greater than $2,500 and the good is not being obtained from a Minority-and Women-Owned Business Enterprise (M/WBE), about which more below. When competitive bidding is required, an agency can either let OGS solicit the bids and select the vendor, or it can request that OGS grant permission for the agency to solicit the bids. For purchases of less than $10,000, agencies generally conduct the process themselves, in part for the sake of speed. For items costing more than $10,000, agencies usually let OGS handle bid solicitation, since the specifications are often more difficult to write and OGS personnel are available to assist.

How long does the purchasing process take? "It takes two days longer than the party will wait before calling to complain!" remarked one purchasing officer. Purchasing goods worth less than $2,500 is a relatively quick and simple process compared to contracting. Yet "somewhere between the request and payment, there's always at least one problem."

The lengthiness of the process has led to frustrations, temptations, and to special emergency procedures. In some agencies, in some areas of the State, "you can go to Smith's, tell them you work for the State, and get anything." The agency is then billed and has no choice but to pay. When such purchases occur frequently, the agency clearly has lost control over expenditures.

In order both to halt such practices and to make them unnecessary, one agency has taken several steps. First, nearby merchants were strongly requested not to maintain an account for the agency. Agency personnel were notified that prior approval from the purchasing office was now necessary to purchase emergency supplies; out-of-pocket purchases would no longer be reimbursed. Finally, in emergency situations a purchase order number would be issued

7.1 Agency Purchase Flow Chart
to be used for purchasing commodities

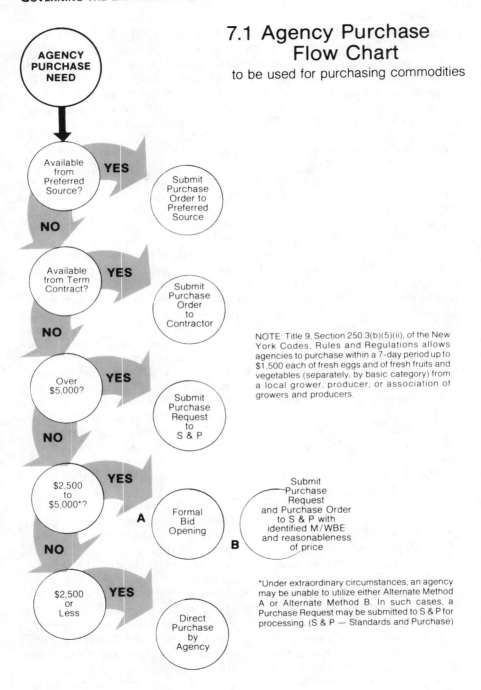

NOTE: Title 9, Section 250.3(b)(5)(ii), of the New York Codes, Rules and Regulations allows agencies to purchase within a 7-day period up to $1,500 each of fresh eggs and of fresh fruits and vegetables (separately, by basic category) from a local grower, producer, or association of growers and producers.

*Under extraordinary circumstances, an agency may be unable to utilize either Alternate Method A or Alternate Method B. In such cases, a Purchase Request may be submitted to S & P for processing. (S & P — Standards and Purchase) immediately to the employee who in turn could give it to the local merchant, thus avoiding the week-long purchase order process. Agencies may sometimes submit purchase orders over the phone when it is essential to speed up the process, then follow the oral request with written confirmation.

Every purchasing officer interviewed stressed that when employees by-pass the normal purchasing channels, the State almost invariably pays a higher price. Central purchasing offices can reduce costs by buying goods in bulk if they know how much of an item will be needed. They keep lists of vendors whom they can call to compare prices. Finally, they often know from experience whether a particular vendor is likely to deliver relatively quickly. As one purchasing officer noted, "We know where to go and whom to go to." (Guidelines for internal control of purchasing procedures can be found in Bulletin G-54, Procurement and Disbursement Guidelines, OSC.)

Prompt Payment Legislation

In 1984 legislation was passed that provided for interest payments to vendors who do not receive payment for goods within forty-five calendar days after the State has received merchandise or proper invoice (whichever date is later). Of these forty-five days, the agency has thirty-three days and OSC twelve to process the payment. Interest charges are charged to whichever organization fails to act within the allowable processing time. Apparently, living up to these time deadlines has not been easy. For the period April 1, 1986, to October 31, 1986, the average monthly interest charges owed by the State totalled $41,604, of which over 99 percent was due to delays within agencies.

The legislation was adopted in order to make the State a more attractive customer. Agencies have now automated many of their payment procedures to reduce processing time, and when delays do occur, the vendors are less displeased because they will be compensated. Another reported effect of the law is that local merchants are less willing to provide goods to State employees who have not obtained a purchase order or purchase order number, as they are eligible for interest under the law only if there was an existing contract (in legal terms, a purchase order qualifies as a contract) in place. The law gave the State until July 1, 1988 to speed its payment procedures even more, to a total of thirty days' processing time.

Minority-and Women-Owned Business Enterprises (M/WBEs)

New York State has long been committed to affirmative action. Executive Order 21, signed in August, 1983, mandates that agencies use the procurement process to promote minority and women-owned businesses' involvement with the State. Agencies have been most successful in this effort in purchases of up to $5,000. In the spirit of Executive Order 21, OGS purchasing guidelines offer agencies a choice of what are referred to as Method A and Method B for procuring goods that cost less than $5,000. Under Method B they need not use competitive bidding for goods costing from $2,500-$5,000 if they buy from a responsible minority or women-owned business. This gives the agencies more flexibility than they had previously, and also permits speedier procurement of goods than can be obtained through Method A, since the bidding process always takes longer than direct purchase.

The Department of Economic Development maintains an extensive listing of certified M/WBEs to which purchasing officers often refer. Recently there has been much stricter enforcement of certification rules for M/WBEs, since some of the firms originally listed were found to be fronts for businesses that were in fact not women

PAYNE

or minority owned. In one extreme case, the new enforcement practices cut by 77 percent the number of M/WBEs from which the Office of Parks, Recreation and Historic Preservation was purchasing.

Contracting

The contracting process moves most smoothly when an agency centralizes the function in one individual. In units likely to have contracting needs, designating a coordinator avoids the necessity for a different person to become familiar with the contracting system each time a need arises. If a manager is obliged to prepare a contract and has no experience with the system, the best advice is to "remember that you are not the first person who has ever done a contract. Find someone who has done it to help." Guidelines published by OSC and the agency's legal staff may also serve as handy references. Managers should also be aware that State policy requires that, before contracting out, agencies must determine that the needed service cannot be provided by the agency itself or by other State personnel.

Contract specialists stress the need for planning. "Everybody wants it yesterday" was a commonly heard phrase in contract offices. Those who process the contracts in the agency, and in the control agencies, are the first to admit that the routine is lengthy and often takes months rather than weeks. When asked why it takes so long, the typical answer referred to the large number of contracts, each of which must be reviewed carefully. Although "every manager thinks his or her contract is the most important thing the Department has going," even agency contract offices must sometimes set and follow priorities. In one large agency, for example, the Commissioner is personally involved in setting priorities for contract office personnel.

When a contract is needed quickly, there are ways to speed the process. "If you lose a building to hurricane Gloria the process moves quickly." On the other hand, OSC is reluctant to push contracts through because it has found that an agency request for quick approval is often a flag that there is something unusual about the contract, and therefore it should be reviewed carefully. When a manager needs a contract quickly, one way to save time is to ask the relevant agency personnel (i.e. in the finance, budget, and legal offices) to meet and discuss the contract, rather than send the proposed contract through the ordinary agency channels step by step. If the contract is a high departmental priority as well as the priority of a particular manager, someone in the agency contract office may be able to convince the appropriate offices at OGS, OSC, or DOB that time is of the essence. Control agencies have been described as being "very responsive" to departmental priorities.

Sometimes, work may even be begun before final approval of the contract has been granted, but this is a risky practice for the contractor. Until the contract has been approved, the State is under no obligation to pay the proposed contractor, and the manager must so advise, preferably in writing. Although it has not yet been tested in court, a personal liability issue may be involved. If a manager "asks, authorizes, or insists" that a contractor begin work before a contract has been approved, failure to pay could result in a suit against the manager. It has happened, although very rarely, that contractors have not been reimbursed for goods or services provided prior to contract approval.

Even after a contract has been fully approved and let, problems may occur during implementation. The manager who contracted with the vendor or some staff member is responsible for monitoring contract implementation. The contract monitor is usually successful in resolving minor day-to-day problems, but sometimes cancellation of the contract becomes the only appropriate course of action. If a manager wishes to terminate a contract (and contracts occasionally are terminated), this should not be attempted singlehandedly. Rather, the person who has regularly processed the contract payments should be notified promptly of intent to terminate.

Competitive Bidding

"Managers sometimes call and say they want to hire so-and-so; they have to understand that competition is required" (Agency contract specialist).

Unlike the purchase of goods, for which OGS most frequently awards contracts, each agency is responsible for awarding its own service contracts. The OSC procurement and disbursement guidelines specify a minimum of five viable bidders for each contract. The most common method of solicitation, the Request For Proposal (RFP), may or may not be accompanied by advertising for bids. At least one agency often advertises in minority publications in hopes of attracting more minority-owned business bids. If the qualified firms are likely to be located in a particular region of the State, the agency may advertise in local publications. The RFPs are usually mailed to organizations drawn from the agency's bidders lists. The Department of Economic Development list of small businesses may be used to supplement agency files.

In most agencies it is the program manager's responsibility to write the RFP. Many of the contracts approved each year repeat services purchased the previous year. When the same or similar services have been required in the past, RFP writing may involve mainly cutting and pasting of existing documents. In any case, the more clearly and fully defined the required services the better, both in terms of competition and ultimately in terms of quality provided by the selected vendor.

Who awards the contract? In most cases, the agency creates a committee to evaluate the bids and select the winner. From what level in the agency the committee members come depends primarily on the dollar value of the contract. Some committees may be formed at the division level, but the largest contracts are usually awarded by a committee involving deputy commissioners and top budget people.

Although in most cases the contract is awarded to the lowest bidder or one of the three lowest bidders, quality factors are also considered in selection. The OSC guidelines state that, for all bids that conform to the essential requirements of the RFP, as a minimum, the agency should consider the bidder's prior experience and financial responsibility as well as the price bid. One agency contracts specialist interviewed said her agency sometimes receives several hundred responses to a single RFP, all of which need to be evaluated in terms of both cost and quality.

Not all RFPs result in such a flood of bids. If an agency knows in advance that only one firm is qualified to provide the needed service, it may choose to initiate a sole-source contract rather than to solicit bids. Sole-source contracts must be carefully justified, or they may face delays, questions, and possible rejection from the agency contract office or control agencies. The following illustrates why sole-source contracts may be questioned by OSC. Faced with a critical delivery date, one agency wished to enter into a sole-source contract for art books and posters at a price of $33,000. The Comptroller's Office insisted on competitive bidding but suggested obtaining quotes over the phone rather than visiting each printer to discuss specifications. The agency subsequently awarded the contract to one of four bidders at a price of $15,600. (The original sole source lowered its price to $30,000, but failed to win the contract.)

If an RFP doesn't elicit enough competition and the prices quoted seem unreasonable, it may be reissued with greater emphasis on advertising. Another option is to enter into negotiation with the available bidders for a lower price.

Negotiating, while more an art than a set of procedures, can prove effective in reducing price. For example, one agency had ordered 15,000 catalogs at a price of $17,800. When it became necessary to order a second set for rush delivery, the agency expected to pay the same price, but OSC argued that the price should be lower, since the printing negatives and composition on the reprint had already been included in the price of the first order. Using negotiation techniques learned at an OSC seminar, agency staff finally paid only $10,600 to print the catalogs, with the same rush delivery provided.

A second example of negotiations that paid off concerns the installation of carpet in an agency. After a purchase order was issued by the agency and the material ordered, the Comptroller's Office was notified that the carpet would be installed on a weekend so it would not interfere with daily operations. The vendor requested an additional $2,700 for the weekend installation. Upon reviewing the vendor's justification for the change, OSC discovered that he was charging the bid price for installation plus double time. Although the double time rate was reasonable, a straight time rate had already been included in the contract bid price. When this was pointed out, the vendor readjusted his price downward.

Whether a department should rent equipment or buy it is a departmental decision, irrespective of the dollar value involved. Copying equipment is by far the most common item rented. When the decision is made to rent, it is the responsibility of the agency's purchasing office to compare different vendors' price lists. OSC will still base its approval on a reasonableness standard.

Although it often makes sense to lease equipment when the need is temporary, the purchase price should always be considered and compared. When one agency sought OSC's approval to lease an electronic mail scale for sixty months, OSC compared the costs of purchasing and of leasing and found that the agency would save $3500 by purchasing the scale outright, which it then did.

In addition to the general service contract guidelines (available from OSC), special guidelines have been established for architectural and engineering service contracts and should be referred to if such a contract is being contemplated.

Space Problems and Centralized Services

Agencies that have space allocation or overcrowding problems work with OGS to find solutions. Specifically, the Space Allocation and Space Planning units are responsible for all of the space in State-owned buildings. The Bureau of Leases attends to problems in rented space. Services supervised by OGS include altering existing office space as well as evaluating current use of available space and allocating more space as needed and available.

The Centralized Services Group in OGS provides about half of the statewide telecommunications services for all State organizations, including an extensive fiber optics system, CAPNET, which transmits both voice and data to more than fifty State office locations. Centralized Services also provides electronic data processing, consultant services, time sharing and data base/data communications services to more than forty agencies. It manages a supply support system to those agencies that maintain a number of facilities statewide (e.g., Department of Correctional Services, Office of Mental Health), which includes linens, laundry, food and paper products.

Additionally, OGS provides a number of interagency services. It manages an automobile fleet, which provides pool vehicles for short-term use as well as autos leased back to agencies for longer time periods. The interagency mail system provides courier service among six locations statewide as well as within each of these locations. OGS maintains a printing shop in Albany for interagency use; it also manages a surplus property program, which disposes of no-longer-needed State property and makes federal surplus property available to agencies for a small processing fee.

APPENDIX 1

Glossary

Agency purchase. Purchase made directly by an agency in accordance with the procedures outlined in the Commissioner of General Service's Rules and Regulations, of the State Finance Law and the State Printing and Document Law.

"As specified" contract. A contract awarded by the Commissioner of General Services for a commodity required by an individual agency or agencies.

Bid. An offer to furnish a described commodity or service at a stated price in accordance with the bid documents.

Bid opening. All bids are opened at a time previously established and are recorded in the bid tabulation.

Bid tabulation. A listing of information from vendors' bids (e.g. names, prices, model numbers, delivery terms) in tabular form which facilitates comparison of bids received and determination of the lowest qualified bidder.

Commodities. Printing, materials, equipment, and supplies.

Contract award. The offering of a contract to the responsible bidder whose offer is found to be most advantageous to the State, price and other factors considered.

Contract monitor. The agency staff member responsible for overseeing implementation of the contract.

General Specifications. An OGS publication stating the terms and conditions that apply to all contracts awarded by any State agency.

Index of Commodities. An OGS publication that contains information identifying particular commodity groups, availability of contracts, preferred sources, and so forth. Codes in the index indicate the method to follow in purchasing particular commodities.

Invitation for bid. Similar to **Request For Proposal.** Bids received will be reviewed and the contract normally awarded to a responsible bidder who offers the lowest price.

M/WBE. Minority-and women-owned business enterprise; a business enterprise owned by (or the stock of which is owned by) at least 51 percent women or members of a minority, where a minority is of Black, Hispanic, Asian or Pacific Islands, American Indian or Alaskan Native designation.

Merchandise/Invoice Received (MIR) date. Generally the date on which the agency receives goods/services or a proper invoice. Used to determine interest due (if any) according to Prompt Payment Legislation.

Petty cash account. An account under direct control of the agency used to meet immediate cash needs (e.g., provide change when the department collects fees) as specified in the *New York State Accounting System User Procedure Manual, Vol. XI.*

Purchase order. The official form to be used by an agency when placing an order for a commodity with a contractor or vendor.

Purchase request. The form used by agencies to state the requirements for the purchase of commodities when such purchase will be handled by OGS.

Request For Proposal (RFP). A package of documents supplied to prospective bidders which contains the rules or general conditions to be followed when submitting a bid for a particular service. Proposals received will be evaluated on a variety of criteria, including bidder expertise, quality, and cost.

Specification. Description of a commodity.

Sole-source contract. A contract that has been awarded without competitive bidding; sole-source contracting is permissible only when competition is not available or feasible. Justification for such a contract (including reasonableness of the cost) must accompany the contract through the approval process.

Term contract. A contract that has been awarded by the Commissioner of General Services for commodities that are made available to State agencies on a continuing basis for a definite period of time.

Chapter VIII

Administrative Law and Agency Limitations

With the expanded and expanding scope of governmental activities, some executive agency decisions will inevitably be challenged by those who are affected by them. On the one hand, through their rule-making, enforcement, licensing (in some cases) and investigatory powers, agencies have a substantial influence over the lives and activities of the citizens of the State. On the other, citizens, backed by imposed constitutional rights and a knowledge of the limitations on administrators, may take virtually any agency decision to court. It is important for managers to have some knowledge of administrative law and to recognize that potentially controversial decisions can be challenged. The agency's counsel's office plays a critical role in this area, but managers also need some perspective on the limits of administrative authority.

Limits on the Exercise of Agency Powers

Within an agency, there are three basic restrictions on administrators in making virtually any type of decision that will have an impact upon the public. These restrictions "are really a way of taking something anti-democratic [agency rulemaking and adjudicatory powers] and making it legitimate," according to a faculty member, SUNY Albany Department of Political Science. The first restriction concerns the agency's realm of authority. Normally, an agency is created by statute and therefore has statutory powers, constraints, and mandates. The law lays out the broad areas that the agency is to be involved in and specifies the particular types of authority to be exercised. The agency itself is then left to fill in the details necessary for implementation and is given discretionary administrative power to do so. If a department is vested with the power to license particular professions, for example, then as long as the enabling act remains on the books, the agency can exercise this authority. It is only with a legislative grant of authority that an agency administrator can go about the business of running programs.

Protection of an individual against "arbitrary and capricious" actions and the requirements of governmental accountability relate directly to the limits of agency authority. When an agency is accused of exceeding its authority, the issue is usually one of differing interpretations of the authority granted, rather than a clear straying beyond the bounds of legislative intent. Even if an agency stays well within the areas established for it by the Legislature, there is a wide grey area in which people acting in good faith may understand the law differently. Sometimes, the Legislature passes broadly phrased laws which leave agencies to set standards that cannot avoid being controversial. Legislators often pass such laws to satisfy various interest groups, each believing the measure will be of direct benefit. As agencies set standards and make rules, they inevitably make decisions that hurt some of these groups, and that may lead to a lawsuit. A recent example is the widely publicized challenge to the Department of Health's issuance of regulations limiting smoking in State offices.

Occasionally, agencies may have difficulty interpreting the law because of the development of new technologies or situations that the Legislature did not anticipate when it passed the law. In the case of *Quotron Systems v. Gallman* (1976), [39 NY2d 428], for example, Quotron argued that the Department of Tax and Finance went beyond its statutory authority by reading too broadly a particular phrase in the law. The law states that any utility which "sells telegraphy or telegraph service" is subject to taxation. Quotron held that their service of providing instantaneous financial market transaction data (using telegraph and telephone lines) did not fall in this category because they purchase, compile, and edit the data they provide, unlike other telegraph companies which merely transmit the data of others. Since the words "telegraphy" and "telegraphic service" are not defined in the law, the case centered around these definitions, and around whether the Department had the authority to define the terms as broadly as it did. In reviewing the case, the court looked at the statement of legislative intent found in the 1941 law from which the current law stems, as well as at a dictionary definition. The court decided against the Department, declaring that it had defined telegraphy and telegraphic service in a way inconsistent with legislative intent, and thus outside of its authority. In fact, the Legislature quite often delegates the power to define a term, leaving the agency more freedom. In this case the Legislature was not intentionally ambiguous; it simply had not anticipated the situation.

A second limit on administrators relates to the rule-making process within agencies. In New York State, it has been the Legislature that has set the standards for this process, but no general standards for rule-making procedures applicable to all agencies in all situations have yet been established (as has been done at the federal level). Certain agencies, such as the Public Service Commission, are required by law to hold hearings prior to rule-making. Where the law does not specifically require the agency to follow a specific process, the courts have refused to set stricter standards.

In adjudicatory proceedings where hearings are held and decisions made after a citizen claims, for example, that a license was unfairly revoked, state law requires that "all parties shall be afforded an opportunity to present written argument on issues of law and an opportunity to present evidence and such argument on issues of fact" [State Administrative Procedures Act, Section 302]. Thus, while agencies have the authority to decide the issue in "any reasonable way," they must first hear all sides of the story.

The last major legal limit on administrators is the broad concept of "reasonableness." In practice, inquiry into the "reasonableness" of a decision is superficial, for the agencies themselves are considered the experts in the field, and judges generally defer to their expertise; the courts do not believe their responsibility is to second guess the agency. In order for a decision to be struck down on the issue of unreasonableness, it has to be shown affirmatively that the decision was irrational, fundamentally flawed, or went against the weight of the evidence.

Constitutional Questions

Historically, the first limits on the procedures that administrators must follow came from court cases dealing with the tension between the citizen's right to due process, and the administrator's legislatively delegated powers. While administrators are granted authority to act in particular areas, the citizen is guaranteed by the fourteenth amendment to the U.S. Constitution that:

> No state shall make or enforce any law which shall abridge the privileges or immunities of citizens of the United States; nor shall any state deprive any person of life, liberty, or property without due process of law; nor deny to any person within its jurisdiction the equal protection of the laws.

Due Process has been defined as a "course of legal proceedings according to those rules and principles which have been established . . . for the enforcement and protection of private rights" (*Black's Law Dictionary*).

For example, prisoners accused of violating prison rules now possess rights to due process. In an attempt to balance the need for secure, orderly facilities with the rights of accused inmates, the Department of Correctional Services traditionally allowed very limited due process for inmates who had been disciplined. Several court cases forced changes in certain aspects of this policy, and the Department realized that unless it made a concerted effort to assure constitutional due process, it would be subject to continuing court reversals. As a result, it rewrote the relevant regulations, changed the standard procedures, and trained hearing officers. Although the agency's legal environment prompted it to make substantial procedural changes to ensure inmates due process, many facility employees now think the Department has gone too far in guaranteeing due process. The Department's understanding of the requirements of due process shapes its response to these expressed employee concerns.

Judicial Restraints: The Civil Practice Law and Rules

Under Article 78 of the Civil Practice Law, citizens can challenge virtually any agency decision that affects the public. Such decisions may relate to the denial of public assistance or other forms of support or subsidy, the refusal of a license, or the issuance of an administrative cease and desist order. Although the percentage of decisions that are challenged is small, a manager can never know which ones will end up in court, and the final court decision will affect future, similar cases. Consequently, the administrator should keep in mind the three questions that a judge would ask:

1. Do you have the authority—what is the statutory reference? (This often involves an examination of the agency's interpretation of the statute and an inquiry as to whether the act is within the bounds set by the Legislature.)
2. Were the proper procedures (as established in State Administrative Procedures Act: see below) followed?
3. Was the decision within the realm of reasonableness?

These questions apply to any agency action whether it stems from the agency's enforcement, investigatory, rule-making, or licensing powers. Appropriate and satisfactory answers are the best defense against ending up on the wrong side of a court decision.

When a decision is challenged, the court's primary resource for determining the boundaries of an agency's authority is the language of the statute. The burden of proof falls on the agency's representatives to demonstrate the link between the agency's action and the statutory enabling act. If the legislative intent is in any way ambiguous, the plaintiff may cite any other official legislative documents to support a different interpretation of legislative intent. These may include the bill sponsor's memorandum in support of the bill, and minutes or transcripts from public or legislative committee hearings, or floor debates. If an agency is found to have overstepped its authority, or to have interpreted the statute too broadly, the court may disallow the agency action.

Although this section has emphasized defending agency decisions, managers may enter the court system as plaintiffs as well as defendants. If individuals continue to operate without a license or refuse to obey an order, agencies have no choice but to turn to the judiciary for enforcement purposes: to obtain a court order and seek imposition of the statutory penalty for noncompliance.

The Legislative Role in Monitoring the Exercise of Agency Authority

Although judicial review of an agency decision is the final check on administrators, other organizations are involved in continually monitoring agency activities to ensure that the agencies are not stepping beyond their authority (as defined in statute) and thus failing to play their proper role.

○ State Administrative Procedures Act (SAPA)

As the body that invests authority in the executive agencies, clearly the Legislature has an interest in seeing that the public is well served by these agencies. When agencies are perceived as responsive and effective, they are a political asset to legislators. The concept of public access to the rule-making process is guaranteed by Article IV Section 8 of the State Constitution which states that:

> no rule or regulation made by any state department [or] officer . . . shall be effective until it is filed in the office of the Department of State. The Legislature shall provide for the speedy publication of such rules and regulations, by appropriate laws.

For these reasons, in the early 1970's, the Legislature looked at the processes that agencies follow in promulgating rules and holding adjudicatory hearings. Although the concept of public access to agency decision-making processes had been established before the passage of SAPA in 1975, case law was the only guide to admin-

PAYNE

istrators regarding those procedures the court would accept as providing citizens with adequate due process. Because there is room for varying interpretations of the court decisions, these principles often were applied inconsistently.

Based on these established principles, SAPA set out explicitly the steps that must be followed in rulemaking proceedings and in adjudicatory hearings. For example, before adopting a rule, unless specifically exempted by SAPA, an agency must publish the proposed rule or regulation in the State Register (a weekly publication of the Department of State) for thirty days. This document, available in libraries and municipal government clerks' offices across the State, ensures that the public can see and comment on proposed rules before they are adopted.

In 1980, Executive Order 100, issued by Governor Carey, called for the preparation of a Regulatory Impact Statement (RIS) with each proposed rule and regulation. The RIS was to include an analysis of the fiscal implications of the rule on State and local government and on all regulated parties, and any other foreseeable economic consequences. Additionally, the statement was to include possible alternatives to the proposed rule or regulation.

In 1983, SAPA was formally amended to include the Executive Order 100 requirement that an RIS be submitted with each proposed rule or regulation. At the same time, a requirement for a Regulatory Flexibility Analysis (RFA) was added, mandating agencies to consider approaches that would minimize the economic impact of rules on small businesses.

(See Appendix 1 to this Chapter for a summary of basic SAPA provisions.)

o Enforcement of SAPA, and The Administrative Regulations Review Commission

Chapter 689 of the Laws of 1978 set up the Administrative Regulations Review Commission (ARRC) composed of three members of each house of the Legislature. The Commission was designed to monitor agencies' compliance with SAPA and is authorized by the statute to "examine rules adopted or proposed by each agency with respect to:

(I) Statutory authority
(II) Compliance with legislative intent
(III) Impact on the economy and on the government operations of the State and its local governments
(IV) Impact on affected parties."

Although the Commission itself has little real power to compel agencies to change their regulations, staff often work informally with the agencies, suggesting alternatives that the agency may not have considered.

Despite its lack of formal powers to force agency compliance, ARRC's authority stems primarily from its links to the Legislature. Agencies put a high priority on being responsive to legislators because they wish to foster and maintain positive relationships. When legislators express concern over a particular rule or regulation, agencies consider their comments seriously.

In about one out of every ten instances of rule-making, Commission staff contact the agency concerning a problem with a proposed rule. Problems are often resolved to the satisfaction of both parties in this informal manner. If a disagreement on an important point is not worked out informally, the co-chairs of the committee can issue a joint letter to the agency. If still unsatisfied, and if there is enough support in both houses, Commission members can seek a legislative remedy, such as removing the agency's authority to act in a particular way.

Implementation of the law often raises questions as to whether the execution is actually in line with legislative intent. On the one hand, the agency must be allowed the flexibility to deal effectively with issues within its mandate; on the other, the public must be safeguarded against possible abuse of this power. If, under the authority of a broadly worded statute, an agency undertakes an action that causes public outcry, the Legislature can pass more restrictive legislation. With this in mind, agencies often anticipate legislative actions in order to retain their discretion.

The Board of Regents and top managers at the State Education Department, for example, had long been of the opinion that high school diplomas should be awarded on the basis of students' ability to meet objective requirements, and the Department's regulations reflected this. As a consequence, many handicapped students who had made heroic efforts to learn never earned diplomas. The Department was able to maintain such a policy for years despite loud interest group protests, but eventually the Legislature (which is generally more sensitive to interest group pressures than are agencies) began to consider changing the law on which the regulations were based. Just as the Legislature "was on the brink of changing the law," according to a State Education Department source, the Board of Regents itself moved to alter the regulations.

The Commission has also been involved with insuring that rules and regulations conform to recent judicial standards. For example, recent court cases have established that agencies must set out adequate standards stating the criteria upon which administrators base particular decisions. Objective standards and criteria help assure that discretion will not be exercised by an agency in an arbitrary, capricious, or discriminatory fashion. Their inclusion in regulations informs the public how discretion will be exercised and may be important in guiding or shaping the action of the regulated party. Without a clear statement of decision-making standards, the regulatory provisions upon which such determinations are based may ultimately be declared illegal.

The problem has been particularly noticeable in regulatory provisions that grant exemptions or waivers from other requirements at the discretion of the administrator. One such case came to ARRC's attention as it reviewed the Department of Social Services' waiver proposal pertaining to supervised independent living programs for children under foster care provided by agency boarding homes. The waiver provision in question, 18 NYCRR 447.3, provided that exemptions to the substantive requirements for agency boarding homes could be made upon approval of the Department. This provision, authorizing the grant of an exception to generally applicable agency boarding home requirements "upon approval," contains no objective standards and thus gives the Department unrestrained discretion in granting or withholding a waiver. The Department's representative offered assurances to the Commission that the issue of standards for the granting of exemptions or waivers would be addressed in a comprehensive fashion in the near future. This action should assure avoidance of the legal standing of the Health Department in the mid-70's, when the court decided in *Levine v. Whalen* [39 NY 2d

519, 384 NYS 2d 721] (1976) that a regulation extending to the Commissioner the right to grant exceptions from requirements of general applicability upon vague and subjective standards was invalid (excerpted from ARRC 1983 Report).

Instances of omission may also draw ARRC attention. If proposed agency rules and regulations do not address an issue that the statute particularly directed the agency to do, ARRC can be expected to point this out to the agency. At the federal level, courts have found in favor of plaintiffs who challenged agencies' refusal to make rules, as well as ruling against agencies that refused to appropriately institute a fact-finding process, withdrew rules arbitrarily, and intentionally delayed taking action (Phillip J. Cooper, "Conflict or Constructive Tension: The Changing Relationship of Judges and Administrators," *Public Administration Review*, November, 1985, pp. 643–651).

Under its continuing bill review process, the Commission examines all bills that grant rule-making authority. The purpose is to consider whether the bill contains either a mandatory or a permissive grant of such authority, and to ensure that the language provides clear, definitive guidance as to the agency's role. If ARRC feels that the bill includes broad, vague, or otherwise unclear language, it may work with the sponsors to improve it.

From the agency perspective, laws are sometimes extremely broad and fail to offer adequate guidance as to the Legislature's real intent. Legislative sponsors occasionally work with the agency as it designs rules to implement the legislation. These efforts could cause problems for the agency if the sponsor's intent differs from the stated or implied intent of the Legislature as a whole in regard to the bill as passed. Also, laws that include grants of mandatory rule-making power sometimes specify effective dates that do not allow the agencies enough time to promulgate the necessary rules. This concern was recently addressed by the Bill Drafting Commission at the Legislature, which issued a directive stating that all bills with rule-making grants were to be drafted to allow adequate time necessary for an agency to adopt rules.

Executive Branch Restraints

The Office of Business Permits and Regulatory Assistance (OBPRA) was created in 1978 to help businesses through the maze of State regulations and red tape. As part of the Governor's 1984 legislative program, the office was granted the power to review proposed regulations and the concerns of regulated parties. This role was established for OBPRA because of a perceived need on the part of regulated parties for a more stringent check on the agencies' rule-making activities.

Proposed regulations are submitted to OBPRA and are reviewed for compliance with the following criteria:

1. The proposed rule is
   a. clearly within the agency's authority as delegated by law;
   b. consistent with and necessary to achieve a specific legislative purpose;
   c. clearly written so that its meaning will be understood by the people it affects;
   d. not unnecessarily duplicative of federal or State statutes or rules;
   e. consistent with State statutes and rules; and
2. The agency has complied with the statutes requiring the preparation of regulatory impact and regulatory flexibility statements and has done so in a way adequate to enable interested people to evaluate the impact of a proposed rule.

If OBPRA concludes that any of the criteria are not met, the agency must respond to OBPRA with changes or clarifications. Frequently, the difficulty is that the proposed rule is too general and will affect more citizens or organizations than were intended. If OBPRA still concludes that any of the criteria remain unmet, the agency must hold a public hearing specifically to address OBPRA's concerns and provide a final forum for objectors. After this hearing, the agency reports to the Governor indicating how it has addressed those concerns and how it intends to proceed with the rule. The comment period on any rule can also be extended by fifteen days and the effective date of a rule delayed for twenty-one days. (The law also provides that ARRC may request OBPRA to extend the comment period on a proposed rule by fifteen days.)

As part of the Executive Branch, OBPRA also has access to the Executive Chamber, and it can often deal with potential problems concerning regulations in an informal manner. Additionally, because OBPRA is much more insulated from partisan politics than is ARRC, it can sometimes act more expeditiously in decision-making.

Based upon study of agency memos and other communications, OBPRA may decide that a particular issue should be promulgated as rules rather than just issued informally; or it may hold that a formal rule is not warranted. Although informal handling of such matters allows the agencies more flexibility, it does not provide citizens a chance to influence the decision-making process. As noted earlier, the SAPA procedures were established to insure that those to be regulated have an active role in the development of administrative rules and regulations.

In an effort to ban gambling-related video games from bars, the State Liquor Authority proposed a rule that, as written, would have excluded all video games. Recognizing this, OBPRA exercised its authority to slow the rule-making process and to allow affected groups to voice objections. Eventually, a revised rule was proposed that both OBPRA and the State Liquor Authority agreed better served the intent.

Whether a body exercising control over agency rule-making activity should be located in the Legislative or Executive Branch became an issue in 1983 in the wake of a Supreme Court decision. One argument for housing such an organization within the Executive Branch was the separation of powers doctrine. Constitutionally, the Legislature is the decision-making body; the Executive implements laws passed by the Legislature and approved by the Governor. The Legislature does not have the legal right to interfere in agency decisions although, in the past, it has attempted to override particular agency rule-making activities.

In June, 1983, the United States Supreme Court, in the case of *Immigration and Naturalization Service v. Chadha* (462 U.S. 919) declared unconstitutional the veto of federal agency rules by one house of Congress. The case arose when, in 1975, the House of Representatives vetoed a decision by the Immigration and Naturalization Service to deport an alien. This "legislative veto" excluded any review and opportunity for approval by the President. In *Chadha*, the Supreme Court found the veto to violate both the principle of separation of powers of the three branches of government and the requirement of the Constitution that Congressional power be exercised by means of a bill passed by both houses and presented to the President for approval. The House's veto brought the legislature too close to the area of execution. (The case is reported in more detail in the ARRC 1983 report.)

While New York does not have a statutory legislative veto, ARRC members and other legislators have for the past several years sponsored bills to establish a legislative veto over agency-promulgated rules. (In contrast, legislative veto provisions are included in more than 160 individual federal laws, and a number of states have adopted legislative veto statutes.) The U.S. Supreme Court's decision in *Chadha* places all such legislative vetoes in jeopardy.

The Agency Hearing and Decision-Making Process

The nature of agency business requires that administrators play quasi-judicial and quasi-legislative roles. The administrative law process merges the adoption of specific standards in rules, the investigation of possible violations, the notice or accusation, the hearing, and the decision in a single agency. Because of this structure, administrators must exercise special care to preserve not only the actuality, but also the appearance of fairness and impartiality encompassed within the legal term "procedural due process."

From their perspectives, agencies strive to make decisions that are consistent with agency mandates and goals as well as with principles of effective management and, in doing so, to avoid litigation whenever possible. In dealing with the public, one of the most imprecise but important concepts that agencies must keep in mind is that of "fairness." If citizens who take part in decision-making proceedings or in adjudicatory hearings are left with a sense that the process was "fair," they are likely to accept the decision; if they believe that somehow the process did not allow them a chance to offer their side of the problem, they may be tempted to seek additional review of the decision through an appeal.

Consider for a moment the situation of the citizen who has received a notice stating that a hearing is scheduled on a particular day to review the possibility of license revocation. This person had to comply with agency guidelines to get the license in the first place; now that the agency is questioning the license, the citizen must appear at the hearing and defend him or herself. The catch is that the agency itself is going to conduct the hearing—the very agency that initiated the proceedings. The question that must run through the licensee's mind is, "How likely am I to get an impartial hearing?"

The Department of State faced such an issue with its licensing unit. This agency licenses certain vocations and, as part of this duty, disciplines, investigates, and maintains a legal staff for the presentation of cases against practitioners. Included in the adjudicatory unit are both presenting attorneys and hearing officers. At one time, the Department was structured in such a way that the attorneys and hearing officers often switched roles in different cases, allowing the possibility that a particular attorney might present the case against a person in one instance, and then play the role of the "impartial" hearing officer in another case a few months later.

After reviewing the system, the Department felt that it could lead to a perception by the public that the proceeding was less than fair. Even if both attorneys and hearing officers acted in a manner that was impeccably fair to the parties involved, the public must not be presented with a system that looks like someone with a grudge could influence the outcome. "The appearance of impartiality is as important as impartiality itself; this is how confidence in the system is built," stated one agency counsel.

In response to this situation, the Department of State restructured its licensing unit so that presenting attorneys and hearing officers are now in completely different units. "The skills involved in the two jobs are completely different," said one department representative. The two groups are independent of each other and receive separate, job-specific training.

Recently, bills have been proposed in the Legislature which call for a completely separate department for hearing officers to ensure that these officers are not under any pressure to decide a case in a particular way. Once an agency has committed itself to a stance, there may be organizational pressures to uphold the decision. If an independent agency were in charge of the process, no such biases would exist. On the other hand, expertise on the topic is also vital. "Expertise is just as important as impartiality, and this expertise is found within the agency. An impartial hearing by an officer who is incompetent in the subject matter is not of much use to the citizen either," stated one source. The issue relates to the philosophy of agency adjudicatory proceedings as well. If the primary purpose is enforcement of agency standards, perhaps hearings should be held by the agency, but if the purpose is judicial, they might be more appropriately conducted by a separate agency.

Other departments (such as the Department of Motor Vehicles) have internal appeals processes so that a citizen unsatisfied with the initial determination can carry the case through several layers of review. No decision can be brought to court unless all levels of agency review have been exhausted, but when a final agency decision is challenged, the court looks at the three questions discussed earlier. Administrators should recognize the importance of creating a complete, well-documented file on each case before a decision is made. When the court considers a case, it looks at the record that existed at the time the decision was taken. Even if the decision is correct, lack of supporting evidence may render it legally unacceptable.

Role of the Attorney General

When an agency decision is challenged, the suit often names administrators individually (and, particularly, commissioners). At the initiation of the suit, the agency and the Attorney General's Office are simultaneously served with the papers. In accord with the description of the Attorney General's duties as set out in Section 63 of the Executive Law, the Attorney General's Office represents agencies and officers named in suits arising from program and policy areas. Because the Office is responsible for prosecuting and defending all actions and proceedings in which the State is interested, it must be notified whenever such an action or proceeding is instituted. Upon notice, the Department of Law looks into the case to determine whether the interests of the State call for the Department's involvement.

Section 17 of the Public Officers Law deals with State employees' rights to counsel. If the action (or failure to act) in question is determined to have been "within the scope of public employment," the Attorney General will represent the employee under Section 17. A few agencies, such as the Department of Agriculture and Markets, are exceptions; they generally handle their own suits as authorized in statute. The State does not represent employees in criminal matters. If for this or some other reason, the Attorney General determines that it is inappropriate to represent the employee or if some conflict of interest is identified, the employee is entitled to private counsel representation with "reasonable" fees and expenses paid by the State.

When the Attorney General's Office does agree to represent, State lawyers review all documentation relevant to the case. Either the agency counsel or the Attorney General's Office works closely with the administrator to prepare an affidavit about the issue in question. The administrator's personal involvement in the case depends on the type of challenge that has been mounted. If the case questions the agency's authority to act, or attempts to force the agency to take action, the administrator may not be as fully involved as he or she would be in a case questioning the procedural or substantive aspects of the action. In such cases, the agency counsel's office acts as the liaison between the agency personnel involved and the Department of Law.

Generally, individual liability is not an issue in these cases. In fact, the question of personal liability on the part of administrators has not yet become a major issue in New York although it has in other states. In New York, most actions taken against individual administrators have involved agencies with law enforcement powers.

In most cases against individuals, the Attorney General's Office and, in consultation with that office, the Office of the State Comptroller decide about indemnification and the payment of costs associated with judgment or settlement of a claim. If compensatory charges are imposed, the individual is indemnified. In cases of indemnification, the law sets forth very specific procedural requirements for notification of the Attorney General's Office and request for representation.

Access to Governmental Activities

In order to keep government responsive to the citizenry, over the past decade, the Legislature has provided a variety of opportunities for direct citizen access to governmental activities. Among these are the Freedom of Information Law and the Open Meetings Law. Recognizing the limits on government access to records, however, for citizens in and out of government, the Personal Privacy Protection Law established State agency obligations in the collection and subsequent disclosure of personal data. The Committee on Open Government has oversight responsibilities for this and for each of the following laws.

The Committee on Open Government (originally established under a different name in 1974) consists of five representatives of government or their designees: the Lieutenant Governor, the Secretary of State, the Director of the Budget, the Commissioner of the Office of General Services, and a representative of local government—two members of the media, and four members of the general public. Housed in the Department of State, the Committee serves to educate, to write opinions when there is an appeal following denial of access, to give oral advice, and to maintain records on agency compliance with open government laws.

Freedom of Information Law

"The Legislature therefore declares that government is the public's business and that the public, individually and collectively and represented by a free press, should have access to the records of government" (Public Officers Law, Article 6 Section 84).

The Freedom of Information Law (FOIL) ensures public access to all public records of the Executive Branch and its agencies (including records stored in a computer) except those that fall into nine identified categories. The exceptions are intended to prevent misuse of information, but not to allow room for "executive privilege." The courts have therefore ruled that the only information not accessible by the public is that which falls into the specific categories listed. For example, a business seeking information regarding a competitor from a regulatory agency is denied access under the law. Anyone seeking agency memos that contain opinions on personnel may be denied access, but if the memos contain statistical data, instructions to staff that affect the public, or agency policy statements, the request must be granted. Although a request for a record about a particular individual might be denied on the ground that it would be an "unwarranted invasion of personal privacy," anyone wishing to obtain information regarding a public employee's job duties or salary must be granted access. Time limits are specific: an agency must respond within five business days of the receipt of a request. If the agency needs more time, it must respond accordingly. Failure to respond indicates denial, which is subject to appeal. Questions about what is excepted by the law should be addressed to the Committee on Open Government. Although the Committee does not have adjudicatory powers—that is, its opinions are not binding—they have been cited in cases that ended up in court. If the appeal is brought to court, the latter has the power to award attorney's fees to the person challenging denial of access when that person "substantially prevails."

The Open Meeting Law

The Open Meeting Law, also referred to as the "Sunshine Law," was passed in 1977 to open meetings of public bodies to members of the public, and thus allow them to observe public policymaking in action. The law does not apply to judicial or quasi-judicial proceedings (except Public Service Commission proceedings or zoning boards of appeals), to political caucuses, or to any matter made confidential by federal or State law. Furthermore, "executive" sessions may be closed to the public when held for specific reasons enumerated in the law. The Committee on Open Government, which oversees implementation of this law as well, can advise as to whether a particular meeting can be closed under the law.

The Influence of the Courts on New York State Policy: Some Examples

The basic principles of administrative law set forth in the preceding sections are well established, but judges' interpretations of law evolve over time. Awareness of this evolution "can help to avoid liability judgments, prevent the waste of time and effort when agency decisions are reversed, avoid loss of control over one's agency to a complex remedial court order, and lead to savings of money as well as time from having to replicate and improve work rejected in judicial review." (Phillip J. Cooper, op. cit.)

A Department of Health official noted, for example, that recent court decisions concerning the legal definition of death and the maintenance of life support mechanisms "constantly enter into our thinking." Although court decisions in the field of education "have not generally shaken the system," the Board of Regents showed responsiveness to the changing legal environment when, following a related court decision, it modified State regulations to assure girls access to boys' sports teams and competitions when no girls' team exists in the same sport.

In the social services field, the 1970 U.S. Supreme Court decision in *Goldberg v. Kelly* (397 U.S. 254) shaped welfare administration procedures not only in New York, where it originated, but nationwide. In this case, the court weighed two competing interests: the interest in avoiding increased cost and administrative burden, and the interest in assuring welfare recipients' rights to a fair hearing before termination of aid after a caseworker has found them ineligible. Because of the consequences to the recipient of a mistake on the caseworker's part—the recipient might be left with no means of support—the court ruled that there must be a hearing before aid is cut off.

Although the judges who dissented in *Goldberg v. Kelly* stated their concern that the decision would lead to more expensive, more exhaustive, more detailed protections being required of the State as new litigation arose, these fears have proven unfounded. Instead, the courts have been increasingly sensitive to cost considerations and have repeatedly refused to rule against the State out of deference to the expertise of agency managers.

The spread of AIDS, for example, has presented challenges to administrators in many agencies at both State and local levels. In considering the response to AIDS cases in prisons, judges have had the opportunity to specify how prisoners and employees should be protected from the disease and what special measures should be taken. They have refrained from making such decisions on the basis that these issues should be resolved at the agency level. The Department of Correctional Services has established policies to handle the problem (inmates who are AIDS victims are now segregated, for example). In contrast, litigation and court decisions in other areas have led directly to major shifts in agency policies.

The courts have played an important role in the development of rights for homeless people, another area that affects administrative decisions in both State and local government. In the landmark case *Callahan v. Carey*, the plaintiff and defendant were able to negotiate a settlement before the court handed down an official judgment*. In the consent judgment, which is legally binding and subject to court oversight, New York City agreed to accept responsibility for the shelter of every homeless man who presented himself to the local Department of Social Services. (The responsibility was extended to women and families in subsequent cases, although at the present time no clear, general right to shelter has been declared.)

Long after the case was settled, the court continued to monitor the settlement, including details such as the number of showers and toilets that must be provided per person. A source at the Department of Social Services describes the court as having imposed "an incredible burden on the Department," but it was not the judge

---

* *Callahan v. Carey*, Index No. 42582/79, (unpublished judgment decree; copy on file at the Rockefeller Institute for Government).

who set the detailed administrative requirements in the consent judgment, but rather the parties themselves.

The Willowbrook consent decree is another example of detailed administrative standards arising from a court case [*New York State Association for Retarded Children, Inc. v. Rockefeller* (357 F. Supp. 752–1973)]. In this instance, they involve minimum health and safety standards in the Willowbrook State School for the Mentally Retarded, a facility then housing 4,727 residents.

Because of the deplorable conditions it found, the court granted preliminary relief to the plaintiffs by requiring such measures as immediate hiring of specified members of staff, a contract with a hospital for medical care, and physical repairs to the buildings. The case was later settled by the parties, with detailed administrative standards enumerated in the consent decree and enforced by the court. Although in both *Willowbrook* and *Callahan* it was the parties involved that set the standards in the settlement, it is fair to say that the consequent administrative burden and the important shifts in department policy would not have taken place if not for the courts.

Judges have had an important impact on every conceivable policy area. At the same time, they have consistently deferred to agency expertise except in the most extreme cases; when detailed standards have resulted from a case, they have often been the result of negotiations between the parties involved rather than dictates from the judges. Finally, judicial decisions serve to define additional limits within which managers must work, limits that sometimes seem more distant from the agency's day-to-day environment, but which are no less real than budgetary limits and limits established by the Legislature.

McKinney's Consolidated Laws of New York and *Consolidated Laws Service* are both good sources for identifying important court decisions if one knows which law is at issue (see Appendix J). They give one or two sentence summaries of relevant decisions following each section of law. *The Index to Legal Periodicals* is also useful, as it references articles on legal issues by subject as well as by case title.

APPENDIX 1

A Summary of SAPA Provisions

NOTICE REQUIREMENTS

The State Administrative Procedures Act (SAPA) provides for five different rulemaking notices: **proposed rule-making, expiration, continuation, adoption,** and **emergency adoption.**

A notice of **proposed rule-making** must be submitted to the Secretary of State's Office for publication in the *State Register* prior to the adoption of a rule. This notice must be published at least thirty days before the adoption of a rule except when a public hearing is mandated by statute. In that instance, the thirty-day period must precede the public hearing. The agency proposing a rule must provide a copy of the notice to any person who had previously submitted a written request to the agency.

A notice of the **expiration** must be published in the *Register* by the Secretary of State whenever a notice of proposed rule-making expires (in most instances 180 days after initial publication in the *Register*).

A notice of **continuation** is used by agencies to extend the expiration date of a notice of proposed rule-making for an additional period of up to ninety days. A notice of proposed rule-making may not be continued more than twice after the original expiration date and an agency may not adopt a rule until thirty days after the notice of continuation appears in the *Register*. A notice of continuation must contain the subject, purpose, and substance of the proposed rule.

When an agency adopts a proposed rule, it must file the rule with the Secretary of State's Office and must submit a notice of **adoption** for publication in the *Register*.

SAPA also provides for a notice of **emergency adoption** to be used for an emergency rule. An agency may file a rule as an emergency if it finds that its immediate adoption is necessary to preserve the public health, safety or general welfare, and that compliance with a previously established provision of SAPA would be contrary to the public interest. An emergency rule expires sixty days from the date it is filed with the Secretary of State's Office, unless otherwise provided by law or when (within the time limit) the agency adopts the rule pursuant to SAPA.

Section 101-a of the Executive Law contains a rule-making notice procedure to inform the Temporary President of the Senate and the Speaker of the Assembly of an agency's rule proposal and emergency rule adoptions. Notice provided to legislative leaders are similar to notices required by SAPA, except that an additional fiscal analysis must be included, setting forth the costs to state and local government of enforcing the rule.

REGULATORY IMPACT STATEMENT

Chapter 344 of the Laws of 1983 requires agencies to prepare a Regulatory Impact Statement (RIS) and, as appropriate, a revised RIS when an agency proposes a rule or adopts an emergency rule. A copy of the RIS must be submitted to the Governor, the Temporary President of the Senate, the

Speaker of the Assembly and the Administrative Regulations Review Commission.

In order to reduce the paperwork burden that completing an RIS imposes, agencies may submit a consolidated RIS for any series of virtually identical rules proposed simultaneously. Furthermore, agencies may claim exemption from submission of an RIS for a rule involving only a technical amendment or a rule defined in Section 102(a)(ii) of SAPA (primarily concerned with rates). Agencies are also required to submit a revised RIS when there are substantive changes in the text of the rule as adopted from the text of rules as proposed.

REGULATORY FLEXIBILITY ANALYSIS

Chapter 910 of the Laws of 1983 requires agencies to consider using different approaches to minimize the regulatory/compliance impact of proposed rules on small business. For this purpose, a small business is defined as any business that is resident in New York State, is independently owned and operated, and employs one hundred or fewer individuals.

Agencies proposing rules that do not impose new reporting, record-keeping or other compliance requirements on small businesses, or rules that are defined in Section 102(a)(ii), are exempt from issuing RFAs. However, the agency must issue a finding that explains its exemption from the RFA requirement in the notice of proposed rulemaking. To avoid duplication, an agency may issue a single RFA for a series of closely related rules.

PUBLICATION OF RULES

The New York State Constitution, Article 4, Section 8, requires that the Legislature, by statute, provide for the speedy publication of agency rules. This is accomplished by Section 102 of the Executive Law which mandates that the Secretary of State publish the *Official Compilation of the Codes, Rules and Regulations of the State of New York (NYCRR)*. The NYCRR is updated monthly and contains the text of all rules adopted by agencies.

Chapter 698 authorizes OBPRA to determine by rule those categories of rules that will not be reviewed. It also makes the following provisions:

1. OBPRA may also extend for fifteen days the comment period on a proposed rule to allow interested parties sufficient time to analyze and comment on it (SAPA, 202-c[8]).
2. Agencies are authorized to prepare a regulatory agenda (SAPA, 202-d).
3. The effective rule date of a new rule may be delayed for twenty-one days after filing when the rule as adopted has substantive changes in comparison with the rule as proposed or when revised regulatory impact or flexibility statements are submitted (SAPA, 203[1]).

More detailed information on each of these procedures is found in McKinney's volume on the State Administrative Procedures Act (see Appendix J).

Chapter IX

State Government in an Intergovernmental Setting

The job of State managers would be difficult enough if their only concerns were with the state systems considered in previous chapters. In reality, the day-to-day operations of State agencies are affected by policies implemented at the federal level, and many actions taken by State managers in turn have substantial effects upon the State's 1612 local governments. It is therefore important for managers to have a clear understanding of the intergovernmental context in which they work, and to be aware of the perspective of the local governments that are affected directly by their decisions.

Local Governments

Geographically, the State is divided into 62 counties (five are boroughs of New York City), and these counties are subdivided into a total of 932 towns. All of the State's 556 villages are located in towns but the 62 cities (with minor exceptions) are wholly outside of the towns. Although towns are sometimes envisioned as being smaller than cities, and providing a more limited array of services, the population has spread from cities to surrounding areas within the past few decades so that this is no longer true. In the most extreme example, the Town of Hempstead currently has more than twice the population of the city of Buffalo. If, in some places, the many local boundaries do not seem entirely rational, it is because they have evolved over the life of the State rather than being planned at one time. In addition to counties, towns, cities and villages, there are many "special districts" that meet local needs for services such as fire or police protection, sewer systems, or any other desired service. Residents in a neighborhood in Queens grew weary of climbing stairs to the train station, for example, and set up a special district to tax themselves to provide for an escalator. School districts, too, have boundaries that usually do not coincide with other units. When all of these special districts are added to the number of towns, counties, cities and villages, the result is more than 9,700 local units, all of which, according to "Dillon's Rule" (ruling by Iowa Supreme Court Judge John F. Dillon in 1868) are creations of the State and subordinate to it (*City of Clinton v. Cedar Rapids and Missouri River Railroad Co.*, 24 Iowa 475, 1868).

The State Constitution (Article IX), as amended in 1963, grants local governments the power to "adopt or amend local laws which are not inconsistent with the provisions of the Constitution or with any general law," and the power to adopt or amend other local laws when not restricted by the Legislature. The 1963 amendment also included a Local Government Bill of Rights. Generally, the State Legislature may not pass any law that affects only one locality rather than a general class of units unless the governing body of that locality has first approved the bill. This approval by a locality is referred to as a home rule request. The State can, however, intervene when a state interest exists, and the State itself makes this determination. Also, the courts usually rule that a bill is "general" even if the class of governments is narrowly defined. For example, laws applying to "cities with a population of over 1,000,000" (only New York City) and "counties, except a county wholly contained within a city" (which excepts only New York City counties) have both passed the test of generality.

To further elaborate on the law-making powers of local government, the Legislature enacted the Municipal Home Rule Law and the Statute of Local Governments. Many other laws also contain provisions related to municipalities, among them the Civil Service Law, the General Municipal Law, the Local Finance Law, and others.

One locality deserves particular mention: New York City. More than 40 percent of the State's residents live there, and the City must contend with a host of unique problems brought on by its size and position as an international center. Its uniqueness earns it separate treatment in most aid programs, where the fairness of distribution between upstate and downstate interests often is contested. In fiscal year 1985, the City's total revenues of $21.2 billion were greater than the combined total of all other counties ($7.2 billion), cities ($1.8 billion), towns ($2.2 billion), villages ($.8 billion), and school districts ($9.1 billion) (*Special Report on Municipal Affairs, 1985,* Office of the State Comptroller, Table 8, p. 412).

State managers and local officials face many challenges peculiar to their level of government. Local officials and administrators experience firsthand the results of state policymaking. For example, when State officials made the decision to move toward relocating mental patients from state institutions into community residential facilities, it was local officials who were required to deal immediately with deinstitutionalization as it directly affected their communities.

While State legislators are constantly concerned with the opinions of their constituents, they are nonetheless more removed from them than are local elected officials. State legislators have the freedom to pass broadly phrased legislation, thus satisfying many interest groups simultaneously and transferring responsibility for development of specific rules or methods of implementation of the law to State agencies. When the laws are finally implemented at the local level, often it is local elected officials (who typically hold full-time jobs in addition to their public responsibilities) who are likely to be flooded with phone calls from angry or uninformed residents.

Unfortunately, the relationship between State administrators and local officials is not always characterized by mutual appreciation. Local officials' expressed concerns are only one of many pressures on State managers, and these concerns cannot necessarily be top priority. Local governments also have a number of concerns about State agency procedures.

State agency personnel have occasionally taken to the press stories concerning specific local governments or programs that directly affect them without first informing local officials. Local elected officials, previously unaware of a problem or question, suddenly find themselves on the news appearing uninformed and not on top of the situation. Such incidents work against the cooperative spirit essential to the effective, efficient provision of services in a decentralized state like New York. In contrast, cooperation is promoted when managers are sensitive to the immediacy of the political environment in which local officials must govern, and when they communicate directly with the top elected or administrative local officials about action to be taken that will involve their locality.

Local representatives also emphasize the necessity of applying State regulations consistently across localities. "We understand that a phenomenon like AIDS is going to change the way the Health Department deals with the counties, but we expect from the State consistent application and enforcement [of the necessary policies]," noted one county representative. The difficulty that State managers face with respect to this expectation is the competing pressure to recognize localities with special situations (perhaps by granting waivers).

Often, State regulators are required to perform a second kind of balancing act. Any change in an established regulation has consequences for those who have planned and invested on the basis of the old standard. Thus, when emission standards were changed as some counties were already in the midst of designing and constructing resource recovery (garbage-burning) plants, the local governments were forced to incur considerable additional costs to meet the new requirements. The result was resentment toward State regulators, who were perceived as being unable to make up their minds about a safe level of emissions. There seems to be no simple resolution to this tension, since scientific knowledge about the effects of pollution and other toxic substances is continually advancing, necessitating refinements or modifications in related regulations. Local sources suggest that regulators need to be aware of the costs imposed and ask that they make every effort to set a standard that will make sense for a long period of time.

While the various types of local governments (and individual localities within them) disagree on many issues, there are at least two ideas that all support. First, program control should accompany fiscal responsibility. The localities believe that for many programs they have far too little discretionary authority, considering their financial contribution. (This issue is addressed further in the section on mandates below.) Second, they believe that, when the decisions affect them, they should be involved in decision-making at the highest level of state government. One way of having input at the highest levels is through an advisory commission on intergovernmental relations. When State officials discuss possible decisions with local representatives informally, a similar purpose is accomplished. (The U.S. Advisory Commission on Intergovernmental Relations serves this purpose at the federal level; its publications are useful sources for anyone interested in a more in-depth study of the field.)

State-Local Interactions

State and local governments interact in almost every imaginable area. Administratively, local governments adhere to paperwork regulations specific to each program, purchase items from State contracts through OGS (although this is optional, most choose to take advantage of it), attend training programs conducted by the Office of the State Comptroller and turn to the State Insurance Department when they lose their liability insurance. (Through its Market Assistance Program, the Insurance Department has so far matched 290 municipalities with new insurers.) The Civil Service Department routinely audits the 110 city and county civil service commissions. In addition, it assists localities that choose to set up their own examination systems, provides some training, and administers some oral exams.

The Departments of Social Services, Health, Education, Transportation, and Motor Vehicles, and Office for the Aging are all deeply involved in programs administered at least partly by local governments.

In the Department of Health (DOH), almost every manager is involved in state-local issues in some way. In the areas of both environmental and preventive health, county health departments are the first-line service providers; however, they work closely with State employees in DOH's six regional offices. The regional offices can be thought of as divided in half: personnel working for the Office of Health Systems Management (OHSM), and those working for the Office of Public Health. While OHSM is primarily regulatory, employees of the Office of Public Health are specialists in preventive health programs and work alongside county health officers to administer programs. Many programs are partially funded by State aid, but there is considerable local variation in the programs and in local law relating to health.

During the 1986 legislative session, the Legislature revamped a key section of the Public Health Law. In exchange for a more liberal State aid reimbursement formula, each county must develop a comprehensive local public health plan, to be reviewed by DOH. Although this appears to be a movement toward greater State control of health policy, the criteria for evaluation of the plans are being developed in conjunction with the Association of County Health Officers (an affiliate of the Association of Counties) in an effort to meet local needs to the greatest extent possible within the law and within the statewide concerns of DOH.

In the area of social services, the county departments of social services (except in New York City) are the major service providers. To incorporate local experience into policy development, work groups made up of local interests are often formed. "They have a real impact on any new policy," reported a source in the Department of Social Services, "because you have to have the county's cooperation to get anything done."

Those who deal with a broad range of state-local issues from a statewide perspective include the Office for Local Government Services in the Department of State, the Division of Municipal Affairs in the Comptroller's Office, the Management and Inter-Governmental Systems Unit in the Division of the Budget, the Legislative Commission on State-Local Relations, and the Local Government and Cities committees in each house of the Legislature. The State Board of Equalization and Assessment is also important, as it administers the State's property tax system, which is the primary source of revenue for most local services. (For additional discussion of technical assistance provided to local governments by these organizations as well as local government associations, see *New York's System of State Aid*, Legislative Commission on State-Local Relations, December, 1982.) Under Governor Cuomo there is also a Deputy Secretary to the Governor for Education, Local Government, and the Arts, and a Program Associate working for the Deputy Secretary, both of whom play key roles in policy formation.

The Office for Local Government Services in the Department of State employs about twenty-four professional and support staff who provide services to local governments. Through the Office, for example, a locality can find out about labor relations contracts recently negotiated by similar jurisdictions in the State. Because water, wastewater and sewer systems are a major local expense, the Office provides information and advice aimed at reducing the costs of these systems. It also supplies training on planning and zoning, and other training as needed, assistance with computerization, work in the area of economic development, and general management consultation. The Department of State's legal staff are also available to answer local officials' questions about setting up cooperative service agreements and about changing the organizational form of their government. Finally, Office staff are often involved in special assignments such as the Liability Insurance Task Force (1985) and the Task Force on Mandates (1986).

The Division of Municipal Affairs within the Office of the State Comptroller wields power as the auditor of local fiscal practices. Whatever form local governments choose to take, they must use specified accounting procedures to report their revenues and expenditures. Since this system includes uniform definitions and methods for all municipalities, the Bureau of Research and Statistics (within the Division) can issue definitive reports on the fiscal status of the State's political subdivisions. "We provide all players with the same ammunition, thus making it easier to concentrate on the issues instead of arguing over the numbers" (Bureau source). The Division also sponsors training for local fiscal managers and provides advice to local governments when they find themselves in financial trouble.

If the fiscal problems of a local government are severe, DOB's Management and Intergovernmental Systems unit may also become involved. Unlike the Comptroller's Office, DOB can authorize emergency State aid when appropriate. The Division also interprets the Executive Budget for local government lobby groups and is involved on an *ad hoc* basis with other groups and issues as they arise.

State agencies provide some services that local governments eagerly take advantage of; regulation and control of local service provision is another major aspect of the state and local relationship that may be greeted quite differently. When State managers can involve their local counterparts in regulatory decisions that will affect them, and can leave them options, or at least provide expert

187

support to implement decisions made at the State level, the "state-local partnership" is strengthened.

The State Commission of Correction, for example, has a legally mandated role in the regulation and oversight of State correctional facilities, county jails, and city lock-ups. As one official there noted, while "local governments are not thrilled at the fact of our existence, the process that we use in establishing regulations does involve feedback" regarding local experience. For example, a jail education law, signed by the Governor in July, 1986, required the Commission to develop regulations for jails to clarify who is to provide education for eligible inmates (those under twenty years of age without a high school diploma), and who is to pay for it. The Commission promptly drafted regulations and distributed them to the appropriate local officials; enforcement was not scheduled to begin until mid-1987, leaving time for local problems with implementation to be identified and resolved.

Local representatives stress that although there often exist formal mechanisms to allow local comment, it is difficult in practice to obtain even minor changes in rules and regulations once the initial rule has been formulated. Rather, they would hope to be consulted in the draft stage, "before the agency position has hardened."

State Aid

The portion of the State budget appropriated to assist local governments is among the highest in the nation. Total aid in 1985 was $10.6 billion—nearly a quarter of total revenue raised by local governments (see Chart 9.1). On the other hand, local governments are required by State law to administer a large number of programs; a 1977 national survey found that New York mandated activities in sixty of seventy-seven functional areas—the highest of any state. Nonetheless, $1.2 billion of the $10.6 billion was distributed as general purpose State aid, which localities may use as they choose, thus providing some flexibility. The rest is earmarked for special purposes (see Chart 9.2).

The question of how much State aid is fair, considering the number of activities local governments are required to engage in, would be a great deal easier to resolve if the requirements could be listed and their costs determined. The problems involved are discussed below in the section on mandates; suffice it to say that the sharp debate over State aid, centered around the issue of fairness, is likely to continue.

Moreover, there are not just two sides to the State aid/fairness issue, but three, four, and sometimes five. Although representatives of towns, counties, cities, and villages all have an interest in working

9.1 State aid as percent of local revenues
Fiscal year 1984

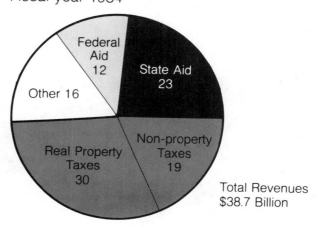

Source: 1985 *State Aid to Local Government,*
Office of the State Comptroller, Exhibit I

together to obtain more State aid (they all want a bigger State aid pie to slice), they also compete for funds and disagree about optimal distribution (they each want a bigger piece). In the spring of 1984, in order to work together on issues where possible, the leaders of the three major local government organizations (the Conference of Mayors and Other Municipal Officials, the Association of Towns, and the Association of Counties) formed an informal "Municipal Council," which meets about twice a month (more frequently when necessary). Working together on issues such as State aid and liability insurance produced results "much better [for the local governments] than what would have happened if we were out there individually and fighting among ourselves" (Council member).

"The revenue limitations and reduced funding levels are forcing public managers to be more creative in their decision-making." (Steven V. Alteri in *NYS Town and Government*, January 1986, p. 24.)

The largest source of revenue for local governments is real property taxes, although this source is limited by the State constitution and by State laws. New York City and Yonkers are subject to tax limits of 2.5 percent of a five year average of the full value of taxable real estate; most other cities are subject to a limit of 2 percent. Tax limits pose a problem: Since 1985, two cities and sixteen

9.2   Distribution of State
STATE FISCAL YEARS ENDED

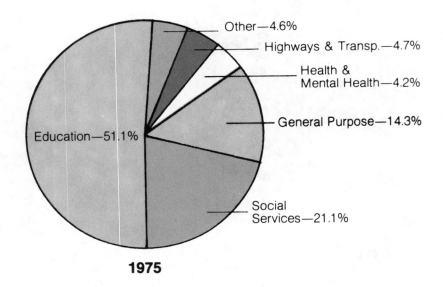

Other—4.6%

Highways & Transp.—4.7%

Health &
Mental Health—4.2%

General Purpose—14.3%

Education—51.1%

Social
Services—21.1%

1975

Although the General Purpose, Social Services and Health and Mental Health categories registered growth in outlays during the above period, all three experienced proportional declines with respect to total disbursements. Source: *1985 State Aid to Local Government,* Office of the State Comptroller, Exhibit VIII

school districts have been taxing at the maximum rate (OSC, *Special Report on Municipal Affairs,* 1985, pp. 44–45).

The three other major sources of revenue are federal aid, State aid and sales taxes (the latter accounts for almost one-sixth of county revenues); special taxes, charges and fees also provide a small portion of local revenue.

While State aid has remained at about one-quarter of local revenue in recent years, federal aid as a percent of revenue has gradually declined (see Chart 9.3), in line with President Reagan's New Federalism policy. The role of the federal government has shifted dramatically from its previous role of innovator. An earlier indicator of this change was the movement in the late sixties and early seventies from categorical grants, which tightly controlled

Aid by Major Category
IN 1975 AND 1985

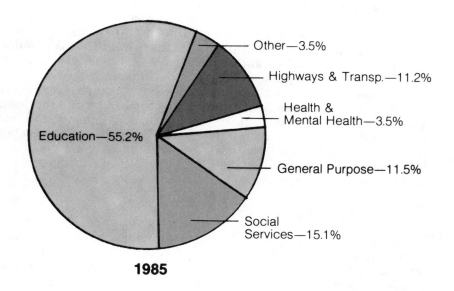

Other—3.5%

Highways & Transp.—11.2%

Health &
Mental Health—3.5%

Education—55.2%

General Purpose—11.5%

Social
Services—15.1%

1985

spending for specific projects, to block grants, which require less paperwork and allowed local governments more freedom, but which are also easier to reduce (or even eliminate).

Local governments' recent loss of $470 million in federal revenue sharing is a second illustration that still stings in many areas. Towns that used the money to cover capital costs may be able to increase their borrowing to cover the loss. Towns that recently experienced a surplus may now only break even. On the other hand, very small municipalities, where federal money comprised a substantial portion of the budget, and localities that used the money to finance a vital local service suffer more. A source in the Governor's Office described the current budget as "a triage process," with many worthy programs not receiving funding because the emergency cases must come first, and does not believe it likely that the State will replace federal cuts.

A key prerequisite to getting any change in aid to pass in the Legislature is that a bill or bills proposed for this purpose hurt no one. Increases in aid may be distributed differently, but bills that result in actual decreases are not likely to pass. To avoid this type of redistribution, the Legislature continued to base its aid distribution on 1970 census data through 1984, even after 1980 population data were available. State aid was capped at that time, so legislators were not able to disguise a redistribution through increases.

Because the level of State aid varies from year to year, many localities face real dilemmas in developing their budgets. Most local governments operate on a fiscal year that begins January 1 (some begin on July 1) rather than April 1, the beginning of the State's fiscal year. Hence, their tax rates are set, and programs planned, based on educated guesses about what will be forthcoming, but without any firm knowledge.

The Mandates Debate

Mandates are activities that local governments have been forced to undertake and pay for because of decisions made at the State level or in the courts. In one instance, State social services staff housed in part of a county office building were forced out of their offices and onto the street in a symbolic protest against program mandates. Tension was also apparent in a protest against State mandated property tax exemption for religious organizations in the town of Hardenburgh (population 236). More than half of the residents became ordained as ministers of the Universal Life Church, a "church" that ordained anyone who could pay a fee to dramatize the effect of the exemption on local government.

Are laws or regulations considered mandates only if they require that something be done under all circumstances? In recent years, one classification effort (the Legislative Commission on Expenditure Review) has categorized regulations of this kind as Type I mandates. Type II mandates are those that, by *allowing* a locality to do something, make it politically difficult to choose not to do it. The late Mayor of Albany, Erastus Corning, once remarked, "Here the Legislature gives a municipality an opportunity to help senior citizens [by exempting them from property tax], so you're damned if you do and damned if you don't. It's not a mandate, but you look like a bum if you don't do it." (Arlene Bigos, "State, Local Governments Argue When Mandated Expenses are Mandatory," *The Knickerbocker News*, Albany, NY, February 23, 1976, p. 2A.) In fact, however, some local governments did choose not to implement this exemption.

9.3 State and federal aid as percent of local revenues (excluding New York City)

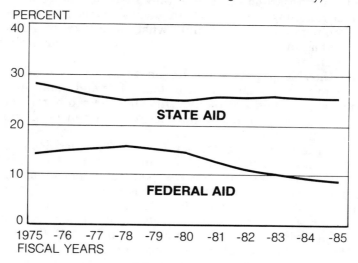

PERCENT

NOTE: Total intergovernmental aid from the State and Federal Governments as a percent of total revenues remained fairly stable through the eleven year period 1975-1985.

Source: *Special Report on Municipal Affairs—1985*, Office of the State Comptroller, Table 1-Aa

Finally, Type III mandates specify that, if a locality chooses to provide a service, that service must be provided subject to the enumerated provisions. (LCER, *State Mandates to Counties*, August 1981.) A city need not have its own police force, for example, but, if it so chooses each officer must have completed four hundred hours of training, and numerous other requirements must be met as well.

Rather than assure availability of State funds for each mandate when it is passed, as happens in some other states, New York addresses the cost of mandates to localities by appropriating relatively generous amounts of general purpose State aid. The question of how much is enough to cover these costs adequately is likely to continue to be hotly debated.

The debate over mandates arises from a fundamental tension between State and local governments concerning who should have how much decision-making power and who should pay how much for the services provided. It is also a clash between the legal reality that local governments are creatures of the State and of the principle of home rule.

Everyone agrees that a balance must be struck between the State's interest in providing residents with a basic level of service and protection regardless of where they live, and the communities' interest in retaining the freedom to govern themselves as they see fit. The problem comes in defining what basic level of service the State should assure. How much autonomy and how much uniformity are appropriate?

While those engaged in debate on these issues often talk as though there were policies that are clearly fair and unfair or clearly right and wrong, they are really struggling for a different balance point between freedom and uniformity, or between local and state financing responsibilities.

Whatever level of mandated services the State decides upon, the mix of State and local funding for mandates raises both economic and political questions, but it is the political implications that are probably the more important in driving the debate. Specifically, neither the State nor local elected officials are anxious to be responsible for expanding their budgets to meet the costs of the mandated programs. Local officials argue that it is politically easier for the State to absorb the costs, since the State's revenues have been increasing naturally, without increases in tax rates, in recent years. In general, the local governments' financial situations require them to raise taxes in order to realize the needed increase in revenue. Either way, if a service is mandated, the funds come from the wallets of State taxpayers. The difference is in who will pay more (State and local tax systems have different impacts on poor and wealthy taxpayers) and which jurisdiction will be held responsible for the cost of the program.

In a few cases, local governments are providing mandated services that they would rather the State both provide and fund. Currently, counties provide and pay for certain education programs for handicapped pre-schoolers, a function they feel should be handled by the State Education Department. Most would also rather not be involved with Medicaid, an $8 billion program administered at the county level, for which counties pay about 20 percent of the costs, and one whose costs have risen rapidly in recent years. Although there has been a trend toward the State's assuming greater financial responsibility in this area, complete financial and administrative assumption by the State is unlikely. Furthermore, as long as the counties administer the program, the State argues, they should be required to share in the costs so they maintain an interest in the efficiency of the operation.

In many cases, however, the complaint of local governments is not with what they are being required to do, but with the additional expenses incurred in doing it. Environmental and health-related

PAYNE

mandates often fall into this category. No one is against healthy people and a clean environment, but the arguments over where responsibility lies for financing such programs are endless.

The Department of Environmental Conservation (DEC), for example, is currently at or near "the top of the list of regulators." Solid waste disposal has become a crisis situation in many localities, as some landfills close because they are out of compliance, while others are beyond their capacity limits. In promulgating and enforcing regulations designed to maintain a safe and healthy environment, DEC has incurred the dissatisfaction of many a local manager who has to cope with mandated costs in this area rising rapidly, without any corresponding increase in financial assistance. In some instances, local irritation with State agencies may be misdirected. Agencies are responsible for furthering their missions by promulgating rules and regulations when necessary, but only the Legislature can appropriate funds.

The fact is, although there are a large number of mandates in existence (the Legislative Commission on Expenditure Review counted 2,632 existing statutory mandates to counties alone in 1977), no one knows what their cost is, and the cost of finding out is in itself prohibitive. The number of mandates continues to grow: new ones are often added, and old ones are seldom replaced or cancelled. Of the mandates counted by the LCER, 1,037 are "ministerial" mandates; that is, they involve the administration of local activities rather than the programmatic aspects of governing. (How does one go about estimating the cost of using form A, which has been mandated, rather than form B?)

Further, it is impossible to know what the level of service in a community would be without any mandates. Although a 1986 Rockefeller Institute of Government survey found that about half of the upstate counties queried estimated the total cost of mandates at between 76 and 100 percent of their expenditures, some of those costs may be for services the county would provide even without a mandate.

Difficulties in determining the costs of mandates, as well as the pervasive tendency to want someone else to pay, frequently reduce arguments over increased funding to "shouting matches." In 1983, in an attempt to increase awareness of the costs of mandates, the Legislature amended the Legislative Law to require that fiscal notes accompany bills imposing a fiscal burden on local governments. Local officials had hoped that legislators' heightened awareness of the costs they were imposing would slow the growth of mandates, but the consensus seems to be that the fiscal notes have not had this effect, perhaps in part because of the previously noted difficulties with obtaining reasonable cost data. Still, "they are better than nothing," comments one lobbyist for local government.

The groups that represent local governments (the Conference of Mayors and Other Municipal Officials, the Association of Towns, the Association of Counties) must be concerned not only with legislative activity, but also with proposed regulations, since these have the force of law. Local representatives often use the comment period following publication in the State Register to try to influence an agency to withdraw or change a proposed rule or regulation.

One legislative change that counties (and New York City) were able to achieve was a partial takeover by the State of long-term care costs for Medicaid patients. Governor Cuomo estimates a total local savings of $1.3 billion from 1983 through 1986. Changes in the other direction have also taken place, however. Since the State began its policy of deinstitutionalization, the number of inpatients has dropped from close to 100,000, during the Rockefeller administration, to approximately 23,000 in 1987. Along with the shift in patient population has come a shift in cost burden from the State to the counties.

The Governor has sometimes opposed the Legislature's attempts to increase the number of mandates. Rockefeller vetoed several bills that would have imposed mandates, and in 1976, the Legislature overrode a veto for the first time in 104 years on a bill that required New York City to appropriate a specific proportion of its budget for education.

The Cuomo administration identified the mandate situation as one of its top priorities and in 1986 set up a task force composed of local and State representatives to identify obsolete and unnecessary mandates. The task force's first progress report was issued in 1987.

Policymakers also need to be aware that mandates can have unintended effects, including no effect at all. Unless strictly enforced, mandates may not be truly requirements; not all mandates are strictly enforced. A 1970 law, for example, requires local governments to adopt a code of ethics, and to create and maintain a board of ethics. The code must be filed with the Office of the State Comptroller. Although the Town of East Greenbush (near Albany) originally complied, a police sergeant who sought the assistance of the board of ethics was told by the Town Supervisor that it had "been inactive since 1974." The Supervisor continued, "I do not even remember who the members were. Two, I believe, have died, and I don't know who may have been the third one." (Laurie Anderson, "Ethics Board Has Faded Away," *The Knickerbocker News,* August 7, 1986, p. 4A.)

On the other hand, some local officials have found that noncompliance with some mandates can have important consequences. Every municipality must file an annual financial report with the Comptroller's Office. If the OSC does not receive the report within ninety days after the due date, a letter is mailed notifying the municipality that willful refusal to comply is a misdemeanor, and that the locality's share of State aid and federal aid is in jeopardy. Fiscal officers have in fact been fired for noncompliance. Similarly, exceeding the constitutional tax limit can result in the loss of State aid. When this situation occurred in 1985, a treasurer and a city manager lost their jobs.

While local governments often oppose State meddling in local affairs, they sometimes seek State assistance. Currently, counties collect sales tax revenues and distribute some to the towns, villages, and cities within their borders. The method of distribution is at the discretion of the county. Not surprisingly, the Association of Towns would like the State to fix the towns' percent of the revenue.

Towns would also like to have some influence in the decision of an area to incorporate itself as a village. The advantages to the people of the village include zoning privileges and more State aid. The town, however, experiences a loss of revenue for activities such as highway maintenance and planning, and so feels legislation should be passed allowing it to participate in the decision to incorporate.

Intergovernmental Cooperation

"Whenever a municipality has the legal authority to perform a certain function but finds difficulties in carrying out the task, a cooperation agreement should be considered" (NYS Conference of Mayors, *Municipal Cooperation Agreements*, 1986, p. 3.).

Especially today, in an atmosphere of fiscal retrenchment at the federal level and fiscal conservatism at the State level, cooperative agreements between levels of local governments (and between neighboring local governments) need to be considered as possible responses to decreased funding. Such agreements are often made in the area of public works (e.g. snow removal) and often are informal rather than written, signed documents. While a local official's primary consideration may be getting the snow off the streets by morning, legal problems and liability questions may ensue if there is no signed agreement between provider and receiver. To highlight this fact, and to point out other legal restrictions on agreements (i.e. in the areas of fire and police protection), the Conference of Mayors and Other Municipal Officials recently published a report entitled *Municipal Cooperation Agreements: Sharing Services Under New York State Law*.

At times, cooperation represents the only alternative to eliminating a program. Two school districts in the Town of Colonie near Albany had been administering a special enrichment program each summer on school property and charging a small fee to cover some of the costs. When the courts declared the fee illegal, the program faced elimination. Instead, the Town was able to take over administration so that a fee could legally be charged and the 1400 students enrolled in the program could continue to participate.

The idea of encouraging intermunicipal cooperation was set out years ago in a section of the Municipal Law, but there has never been funding to provide incentives. Nevertheless, the Office of the State Comptroller lists 222 formalized joint activities in its 1985 *Special Report on Municipal Affairs*. The Legislative Commission on State-Local Relations believes that the potential for savings from cooperative agreements is still not being fully realized, in part because of start-up costs and political inertia. The Commission supports proposed legislation to financially encourage cooperation in such areas as sharing computer services, tax assessors, and landfill arrangements.

"The question of 'who should be providing what services?' will be a major research question for the next couple of decades," according to a Legislative Commission source. A first step toward finding answers involves cataloging the services that are currently being provided by each level of government. Doing so reveals a variation in services provided by towns, for example, that is as great as the variation between towns and villages. The Legislative Commission on State-Local Relations is working in conjunction with researchers at Cornell University to examine the issue of service provision and to identify any appropriate, politically viable changes that could be made.

One area certain to be identified is solid waste management. In recent years, responsibility for this area has tended to evolve up to the county level, but even this has proven unsatisfactory. "The nature of our solid waste management problems require that we look for regional solutions" (Governor Mario Cuomo, *Message to the Legislature*, January 7, 1987, p. 48.).

Although, as Cuomo points out, the nature of the solid waste problem makes regional cooperation absolutely essential, regional provision of other services that are not yet posing critical problems may also be more efficient. "Certainly there needs to be some service consolidation," remarked one county official. Yet political boundaries are slow to break down, and cooperative ventures are dependent on the spirit of those involved. "You can't go into an agreement without trust," observed one source, and "fiefdom issues" often prevent cooperation. A 1985 survey conducted by the Legislative Commission on Rural Resources found that many local governments recognize problems in setting up cooperation agreements. "A large number of problems, however, were neither legal nor logistical; they were either political or parochial" (Legislative Commission on Rural Resources, *Intermunicipal Cooperation: A Survey of Local Governments*, August, 1985, p. 14.).

In addition to cooperative agreements between local governments, regional issues are often addressed through regional bodies independent of any one government. The activities of the eleven regional planning commissions around the State include coordinating projects, providing technical assistance for local planning activities, collecting and reporting regional data, and undertaking special studies such as a study of aviation activities at the Albany County Airport since deregulation.

Other regional bodies independent of local boundaries include "authorities" such as transportation authorities, urban renewal agencies, and industrial development authorities. Besides allowing an area to address a regional need directly, these public authorities operate free from many of the restrictions on governments. Civil service rules often do not apply, and although they are not backed by the full faith and credit of the State, public authorities have easier access to some types of loans than do local governments and can issue bonds more easily. Since these entities are not subject to constitutional tax limits, they can apply rents or user fees to finance the service without raising the area's taxes.

Because of these advantages, the number of local public authorities continues to increase. As of fiscal year 1984, there were over five hundred such bodies throughout the State.

State-Federal Relations

Responsibility for the provision of many services is shared among local, state, and federal levels of government. The State relies on federal funding for many programs. New York also receives large amounts of federal aid relative to other states. In fiscal year 1984, New York ranked fourth in the country in federal aid obtained, and second in aid for public welfare. The total: $10.9 billion, $337 million of which was for public welfare.

The New York State Office in Washington (Washington Office) serves as the eyes and ears of the Governor in the nation's capital. Just as local governments try to influence the development of State policy, so Washington Office staff try to affect national policy. Although occasionally staff become involved in developing new proposals, generally the Office finds its work thrust upon it by the Congressional agenda. An exception was legislation recently passed allowing fiber optics to be installed along interstate highways. Communications companies asked that an exception be made to the restrictive law then in effect that prohibited locating the new lines along the interstate. They argued that installing fiberoptics along the New York State Thruway just between Albany and Schenectady, for example, would save $5 million. The Office seized the opportunity to develop more general legislation regarding fiber optics installation nationwide.

Washington Office staff are also responsible for analyzing new proposals that may affect the State as they are introduced in Congress, and for interpreting certain laws after they are passed. When the recent immigration reform bill was passed, Office staff summarized the problems with it as well as issues concerning the implementation of the act and promulgation of regulations; in effect they answered the question, "What does this law mean for New York State?" However, the Office's efforts are mainly focused on influencing bills that will affect the State as they pass through the legislative process before they become law.

The Washington Office and State agencies interact in two main ways. The Washington Office often seeks program information from the agencies, either in order to answer program-related inquiries by members of Congress, or to develop arguments for use in Congressional debate; providing information to support favored bills and discredit those it opposes is part of the lobbying effort. Second, some State agencies (for example, the Department of Social Services and the Department of Health) frequently find themselves in need of waivers. One source at DSS expressed frustration at being so heavily regulated. Although the problem was worse before block grants were instituted, "we are still sometimes prevented from doing things that make sense for New York, administratively." In such cases, Washington Office staff use their contacts and, on occasion, the press to provide reasonable arguments as to why federal agencies should grant the necessary waivers.

Occasionally, Commissioners and other high-level State officials are asked to testify before Congress. In developing their testimony, it helps to know where Congressional committee members stand in terms of background knowledge and opinion on the issue. Washington Office staff are helpful in providing this information since they are constantly in touch with committee activity.

Some agencies also hire their own representatives to lobby in Washington. For example, the Department of Social Services has a federal legislative liaison who works closely with his counterpart in the Washington Office. The State Education Department, in line with its independent status, maintains a small office in Washington, the purpose of which is to disseminate information to Congress and to report information on Congressional activities relating to education.

Contact between Federal and State Agencies

The nature of contact between federal and State agencies differs from agency to agency. For many programs, federal agencies serve mainly in a supervisory capacity enforcing regulations they have promulgated. For others, they become more directly involved, providing staff to work with State staff on particular problems. In a few instances, a very cooperative relationship exists, and programs are both jointly funded and jointly administered. An example of this last type is the relationship of the US Geological Survey (part of the US Department of the Interior) with the Department of Environmental Conservation (DEC) and some local governments. At least two-thirds of USGS's work is completed at the request of the agency or jurisdiction, and matching funds are provided. Current joint programs with DEC include the defining of State water resources, studies of PCBs in the Hudson, the Hudson River as a resource, and of water use (where it's going and how it's used). The relationships here are very cooperative. Other examples of cooperation include the exchange of completed tax data between the State Department of Tax and Finance and the Internal Revenue

Service, and implementation of federal regulations that declare the crossing of a State border by a State criminal a federal offense.

The Federal Highway Administration (FHWA) and the State Department of Transportation (DOT) interact through an $800 million aid program, financed by funds collected from highway user fees and gas taxes, and then distributed to states according to a formula. Once the money has been "apportioned" to the State, the latter may spend it on whatever transportation programs it chooses, as long as these programs are in compliance with federal standards. The Highway Administration's role is to review programs to ensure compliance. In the process, however, their engineers assist in project design and planning. When some of the aid money is passed to local governments, the latter are responsible to DOT which is, in turn, responsible to FHWA. Thus FHWA serves as much more of a regulator than does the Geological Survey, although there is frequent professional involvement as well.

The State Department of Social Services administers many programs that are largely federally funded and heavily regulated by the federal government. Interaction with the federal Department of Health and Human Services (HHS) takes place on a program-by-program basis between program staff and the regional HHS office. For some programs the Department has less latitude in its decision-making than the DOT example described above, and the role of HHS in these cases is thus more supervisory.

The State Department of Labor receives about 95 percent of its funding from the federal Department of Labor (DOL). As in other departments, the role of the federal government has been evolving. Some programs are much less tightly regulated than a few years ago, but the new freedom presents its own concerns. Although the State appears to have a great deal of programmatic latitude (under the Job Training Partnership Act, for example) a source in the Department worries that the real message from the federal government might be "go ahead and try it. We'll let you know if we disapprove."

Within this general trend of reduced federal involvement, programs that require more federal dollars also comply with more regulations (including prescribed methods, quality control mechanisms, and reporting requirements). When a decision at the federal level declared that veterans' separation pay should be counted as income and employment, the State Legislature had to amend the Unemployment Insurance Law in order to remain in compliance. Thus, according to a State DOL source, "what would seem to be a State issue in terms of eligibility for unemployment insurance is really regulated by the federal government."

Suggestions for Incorporating the State-Local Partnership into Day-to-Day Agency Activities

Several suggestions for strengthening the cooperation of State and local governments emerged from discussions with managers and policy makers at all levels:

○ Consult with appropriate local officials early in the planning stages of projects or regulations that will affect them.

○ Keep local officials informed about State activities in their jurisdiction (local officials need to be kept up-to-date in order to respond accurately when constituents call).

○ Over time, identify and communicate with the local personnel who hold the real power; as in any organization, actual power and influence are not likely to correspond to any printed chart.

○ Make use of the following sources of information on New York State's local governments as needed:

Information on Structure and Function
• *Local Government Handbook*, 4th edition, Department of State, 1987.
• *New York's Local Government Structures—The Division of Responsibility*, Legislative Commission on State-Local Relations, 1983 (soon to be updated).
• *County Directory*, New York State Association of Counties (annual).

Financial Information
• *Special Report on Municipal Affairs*, Office of the State Comptroller (statistical annual).
• *Catalogue of State and Federal Programs Aiding New York's Local Governments*, Legislative Commission on State-Local Relations, 1986.
• *State Aid to Local Governments*, Office of the State Comptroller (annual).

APPENDIX*

A Typology of Mandates

Should all State mandates upon local governments be reimbursable in full? Rational analysis of the different types of mandates levied by the fifty state governments leads to the conclusion that not all mandates should be reimbursed in full or in part.

State mandates upon local governments may be classified by type as follows:

Due Process mandates contain directives relative to notices of proposed local government actions and public hearings.

Entitlement mandates stipulate that specified classes of citizens are entitled to receive a specific benefit. Examples include property tax exemptions for veterans of the armed forces and senior citizens.

Equal Treatment mandates are designed to ensure that citizens and employees are treated fairly.

Ethical mandates require local governments to adopt codes of ethics promoting the highest possible moral standards in the public service.

Good Neighbor mandates seek to prevent individual local governments from spilling problems and resulting costs over local boundary lines to neighboring units. Minimum state environmental standards are examples of good neighbor mandates.

Informational mandates seek to keep citizens well informed as to the activities of their local governments by requiring public meetings of official bodies, guaranteeing public access to local government records, and requiring notices of public meetings of public bodies.

Personnel mandates relate to hours of work, including shifts, fringe benefits, compulsory binding arbitration of impasses in labor-management negotiations, and retirement benefits.

Record-keeping mandates pertain to accounting standards, and financial and other records maintenance.

Structural mandates deal with the organizational structure of local governments.

Service level mandates require the performance of services by local governments meeting minimum State standards. In the area of education, State mandates cover instructional and noninstructional matters and it may be important to make a distinction between the two types of mandates.

---

* Excerpted from Joseph F. Zimmerman, "The State Mandate Problem," prepared for "State Mandates: Room for Reform," conference at the Rockefeller Institute of Government, State University of New York, Albany, September 9, 1986, pp. 22–24. This provides a different way of typing from that of the Legislative Commission on Expenditure Review.

Tax base mandates grant exemptions from the real property tax.

Clearly several types of mandates overlap as illustrated by entitlement mandates and tax base mandates. The above types are suggestive and other types can be developed.

A strong case can be made that the following mandates should not be subject to State reimbursement for added costs imposed upon local governments: **due process, equal treatment, ethical, good neighbor, informational,** and **record-keeping.** These types of mandates serve the purposes of ensuring that local governments conduct their activities in accord with the highest ethical standards, do not discriminate in the provision of services, keep citizens fully informed, and do not cause problems for neighboring local jurisdictions.

One can argue, however, that many record-keeping mandates cumulatively place a financial burden upon local governments exceeding the cost of what these governments may consider to be adequate record-keeping. The cost of record-keeping is difficult to determine.

Structural mandates usually do not impose substantial cost upon local governments and in general do not merit reimbursement.

The costly mandates are **personnel, service level,** and **tax base** ones.

Selected Bibliography

Abdo Baaklini, *The Politics of Legislation in New York State* (Albany: Graduate School of Public Affairs, SUNY at Albany, 1979).

Gerald Benjamin and T. Norman Hurd, eds., *Making Experience Count* (Albany: Rockefeller Institute of Government, SUNY, 1985).

Peter Colby, ed., *New York State Today* (Albany: SUNY Press, 1985).

Alan Hevesi, *Legislative Politics in New York State* (New York: Praeger Publishers, 1975).

Robert Kerker, *The Executive Budget in New York: A Half-Century Perspective* (Albany: NYS Division of the Budget, 1981).

Aaron B. Wildavsky, *The Politics of the Budgetary Process*, 3d ed. (Boston: Little, Brown and Company, Publishers, 1979).

Aaron B. Wildavsky, *The New Politics of the Budgetary Process* (Glenview, Ill.: Scott, Foresman and Company, 1988).

Joseph Zimmerman, *Government and Politics of New York State* (New York: New York University Press, 1981).

Appendices

Preface to the Appendices

Appendix A: State Executive Agencies

Although structurally New York State has twenty departments as limited by its constitution, there have been hundreds of bodies created by the State Legislature and by Executive Order to accomplish the State's goals. This list includes the twenty departments, as well as divisions, offices and other organizations that were created within the departments and are directly responsible to the Governor. It does not include all of the publicly supported policymaking bodies in the State.

We have distinguished commissions from agencies because generally, their missions are narrower in scope. They are listed in a separate appendix. A few well-known, well-established boards and councils are included for convenient reference; however, most were excluded because they are often temporary, quite focused in their mission, and sometimes function without full-time staff. For a brief statement of each agency's purpose and a more inclusive listing of New York's policymaking bodies, see the *Legislative Manual*, published biennially by the Department of State. See also "Something for Everyone: An Inventory of New York State Agencies," by Mary Eileen Kirchgraber, 1984, in NYS Legislative Commission on Economy and Efficiency in Government, *Annual Report*, 1984–85, which includes in chart format, information on the head of each agency, whether it has rule making powers, whether it is covered by civil service laws, the number of filled staff positions, and the 1983–84 appropriation. It is the only such inventory we have been able to locate.

Appendix B: Independent and Executive Branch Commissions with Statewide Missions

Commissions were excluded that were local in scope (with a particular locality or region in their title or mission). Also excluded were "temporary" commissions established after January 1, 1978. All existing commissions and their addresses are listed in the *Legislative Manual*.

Appendix C: State Agencies, Legislative Committees, and Commissions Grouped by Mission and Responsibility

State agencies, Executive Branch and independent commissions, and legislative committees and commissions have been combined in this list by broad topical area of responsibility to facilitate quick, easy identification of the major actors in each policy area.

While other groups have important influences on policy in the subject areas listed, the agencies, commissions and committees included will serve as useful, general sources, and can refer the interested reader to the other relevant organizations.

Appendix D: Inter-Agency Statewide Councils and Committees

We have included those councils and committees that have membership open to State employees in any agency and that are not open to private sector counterparts. Only organizations with career-related criteria for membership are listed. State employees are, of course, members of other career-related organizations, some national, some involving only a few State agencies, and some that include private sector employees as well.

Appendix E: Members of the Legislature

Appendices F, G and H: Legislative Committees and Commissions

Although joint legislative commissions are created to serve the needs of both houses, and are often thought of as nonpartisan, care should be taken to note whether staff serve at the pleasure of one house leader or the other. At least three commissions, the Legislative Bill Drafting Commission, the Legislative Commission on Expenditure Review, and the Administrative Regulations Review Commission, were set up with a rotating chair or co-chair to equalize the influence of the Senate and Assembly. The telephone number of each commission's executive director has been provided since commission staff are usually more directly involved in the commissions' day-to-day projects than are the legislators themselves.

Appendix I: Public Authorities with Statewide Missions

Only those authorities with statewide missions were included to save space and remain consistent in our approach to organizational listings. Regional authorities in some cases have considerable impact on policy and service delivery in their area, particularly in the New York City region. For a complete listing of authorities, see *Directory of New York State Public Authorities, 1985*, available from the Assembly Standing Committee on Corporations, Authorities and Commissions. The biennial *Legislative Manual*, lists the larger public authorities but is not complete.

Appendix J: Handy References

The references listed here represent a good starting place for anyone seeking further detailed information on almost any aspect of New York State Government.

APPENDIX A

State Executive Agencies

Executive Chamber
State Capitol
Albany, NY 12224
(518) 474-8390

2 World Trade Center
Floor 57
New York, NY 10047
(212) 587-2100

Additional Office:
Washington, DC

Office of the Lieutenant Governor
State Capitol, 3rd Floor
Albany, NY 12224

(518) 474-4623

Adirondack Park Agency
P.O. Box 99
Ray Brook, NY 12977

(518) 891-4050

Office for the Aging
2 Empire State Plaza
Albany, NY 12223
(518) 474-8675

2 World Trade Center
Floor 27
New York, NY 10047
(212) 488-6405

(Toll-free hotline: 1-800-342-9871)

Department of Agriculture and Markets
Capital Plaza, 1 Winners Circle
Albany, NY 12235
(518) 457-3880
Regional Offices:
Buffalo
New York City
Riverhead

Rochester
Syracuse

Division of Alcoholic Beverage Control
250 Broadway
New York, NY 10007
(212) 587-4002
Regional Offices:
Albany

Buffalo

Council on the Arts
915 Broadway
New York, NY 10010

(212) 614-2900

Banking Department
2 Rector Street
New York, NY 10006   **(212) 618-6220**
    Regional Offices:
      194 Washington Avenue
      Albany, NY 12210
      (518) 474-2364
      Buffalo   Syracuse
      Rochester   Europe (London)

Division of the Budget
State Capitol
Albany, NY 12224   **(518) 474-2300**

Office of Business Permits and Regulatory Assistance
Alfred E. Smith State Office
Building
17th Floor
Albany, NY 12225   **(518) 474-4357**
   (Toll-free number: 1-800-342-3464)

Department of Civil Service
Building 1, State Office Building
Campus
Albany, NY 12239   **(518) 457-2487**
    Regional Offices:
      Buffalo   New York City

Department of Economic Development
1 Commerce Plaza
Albany, NY 12245   **(518) 474-1431**
    Regional Offices:
      Albany   New York City
      Binghamton   Ogdensburg
      Buffalo   Rochester
      Kingston   Syracuse
      Long Island   Utica
      Canadian Offices (Montreal, Toronto)
      Europe (London)
      European Sub-office (Wiesbaden)
      Far East (Tokyo)

State Consumer Protection Board
99 Washington Avenue   250 Broadway
Albany, NY 12210   New York, NY 10007
 (518) 474-8583   **(212) 587-4482**

Department of Correctional Services
Building 2, State Office Building
Campus
Albany, NY 12226   **(518) 457-7329**

Council on Children and Families
Corning Tower, 28th Floor
Empire State Plaza
Albany, NY 12223   **(518) 474-8038**

Crime Victims Board
97 Central Avenue
Albany, NY 12206   **(518) 473-9649**

Division of Criminal Justice Services
Executive Park Tower
Stuyvesant Plaza
Albany, NY 12203   **(518) 457-6113**

Developmental Disabilities Planning Board
1 Empire State Plaza
Albany, NY 12223   **(518) 474-3655**

Office of the Advocate for the Disabled
1 Empire State Plaza
Albany, NY 12223
(518) 473-4538   **(518) 473-4231**
(voice only)   (TTY/TDD only)
(Toll-free number: 1-800-522-4369)

State Education Department
State Education Building
Washington Avenue
Albany, NY 12234   **(518) 474-1201**
Regional Office:
New York City

State Board of Elections
1 Commerce Plaza
P.O. Box 4
Albany, NY 12260   **(518) 474-1953**
Regional Office:
New York City

Governor's Office of Employee Relations
2 Empire State Plaza
Albany, NY 12223   **(518) 473-8766**

State Energy Office
2 Empire State Plaza
Albany, NY 12223   **(518) 473-4375**
(Energy hotline: 1-800-342-3722)

Appendix A

Department of Environmental Conservation
50 Wolf Road
Albany, NY 12233   **(518) 457-5400**
    Regional Offices:
      Stony Brook   Watertown
      New York City   Liverpool
      New Paltz   Avon
      Schenectady   Buffalo
      Ray Brook

Division of Equalization and Assessment
4 Empire State Plaza
Albany, NY 12223   **(518) 474-2982**
    Regional Offices:
      Batavia   Syracuse
      Long Island   Troy
      Newburgh

Office of General Services
Corning Tower
Empire State Plaza
Albany, NY 12242   **(518) 474-3899**

Department of Health
Corning Tower
Empire State Plaza
Albany, NY 12237   **(518) 474-7354**
    Area Offices:
      Albany   New York City
      Buffalo   Rochester
      New Rochelle   Syracuse
    District Offices:
      Amsterdam   Monticello
      Geneva   Oneonta
      Glens Falls   Saranac Lake
      Hornell   Utica
      Massena   Watertown

Division of Housing and Community Renewal
1 Fordham Plaza
Bronx, NY 10458   **(212) 519-5800**
    Regional Offices:
      Albany   Nassau County
      Buffalo   White Plains

Division of Human Rights
55 W. 125th Street
New York, NY 10027   **(212) 870-8400**

Regional Offices:
   Albany
   Binghamton
   Buffalo
   Nassau County
   New York City

   Rochester
   Suffolk County
   Syracuse
   White Plains

Insurance Department
160 W. Broadway
New York, NY 10013
(212) 602-0434

220 Delaware Avenue
Suite 229
Buffalo, NY 14202
(716) 847-3691

1 Empire State Plaza
Albany, NY 12257
(518) 474-6600
   (Toll-free number: 1-800-342-3736)

Department of Labor
Building 12
State Office Building Campus
Albany, NY 12240
(518) 457-5519
   District Offices:
      Albany
      Binghamton
      Buffalo
      Hempstead
      New York City

1 Main Street
Brooklyn, NY 11201
(718) 797-7820

   Rochester
   Syracuse
   Utica
   White Plains

Department of Law
State Capitol
Albany, NY 12224
(518) 474-7124
   District Offices:
      Binghamton
      Buffalo
      Harlem
      Nassau County
      Plattsburgh
      Poughkeepsie

120 Broadway
New York, NY 10271
(212) 341-2000

   Rochester
   Suffolk County
   Syracuse
   Utica
   Westchester County

Division of the Lottery
Swan Street Building, Core 1
Empire State Plaza
Albany, NY 12223

(518) 474-2744

Office of Management and Productivity (Executive Chamber)
Executive Chamber
State Capitol
Albany, NY 12224

(518) 473-9330

Department of Mental Hygiene
(Consists of three offices: Mental Health, Mental Retardation and
Developmental Disabilities, and Alcoholism and Substance Abuse)

Office of Mental Health
44 Holland Avenue
Albany, NY 12229   **(518) 474-6540**

Regional Offices:

Central New York (Syracuse)

Hudson River (Poughkeepsie)

Long Island (Brentwood)

New York City

Western New York (Buffalo)

Office of Mental Retardation and Developmental Disabilities
44 Holland Avenue
Albany, NY 12229   **(518) 473-9689**

Office of Alcoholism and Substance Abuse
(Consists of the Division of Alcoholism and Alcohol Abuse and the
Division of Substance Abuse Services)

Division of Alcoholism and Alcohol Abuse
194 Washington Avenue
Albany, NY 12210   **(518) 474-3377**

Division of Substance Abuse Services
Executive Park South
Albany, NY 12203   **(518) 457-4176**

250 Broadway
New York, NY 10007
(212) 587-2238

55 W. 125th Street
New York, NY 10027
(212) 870-8365

Division of Military and Naval Affairs
Public Security Building
State Office Building Campus
Albany, NY 12226   **(518) 786-4581**

Department of Motor Vehicles
South Swan Street Building
Empire State Plaza
Albany, NY 12228
(518) 474-0877

141-155 Worth Street
New York, NY 10013
(212) 587-4549

Office of Parks, Recreation and Historic Preservation
1 Empire State Plaza
Albany, NY 12238   **(518) 474-0456**

Regional Offices:

Allegany State Park

Central New York State Park

Finger Lakes State Park

Genesee State Park

Long Island State Park

New York City
Niagara Frontier State Park
Palisades Interstate Park Commission
Saratoga-Capital District State Park
Taconic State Park
Thousand Islands State Park

Division of Parole
97 Central Avenue
Albany, NY 12206 **(518) 473-9400**
Regional Offices:
Albany   New York City
Buffalo   Poughkeepsie
Canton   Rochester
Elmira   Syracuse
Hempstead
New York City Area Offices:
Bronx   Queens
Mt. Vernon   Suffolk

Division of Probation and Correctional Alternatives
60 S. Pearl Street
Albany, NY 12207 **(518) 473-0684**
Regional Offices:
Albany   New York City
Buffalo   Syracuse
Montgomery County

Public Employment Relations Board
50 Wolf Road
Albany, NY 12205 **(518) 457-2854**
Regional Offices:
Buffalo   New York City

Public Service Commission
3 Empire State Plaza
Albany, NY 12223 **(518) 474-7080**
(Energy hotline for gas or electric shutoffs: 1-800-342-3355)
Additional Offices:
New York City   Buffalo

New York State Racing and Wagering Board
400 Broome Street
New York, NY 10013 **(212) 219-4230**

Office of Rural Affairs
Executive Chamber
State Capitol
Albany, NY 12224 **(518) 473-9003**

Appendix A

Department of Social Services
40 N. Pearl Street
Albany, NY 12243   **(518) 474-9516**
   Regional Offices:
     Albany   New York City
     Buffalo   Rochester

Board of Social Welfare
40 N. Pearl Street
Albany, NY 12243   **(518) 474-4357**

Department of State
162 Washington Avenue   270 Broadway
Albany, NY 12231   New York, NY 10007
  (518) 474-4750   **(212) 587-5794**
  (Toll-free DOS Ombudsman number: 1-800-828-2338)

Office of the State Comptroller (Department of Audit and Control)
Alfred E. Smith State Office
Building
Albany, NY 12236   **(518) 474-6046**
270 Broadway   65 Court Street
New York, NY 10007   Buffalo, NY 14202
  (212) 587-5003   **(716) 847-7122**
  Regional Offices: **Division of Municipal Affairs**
     Albany   Hauppauge
     Binghamton   Rochester
     Buffalo   Syracuse
     Glens Falls

Division of State Police
Building 18, State Office Building
Campus
Albany, New York 12226   **(518) 457-2180**
  Regional Offices:
     Albany   Oneida
     Batavia   Poughkeepsie
     Canandaigua   Ray Brook
     Islip Terrace   Sidney
     Middletown   Thruway Troop

State University of New York
State University Plaza
Albany, NY 12246   **(518) 443-5555**

Department of Taxation and Finance
Building 9, State Office Building
Campus
Albany, NY 12227   **(518) 457-4242**
  (Toll-free number for tax information: 1-800-342-3536)
  (Toll-free number for tax forms: 1-800-462-8100)

District Offices:

Albany
Binghamton
Buffalo
Nassau County
New York City

Rochester
Suffolk County
Syracuse
Utica
White Plains

Department of Transportation
Building 5, State Office Building
Campus
1220 Washington Avenue
Albany, NY 12232 **(518) 457-6195**
Regional Offices:

Albany
Binghamton
Buffalo
Hauppauge
Hornell
New York City

Poughkeepsie
Rochester
Syracuse
Utica
Watertown

Division of Veterans' Affairs
194 Washington Avenue
Albany, NY 12210 **(518) 474-3752**
Regional Offices:
Eastern Area (Albany)
Metropolitan Area (New York City)
Western Area (Buffalo)

Division for Women
State Capitol, 2nd Floor
Albany, NY 12224
(518) 474-3612

2 World Trade Center
Floor 57
New York, NY 10047
(212) 587-4408

Division for Youth
84 Holland Avenue
Albany, NY 12208 **(518) 473-7793**
Field Representatives: Local Services

Albany
Binghamton
Buffalo
Elmira
New Paltz

New York City
Rochester
Syracuse
Utica

Regional Offices:
Western New York (Rochester)
Central New York (Syracuse)
Eastern New York (Albany)
Middletown
New York City

APPENDIX B

Independent and Executive Branch Commissions with Statewide Missions

(Either permanent or created prior to January 1, 1978 and still in existence)

Temporary State Commission on Investigation
270 Broadway
New York, NY 10007　　　　　　　　　**(212) 577-0700**

Conducts investigations on (a) the faithful execution and effective enforcement of the laws of the State, (b) the conduct of public officials and public employees (including those of public corporations and authorities), and (c) any matter concerning the public peace, public safety, and public justice.

Temporary State Commission on Lobbying
99 Washington Avenue
Suite 304
Albany, NY 12210　　　　　　　　　**(518) 474-7126**

Seeks to preserve and maintain the integrity of the governmental decision-making process by monitoring lobbyists and disclosing their identities, expenditures, and activities.

Law Revision Commission
488 Broadway
Albany, NY 12207　　　　　　　　　**(518) 474-1181**

Examines the common law and statutes of the State and current judicial decisions for the purpose of discovering defects and anachronisms in the law and recommending needed reforms. Also receives and considers proposed changes in the law, recommends needed modernization, and reports annually to the Legislature.

Permanent Commission on Public Employee Pension and Retirement Systems
270 Broadway
New York, NY 10007　　　　　　　　　**(212) 587-5033**

Investigates provisions for retirement and related benefits for employees of the State and any of its civil divisions.

State Commission on Judicial Conduct

801 Second Avenue	**1 Empire State Plaza**
New York, NY 10017	**Albany, NY 12223**
(212) 949-8860	**(518) 474-5617**

Receives and investigates complaints against judges of the state unified court system.

Commission on Cable Television
Corning Tower
Empire State Plaza
Albany, NY 12223   (518) 474-4992

Created to promote adoption of cable television on a statewide basis, encourage public and educational affairs programming, develop a statewide communications policy, develop and implement standards for cable television systems and provide assistance to municipalities during the purchasing process.

Disaster Preparedness Commission
Public Security Building
State Campus
Albany, NY 12226   (518) 457-2222

Studies both man-made and natural disaster prevention, response and recovery, and prepares State disaster and preparedness plans which are reviewed by the Governor.

Commission on Quality Care for the Mentally Disabled
99 Washington Avenue
Suite 730
Albany, NY 12210   (518) 473-4057

Reviews the operation and organization of the Offices within the Department of Mental Hygiene and assists the Governor in mental hygiene policy development.

State Commission of Correction
60 South Pearl Street
Albany, NY 12207
(518) 474-1416

State Office Building,
Room 412
165 W 125th Street
New York, NY 10027
(212) 870-4315

Advises and assists the Governor in the development of programs, plans and policies to improve the administration of correctional facilities. Also visits, inspects and appraises the facilities, and promulgates rules and regulations establishing minimum standards.

Governor's Traffic Safety Committee
South Swan Street Building
Empire State Plaza
Albany, NY 12228   (518) 474-5777

Approves and coordinates state and local agencies' highway safety programs and those of other public and private agencies and interested individuals and organizations. Also serves as liaison with the National Highway Traffic Safety Administration and the Federal Highway Administration.

APPENDIX C

State Agencies, Legislative Committees, and Commissions Grouped by Mission and Responsibility

(See other listings for addresses and telephone numbers.)

Agriculture/Rural Resources

Department of Agriculture and Markets
Office of Rural Affairs
Senate Standing Committee on Agriculture
Assembly Standing Committee on Agriculture
Legislative Commission on Dairy Industry Development
Legislative Commission on the Development of Rural Resources

Arts/Recreation

Council on the Arts
Office of Parks, Recreation and Historic Preservation
Senate Standing Committee on Tourism, Recreation and Sports
    Development
Assembly Standing Committee on Tourism, Arts and Sports Development

Business/Consumer Affairs

Office of Business Permits and Regulatory Assistance
State Consumer Protection Board
Department of Economic Development
Department of State
Office of General Services
Division of Alcoholic Beverage Control
Banking Department
Insurance Department
Senate Standing Committee on Consumer Protection
Assembly Standing Committee on Consumer Affairs and Protection
Assembly Standing Committee on Small Businesses
Legislative Commission on Public/Private Cooperation

Criminal Justice

State Commission of Correction
Department of Correctional Services
Crime Victims Board
Division of Criminal Justice Services
Division of Parole
Division of Probation and Correctional Alternatives
Division of State Police
Senate Standing Committee on Crime and Correction
Assembly Standing Committee on Correction

Education

State Education Department
State University of New York
Senate Standing Committee on Education
Assembly Standing Committee on Education
Senate Standing Committee on Higher Education
Assembly Standing Committee on Higher Education
Legislative Commission on Skills Development and Vocational Education

Employment/Labor Relations

Department of Civil Service
Governor's Office of Employee Relations
Department of Labor
Permanent Commission on Public Employee Pension and Retirement Systems
Public Employment Relations Board
Senate Standing Committee on Civil Service and Pensions
Senate Standing Committee on Labor
Assembly Standing Committee on Labor

Energy

State Energy Office
Public Service Commission
Senate Standing Committee on Energy
Assembly Standing Committee on Energy

Environment

Adirondack Park Agency
Department of Environmental Conservation
Office of Parks, Recreation and Historic Preservation
Legislative Commission on Solid Waste Management
Legislative Commission on Toxic Substances and Hazardous Wastes
Legislative Commission on Water Resource Needs of Long Island
Senate Standing Committee on Environmental Conservation

Financial/Fiscal

Banking Department
Division of the Budget
Legislative Commission on Expenditure Review
Legislative Commission on the Modernization and Simplification of Tax Administration and the Tax Law
Senate Standing Committee on Banks
Assembly Standing Committee on Banks
Senate Finance Committee
Assembly Ways and Means Committee

Appendix C

Senate Standing Committee on Investigations, Taxation and Government
 Operations
Assembly Standing Committee on Real Property Taxation
Office of the State Comptroller
Department of Taxation and Finance

Health/Mental Hygiene

Department of Health
Department of Mental Hygiene, composed of the following three Offices:
 - Office of Mental Health
 - Office of Mental Retardation and Developmental Disabilities
 - Office of Alcoholism and Substance Abuse, composed of the
   following two divisions:
   - Division of Alcoholism and Alcohol Abuse
   - Division of Substance Abuse Services
Commission on Quality Care for the Mentally Disabled
Senate Standing Committee on Health
Assembly Standing Committee on Health
Senate Standing Committee on Mental Hygiene
Assembly Standing Committee on Mental Hygiene
Council on Health Care Financing (Legislative)
Legislative Commission on Toxic Substance and Hazardous Wastes
Senate Standing Committee on Alcoholism and Drug Abuse
Assembly Standing Committee on Alcoholism and Drug Abuse

Housing/Economic Development/Urban Development

Department of Economic Development
Division of Housing and Community Renewal
Senate Standing Committee on Cities
Assembly Standing Committee on Cities
Senate Standing Committee on Commerce, Economic Development and
 Small Business
Assembly Standing Committee on Commerce, Industry and Economic
 Development
Senate Standing Committee on Housing and Community Development
Assembly Standing Committee on Housing

Human Services

Office for the Aging
Council on Children and Families
Office of the Advocate for the Disabled
Department of Social Services
State Board of Social Welfare
Division for Youth
Division for Women
Division of Human Rights
Senate Standing Committee on Aging

Assembly Standing Committee on Aging
Senate Standing Committee on Child Care
Assembly Standing Committee on Children and Families
Senate Standing Committee on Social Services
Assembly Standing Committee on Social Services

Law/Courts

Office of Court Administration
Temporary State Commission on Investigation
Department of Law
Law Revision Commission
Legislative Bill Drafting Commission
Temporary State Commission on Lobbying
Administrative Regulations Review Commission (Legislative)
Senate Standing Committee on Codes
Assembly Standing Committee on Codes
Senate Standing Committee on the Judiciary
Assembly Standing Committee on the Judiciary

Military/Veterans' Affairs

Division of Military and Naval Affairs
Division of Veterans' Affairs
Senate Standing Committee on Veterans' Affairs
Assembly Standing Committee on Veterans' Affairs

Transportation

Department of Motor Vehicles
Department of Transportation
Governor's Traffic Safety Committee
Senate Standing Committee on Transportation
Assembly Standing Committee on Transportation
Legislative Commission on Critical Transportation Choices

Government

Office of General Services
Office of Management and Productivity (Executive Chamber)
Assembly Standing Committee on Governmental Employees
Assembly Standing Committee on Government Operations
Senate Standing Committee on Corporations, Authorities and
    Commissions
Assembly Standing Committee on Corporations, Authorities and
    Commissions
Senate Standing Committee on Elections
Assembly Standing Committee on Election Law
Senate Standing Committee on Investigations, Taxation and Government
    Operations
Senate Standing Committee on Local Government

Appendix C

Assembly Standing Committee on Local Government
Legislative Commission on Public Management Systems
Legislative Commission on State-Local Relations

APPENDIX D

Inter-Agency Statewide Councils and Committees

State Affirmative Action Advisory Council

Consists of the affirmative action officers of each State agency. The Council advises the President of the Civil Service Commission in all matters affecting affirmative action.

The Council chair rotates annually.
1988 Chair: Mitzi J. Glenn
Banking Department
(518) 473-6160

New York State Comptrollers' Advisory Committee

Composed of fiscal representatives from a broad range of State agencies. The Committee considers fiscal and payroll operational practices that affect all State agencies and assists the State Comptroller in determination and refinement of policies in these areas.

Contact: James McGill
Office of the State Comptroller
(518) 474-2455

State Council of Fiscal Administrators

The Council's mission is to promote the professional development of members in order to enhance the financial management of New York State's agencies. Membership is open to fiscal officers of agencies, commissions, authorities, public benefit corporations and divisions "which are considered autonomous in conducting their financial affairs."

The Council chair is elected biennially.
1988 Chair: Michael McHale
Division for Youth
(518) 473-4590

Inter-Departmental Committee on Electronic Data Processing

Composed of State agency directors of electronic data processing (EDP). The Committee is designed to facilitate the sharing of information, ideas, and experience regarding purchase and utility of hardware and software, as well as organizational and management issues related to EDP.

The Committee holds an annual conference that addresses issues of major concern as identified by the membership. The conference is open to all interested EDP staff at State agencies, local governments, and universities.

The Committee chair rotates annually.
1988 Chair: Vincent Kugler
SUNY Central
(518) 443-5542

Appendix D

New York State Personnel Council

Composed of State agency directors of human resource management and personnel. The Council acts in an advisory and consultative capacity to the Department of Civil Service regarding State personnel policies.

The Council holds an annual institute with an identified theme of importance to its membership.

The Council chair rotates annually.

1988 Chair: Martha Sherwood
Office of General Services
(518) 474-1589

New York State Printing Advisory Committee

Provides a continuing forum for improvement of the State's printing operations, and assists agency personnel in carrying out their printing responsibilities in an efficient and economical manner. Membership includes representatives of State departments, divisions, offices, corporations, authorities, and agencies.

The Committee chair is elected annually.

1988 President: Truman Hoffman
Office of the State Comptroller
(518) 474-4465

APPENDIX E

Members of the Legislature

(1988)

DIRECTORY OF SENATORS

Name	Telephone	Room	Party
	(518) 455-		
Anderson, Warren M.	2276	910 LOB	R
	2276	330 CAP	
Babbush, Howard E.	3536	504 LOB	D
Bartosiewicz, Thomas J.	3531	304 LOB	D
Bernstein, Abraham	2691	420 CAP	D
Bruno, Joseph L.	3191	915 LOB	R
Connor, Martin	2451	415 LOB	D
Cook, Charles D.	3181	902 LOB	R
Daly, John B.	2024	413 CAP	R
Donovan, James H.	2631	504 CAP	R
Dunne, John R.	2831	505 CAP	R
Farley, Hugh T.	2181	706 LOB	R
Floss, Walter J., Jr.	3161	905 LOB	R
Galiber, Joseph L.	2061	414 CAP	D
Gold, Emanuel R.	3431	313 LOB	D
Goodhue, Mary B.	3111	803 LOB	R
Goodman, Roy M.	2211	708 LOB	R
Halperin, Donald M.	3241	918 LOB	D
Hoffman, Nancy Larraine	2665	606 LOB	D
Jenkins, Andrew	2195	604 LOB	R
Johnson, Owen H.	3411	310 LOB	R
Kehoe, L. Paul	2366	812 LOB	R
Knorr, Martin J.	3281	806 LOB	R
Kuhl, John R., Jr.	2091	802 LOB	R
Lack, James J.	2071	815 LOB	R
LaValle, Kenneth P.	3121	805 LOB	R
Leichter, Franz S.	2041	517 LOB	D
Levy, Eugene	3261	946 LOB	R
Levy, Norman J.	3341	811 LOB	R
Lombardi, Tarky, Jr.	3511	612 LOB	R
Marchi, John J.	3215	913 LOB	R
Marino, Ralph J.	2392	412 LOB	R
Markowitz, Marty	2431	406 LOB	D
Masiello, Anthony M.	3371	306 LOB	D
McHugh, John M.	2346	814 LOB	R
Mega, Christopher J.	3255	947 LOB	R
Mendez, Olga A.	3361	302 LOB	D
Montgomery, Velmanette	3451	608 LOB	D

DIRECTORY OF SENATORS

Name	Telephone	Room	Party
	(518) 455-		
Nolan, Howard C., Jr.	2657	711B LOB	D
Ohrenstein, Manfred	2701	907 LOB	D
	2701	314 CAP	
Onorato, George	3486	315 LOB	D
Oppenheimer, Suzi	2031	515 LOB	D
Padavan, Frank	3381	307 LOB	R
Paterson, David A.	2441	413 LOB	D
Perry, John D.	3575	506 LOB	D
Present, Jess J.	3563	509 LOB	R
Quattrociocchi, Ralph	3444	615 LOB	D
Rolison, Jay P., Jr.	2411	512 LOB	R
Ruiz, Israel, Jr.	3395	617 LOB	D
Schermerhorn, Richard E.	2461	409 LOB	R
Seward, James L.	3131	809 LOB	R
Skelos, Dean G.	3171	903 LOB	R
Solomon, Martin M.	2437	408 LOB	D
Spano, Nicholas A.	2231	817 LOB	R
Stachowski, William T.	2426	508 LOB	D
Stafford, Ronald B.	2811	502 CAP	R
Stavisky, Leonard P.	3461	613 LOB	D
Trunzo, Caesar	2111	711 LOB	R
Tully, Michael J., Jr.	2471	848 LOB	R
Velella, Guy J.	3264	944 LOB	R
Volker, Dale M.	3471	609 LOB	R
Weinstein, Jeremy S.	2177	513 LOB	D

ADDRESS CORRESPONDENCE TO: Senator_____
Room_____
Legislative Office Building
or Capitol
Albany, NY 12247

DIRECTORY OF ASSEMBLY MEMBERS

Name	Telephone	Room	Party
	(518) 455-		
Abbate, Peter J., Jr.	3053	725 LOB	D
Abramson, Edward	4203	727 LOB	D
Barbaro, Frank J.	5828	713 LOB	D
Barnett, Henry William	5348	417 LOB	R
Barraga, Thomas F.	4611	629 LOB	R
Becker, Gregory R.	4656	718 LOB	R
Behan, John L.	5997	719 LOB	R

DIRECTORY OF ASSEMBLY MEMBERS

Name	Telephone	Room	Party
	(518) 455-		
Bennett, Lawrence E.	5762	535 LOB	D
Bianchi, I. William, Jr.	4901	601 LOB	D
Boyland, William F.	4466	654 LOB	D
Bragman, Michael J.	4567	828 LOB	D
Brennan, James	5377	433 LOB	D
Brodsky, Richard L.	5753	537 LOB	D
Burrows, Gordon W.	3662	446 LOB	R
Bush, William E.	5383	458 LOB	R
Butler, Denis J.	5014	729 LOB	D
Casale, Anthony J.	5393	450 LOB	R
Catapano, Thomas F.	5821	553 LOB	D
Chesbro, Ray T.	5841	529 LOB	R
Clark, Barbara M.	4711	549 LOB	D
Cochrane, John C.	4141	444 CAP	R
Colman, Samuel	5118	327 LOB	D
Conte, James R.	5732	426 LOB	R
Connelly, Elizabeth A.	4677	826 LOB	D
Conners, Richard J.	4178	524 CAP	D
Connor, Robert J.	5735	542 LOB	D
Cooke, Audre Pinny	5373	430 LOB	R
Coombe, Richard I.	5355	426 LOB	R
Crowley, Joseph	4755	432 LOB	D
D'Andrea, Robert A.	5404	320 LOB	R
Daniels, Geraldine L.	4521	844 LOB	D
Davidsen, Donald	5791	325 LOB	R
Davis, Gloria	5272	419 LOB	D
Dearie, John C.	5102	712 LOB	D
Del Toro, Angelo	4781	501 LOB	D
Diaz, Hector L.	5253	642 LOB	D
DiNapoli, Thomas P.	5192	528 LOB	D
Dugan, Eileen C.	5426	744 LOB	D
Eannace, Ralph	5454	324 LOB	R
Engel, Eliot L.	5296	734 LOB	D
Eve, Arthur O.	5005	736 LOB	D
Farrell, Herman D., Jr.	5491	424 LOB	D
Faso, John	5314	827 LOB	R
Feldman, Daniel	5214	452 LOB	D
Flanagan, John, Jr.	5952	523 LOB	R
Friedman, George	5844	548 LOB	D
Frisa, Daniel	4684	545 LOB	R
Gaffney, Robert J.	4804	921 LOB	R
Gantt, David F.	5606	519 LOB	D
Genovesi, Anthony J.	5211	834 LOB	D

231

Appendix E

DIRECTORY OF ASSEMBLY MEMBERS

Name	Telephone (518) 455-	Room	Party
Gottfried, Richard N.	4941	941 LOB	D
Graber, Vincent J., Sr.	4601	830 LOB	D
Grannis, Alexander B.	5676	522 LOB	D
Green, Roger L.	5325	441 LOB	D
Greene, Aurelia	5671	555 LOB	D
Griffith, Edward	5912	739 LOB	D
Hannon, Kemp	5341	937 LOB	R
Harenberg, Paul E.	5937	724 LOB	D
Harris, Glenn H.	5565	521 LOB	R
Hasper, John	5662	821 LOB	R
Hawley, R. Stephen	5363	402 LOB	R
Heaely, Philip B.	5305	329 LOB	R
Hevesi, Alan G.	4926	943 LOB	D
Hikind, Dov	5721	551 LOB	D
Hill, Earlene	5861	433 LOB	D
Hillman, Morton C.	5172	429 LOB	D
Hinchey, Maurice D.	4436	625 LOB	D
Hoyt, William B.	4886	626 LOB	D
Jacobs, Rhoda S.	5385	435 LOB	D
Jenkins, Cynthia	4451	650 LOB	D
Keane, Richard J.	4691	939 LOB	D
Kelleher, Neil W.	5777	448 LOB	R
King, Robert	5878	820 LOB	R
Koppell, G. Oliver	5965	831 LOB	D
Kremer, Arthur J.	3028	648 LOB	D
Lafayette, Ivan C.	4545	627 LOB	D
Larkin, William J., Jr.	5441	443 LOB	R
Lasher, Howard L.	4811	841 LOB	D
Leibell, Vincent L.	5783	533 LOB	R
Lentol, Joseph R.	4577	621 LOB	D
Lopez, Vito	5537	428 LOB	D
MacNeil, H. Sam	5444	431 LOB	R
Madison, George H.	4627	819 LOB	R
Marshall, Helen M.	4561	619 LOB	D
Martinez, Israel	5414	983 LOB	D
Mayersohn, Nettie	4404	637 LOB	D
McCann, John W.	4807	919 LOB	R
McGee, Patricia	5241	940 LOB	R
McNulty, Michael R.	4474	656 LOB	D
McPhillips, Mary M.	5991	454 LOB	D
Miller, Hyman M.	4505	437 LOB	R
Miller, Mel	3791	349 CAP	D
Miller, Richard	5526	511 CAP	R

DIRECTORY OF ASSEMBLY MEMBERS

Name	Telephone (518) 455-	Room	Party
Murphy, Matthew J.	5511	526 LOB	D
Murtaugh, John Brian	5807	746 LOB	D
Nadler, Jerrold	5802	845 LOB	D
Nagle, James F.	5784	531 LOB	R
Nolan, Catherine T.	4851	833 LOB	D
Norman, Clarence, Jr.	5262	417 LOB	D
Nortz, H. Robert	5545	525 LOB	R
Nozzolio, Michael F.	5655	544 LOB	R
O'Neil, John G.	5797	532 LOB	R
Ortloff, Chris	5943	722 LOB	R
O'Shea, Charles, J.	4633	523 LOB	R
Parment, William L.	4511	638 LOB	D
Parola, Frederick E.	5411	318 LOB	R
Passannante, William F.	4841	837 LOB	D
Pataki, George	4166	534 LOB	R
Paxon, L. William	5741	543 LOB	R
Pheffer, Audrey I.	4292	549 LOB	D
Pillittere, Joseph T.	5284	730 LOB	D
Pordum, Francis J.	4462	652 LOB	D
Prescott, Douglas	5425	323 LOB	R
Proskin, Arnold	5931	723 LOB	R
Proud, Gary	4527	702 LOB	D
Rappleyea, C.D.	3751	340 CAP	R
Robach, Roger J.	4664	824 LOB	D
Saland, Stephen M.	5725	550 LOB	R
Sanders, Steven	5506	622 LOB	D
Sawicki, Joseph	5294	721 LOB	R
Schimminger, Robin L.	4767	847 LOB	D
Schmidt, Frederick D.	5668	732 LOB	D
Seabrook, Larry	4800	938 LOB	D
Sears, William R.	5334	438 LOB	R
Seminerio, Anthony S.	4621	818 LOB	D
Serrano, Jose E.	4717	836 LOB	D
Sheffer, John B., II	4618	635 LOB	R
Siegel, Mark Alan	4794	842 LOB	D
Silver, Sheldon	4477	659 LOB	D
Straniere, Robert A.	4495	326 LOB	R
Sullivan, Edward C.	5603	717 LOB	D
Sullivan, Peter M.	5397	631 LOB	R
Sweeney, Robert	5787	833 LOB	D
Tallon, James R., Jr.	4646	822 LOB	D
Talomie, Frank G., Sr.	5772	546 LOB	R
Tedisco, James	5811	530 LOB	R

DIRECTORY OF ASSEMBLY MEMBERS

Name	Telephone	Room	Party
	(518) 455-		
Tocci, Ronald	4897	940 LOB	D
Tokasz, Paul	5921	432 LOB	D
Tonko, Paul	5197	456 LOB	D
Vann, Albert	5474	422 LOB	D
Vitaliano, Eric N.	5716	539 LOB	D
Warren, Glenn E.	5177	527 LOB	R
Weinstein, Helene E.	5462	741 LOB	D
Weprin, Saul	3851	923 LOB	D
Wertz, Robert C.	5185	404 LOB	R
Winner, George H., Jr.	4538	633 LOB	R
Yevoli, Lewis J.	5456	742 LOB	D
Young, Gregory P.	5291	640 LOB	D
Zaleski, Terrence	5585	628 LOB	D
Zimmer, Melvin N.	4826	839 LOB	D

ADDRESS CORRESPONDENCE TO: Assembly Member _____
Room _____
Legislative Office Building
or Capitol
Albany, NY 12248

APPENDIX F
Senate Standing Committees and Chairs, 1988
(To discuss committee issues, contact the office of its chair)

Committee	Chairperson
Aging	Skelos
Agriculture	Kuhl
Alcoholism and Drug Abuse	Velella
Banks	Marino
Child Care	Goodhue
Cities	Padavan
Civil Service and Pensions	Trunzo
Codes	Volker
Commerce, Economic Development, and Small Business	Floss
Consumer Protection	Kehoe
Corporations, Authorities and Commissions	Schermerhorn
Crime and Correction	Mega
Education	Donovan
Elections	E. Levy
Energy	Seward
Environmental Conservation	Farley
Ethics	Present
Finance	Marchi
Health	Lombardi
Higher Education	LaValle
Housing and Community Development	Daly
Insurance	Bruno
Investigations, Taxation, and Government Operations	Goodman
Judiciary	Stafford
Labor	Lack
Local Government	Cook
Mental Hygiene	Spano
Rules	Anderson
Social Services	Johnson
Tourism, Recreation, and Sports Development	McHugh
Transportation	N. Levy
Veterans	Tully

Other Legislative Contacts

Assembly Switchboard	(518) 455-4100
Senate Switchboard	(518) 455-2800
Bill Status Hotline	(1-800) 342-9860
Legislative Digest	(518) 455-7625
Assembly Public Information Office	(518) 455-4218
Secretary of the Senate	(518) 455-2051
Assembly Documents Room	(518) 455-5165
Senate Documents Room	(518) 455-2311
Legislative Library	(518) 455-2087

APPENDIX G

Assembly Standing Committees and Chairs, 1988*

(To discuss committee issues, contact the office of its chair)

Committee	Chairperson
Aging	Harenberg
Agriculture	Bragman
Alcoholism and Drug Abuse	Engel
Banks	Farrell
Children and Families	Vann
Cities	Dearie
Codes	Silver
Commerce, Industry and Economic Development	Yevoli
Consumer Affairs and Protection	Nadler
Corporations, Authorities and Commissions	Siegel
Correction	Feldman
Education	Serrano
Election Law	Sanders
Energy	Hoyt
Environmental Conservation	Hinchey
Ethics and Guidance	Pordum
Governmental Employees	Lentol
Governmental Operations	Zimmer
Health	Gottfried
Higher Education	E. Sullivan
Housing	Grannis
Insurance	Lasher
Judiciary	Koppell
Labor	Barbaro
Local Governments	Pillittere
Mental Health	Connelly
Oversight, Analysis and Investigation	Murtaugh
Racing and Wagering	Lafayette
Real Property Taxation	Friedman
Rules	M. Miller
Small Business	Schimminger
Social Services	Jacobs
Tourism, Arts, and Sports Development	Murphy
Transportation	Graber
Veterans' Affairs	Conners
Ways and Means	Weprin

---

* There are also a number of special committees and task forces in each house which vary from session to session. Contact information can be obtained from the Assembly Public Information Office or from the Secretary of the Senate.

APPENDIX H

Legislative Commissions

Administrative Regulations Review Commission
146 State Street, Room 301
Albany, NY 12207   (518) 455-2731

Legislative Bill Drafting Commission
State Capitol, Room 308
Albany, NY 12224   (518) 455-7500

Council on Health Care Financing
4 Empire State Plaza, 16th Floor
Albany, NY 12223   (518) 455-2067

Legislative Commission on Critical Transportation Choices
146 State Street, Room 302
Albany, NY 12207   (518) 455-3155

Legislative Commission on Dairy Industry Development
146 State Street, Room 305
Albany, NY 12207   (518) 455-2983

Legislative Commission on the Development of Rural Resources
146 State Street, Room 203
Albany, NY 12207   (518) 455-2544

Legislative Commission on State-Local Relations
State Capitol, Room 504
Albany, NY 12224   (518) 455-5035

Legislative Commission on Toxic Substances and Hazardous Wastes
146 State Street, Room 303
Albany, NY 12207   (518) 455-2100

Legislative Commission on Water Resource Needs of Long Island
Room 2B42, State Office Building
Veterans Memorial Highway
Hauppauge, NY 11788   (516) 360-6206

Legislative Task Force on Demographic Research and
  Reapportionment
146 State Street, Room 208
Albany, NY 12207   (518) 455-4781

Appendix H

Legislative Commission on Skills Development and Vocational
   Education
Legislative Office Building, Room 815
Albany, NY 12248   (518) 465-4118

Legislative Commission on Expenditure Review
111 Washington Avenue
Albany, NY 12210   (518) 455-7410

Legislative Commission on the Modernization and Simplification of
   Tax Administration and the Tax Law
Legislative Office Building, Room 803
Albany, NY 12248   (518) 455-3111

Legislative Commission on Public/Private Cooperation
Legislative Office Building, Room 708
Albany, NY 12248   (518) 455-2211

Legislative Commission on Science and Technology
146 State Street, Room 207
Albany, NY 12207   (518) 455-5081

Legislative Commission on Solid Waste Management
146 State Street, Room 307
Albany, NY 12207   (518) 455-2771

APPENDIX I

Public Authorities with Statewide Missions

(Listed with Main Function)

Agriculture and New York State Horse Breeding Development Fund
90 State Street
Room 805
Albany, NY 12207   **(518) 436-8713**

Promotes horse breeding, agriculture, and funding of related research.

Community Facilities Project Guarantee Fund
40 North Pearl Street
15th Floor
Albany, NY 12243   **(518) 473-7453**

Guarantees mortgages for senior citizen centers, day-care centers, and foster care institutions.

Dormitory Authority of the State of New York
Normanskill Boulevard
Elsmere, NY 12054   **(518) 474-5350**

Provides financing and construction services for health care facilities, institutes of higher education, and certain other non-profit organizations.

Facilities Development Corporation
44 Holland Avenue
Albany, NY 12208   **(518) 474-4389**

Acquires, designs, constructs, improves and rehabilitates facilities for the Department of Mental Hygiene, Department of Correctional Services, municipalities, and other non-profit organizations.

Industrial Exhibit Authority
New York State Fairgrounds
Syracuse, NY 13209   **(315) 487-7711**

Promotes agriculture and assists in presenting the New York State Fair.

Natural Heritage Trust
1 Empire State Plaza
Albany, NY 12238   **(518) 474-0697**

Administers and receives bequests and gifts of property donated for historic preservation, outdoor recreation and conservation.

New York Job Development Authority
605 Third Avenue
New York, NY 10158   **(212) 818-1700**

Assists with the financial needs of companies wishing to expand, build new facilities, or locate in the State.

New York State Bridge Authority
Mid-Hudson Bridge Plaza
P.O. Box 1010
Highland, NY 12528   **(914) 691-7245**

Finances, maintains, operates, rehabilitates or reconstructs vehicular toll bridges over the Hudson River.

New York State Energy Research and Development Authority
2 Empire State Plaza
Albany, NY 12223   **(518) 465-6251**

Promotes the conservation of energy and energy resources and the development and use of safe, renewable, dependable and economic energy sources.

New York State Environmental Facilities Corporation
50 Wolf Road
Albany, NY 12205   **(518) 457-4100**

Plans, constructs, finances, maintains, and operates environmental facilities (i.e., sewage treatment, air pollution control, solid waste disposal, hazardous waste treatment facilities).

New York State Housing Finance Agency
3 Park Avenue
33rd Floor
New York, NY 10016   **(212) 686-9700**

Provides financing to increase or preserve the supply of: housing for low-moderate income families; State University facilities; child-care facilities; mental health facilities; senior citizen facilities, medical care facilities, and others.

New York State Medical Care Facilities Finance Agency
3 Park Avenue
33rd Floor
New York, NY 10016   **(212) 686-9700**

Finances construction for non-profit hospitals, health-maintenance organizations and nursing homes.

New York State Project Finance Agency
3 Park Avenue
33rd Floor
New York, NY 10016   **(212) 686-9700**

Sells bonds and notes for the long-term financing of New York State Urban Development Corporation projects.

New York State Science and Technology Foundation
99 Washington Avenue
Albany, NY 12210   **(518) 474-4349**

Supports the growth of university-industry cooperative research ventures, technological enterprise and regional technology development councils. Promotes excellence in scientific research and scientific and technological education.

New York State Thoroughbred Breeding and Development Fund
   Corporation
575 Lexington Avenue
Suite 2605
New York, NY 10022   **(212) 832-3700**

Promotes the breeding of high-quality thoroughbred horses in New York State.

New York State Thruway Authority
200 Southern Boulevard
P.O. Box 189
Albany, NY 12201-0189   **(518) 436-2700**

Constructs, operates and maintains the New York State Thruway system.

New York State Urban Development Corporation
1515 Broadway
New York, NY 10036   **(212) 930-9000**

Develops, acquires, constructs and rehabilitates industrial and commercial facilities in order to generate industrial and commercial development in distressed urban areas.

Power Authority of the State of New York
10 Columbus Circle
New York, NY 10019   **(212) 397-6200**

Operates and constructs electric generating and transmission facilities, and produces, sells, purchases and resells electricity.

Appendix I

State of New York Mortgage Agency
260 Madison Avenue
9th Floor
New York, NY 10016   **(212) 340-4200**

Acts as a secondary money market vehicle when there is not adequate
private sector credit available for new residential mortgage loans.

State University Construction Fund
The State University Plaza
P.O. Box 1946
Albany, NY 12201-1946   **(518) 473-1134**

Finances, plans, constructs, operates and maintains facilities of the State
University of New York.

New York State Higher Education Services Corporation
99 Washington Avenue
Albany, NY 12255   **(518) 474-4898**

Administers New York State financial aid and loan programs to improve
the opportunities in post-secondary education for eligible students.

APPENDIX J
Some Handy References

GENERAL REFERENCES

Manual for the Use of the Legislature of the State of New York (Blue Book)—issued biennially by the Department of State, includes texts of the State and federal constitutions, other documents, information on New York Congressional and State legislative district boundaries, on executive agencies, commissions, authorities, the Legislature, and local government officials. It also provides electoral and population data relevant to the State. The volume is also referred to as the *Legislative Manual.*

The New York Red Book—issued biennially by Williams Press, provides information about the Legislature, State agencies, the courts, and local government associations. It includes biographic data about all State legislators, many executive branch officials, and New York members of Congress and Senators.

The New York State Executive Budget—submitted annually by the Governor to the Legislature, issued by the Division of the Budget. The volume provides a wealth of information about the State's financial plan, revenues and expenditures, debt service and budgeting by State agency. It includes the Governor's Budget Message, setting forth the administration's priorities for the next fiscal year. It offers a concise description of each agency's major responsibilities as well as those of a large number of public corporations, commissions, committees and other entities requesting State funding. Budgeting for both the judiciary and the Legislature (not detailed) are included.

New York State Statistical Yearbook—published annually by the Rockefeller Institute of Government, State University of New York. Provides a wealth of economic and social data about the State, including health and human services, education, commerce and industry, transportation, law enforcement, and agriculture. It also includes information about whom to contact in State agencies for additional data.

TEXTS AND COMMENTARIES

Official Compilation of the Codes, Rules and Regulations of the State of New York (NYCRR)—issued through the Secretary of State's office. There currently are twenty-two volumes organized by subject (banking, health, public service, etc.). Cumulative indexes are published annually and volumes are updated and republished periodically.

McKinney's Consolidated Laws of New York—Annotated; currently composed of more than eighty titles, organized by subject, most multivolumed (e.g., civil practice law and rules, employers' liability, public officers) and including governments at all levels. Each volume is updated cumulatively and annually by pocket supplements. General indexes are updated periodically.

Consolidated Laws' Service—an annotated, multi-volumed collection, covering the same topics as McKinney's. It provides somewhat different annotations and practice commentaries, and therefore serves as an alternative source of detail in legal interpretation. Each volume is updated annually and cumulatively. New volumes are issued as appropriate.

LEGISLATIVE MATERIALS

McKinney's Session Laws of New York—issued annually, provides detail on all legislation passed in the legislative session for that year. It serves as a valuable resource for precise texts of legislation as passed as well as for texts of amendments to existing legislation passed during the legislative session.

Legislative Digest—an annual subscription service issued by the Legislative Bill Drafting Commission. It provides daily and weekly cumulative (while the legislature is in session) and annual volumes on the status of all bills (and summaries) as they pass through the legislative process, including the Governor's action on each as appropriate.

The Legislative Bill Drafting Commission also conducts a computerized *Legislative Retrieval Service*, providing subscribers with dial-up access to various legislative data bases, including bill status, legislative and committee calendars, and texts of bills, laws, and amendments.

Rogers' Pocket Dictionary of the New York State Legislature and Members of Congress—includes pictures, names, districts, party identification, Albany or Washington office and district office locations and phone numbers of all State legislators and New York State members of Congress. Price: $2.00 plus postage and tax. Issued annually. Available from:

Ray Rogers Printing, Inc.
300 Ninth Street
P.O. Box 175
Troy, NY 12181
(518) 273-2505

Index

Index

Index

Index